David Gommon

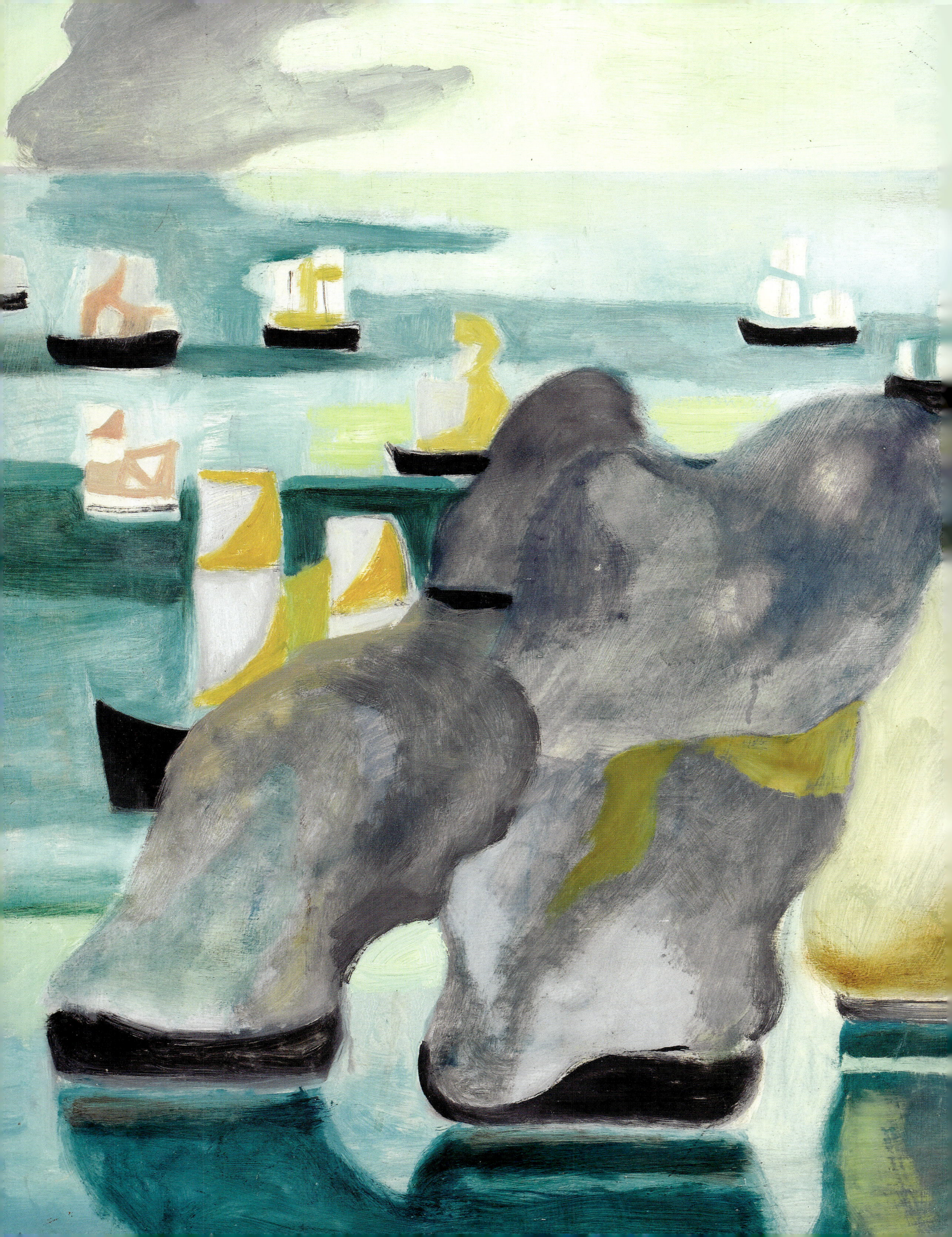

David Gommon

Philip Vann

with
Karen Taylor

Sansom &
Company

First published in 2025 by Sansom & Company,
a publishing imprint of Redcliffe Press Ltd.,
www.sansomandcompany.co.uk / info@sansomandcompany.co.uk

ISBN 978-1-911408-63-5

Text © the contributors / Images © the estate of David Gommon

British Library cataloguing-in-publication data:
A catalogue record for this book is available from the British Library.

Commissioning editor: Paul Deaton
Copyediting: Ann Kay / Design and typesetting: eandp.co.uk
Printed by Short Run Press Ltd, Exeter EX2 6LW / www.shortrunpress.co.uk

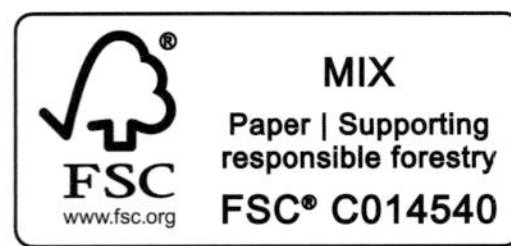

Sansom & Company is committed to being an environmentally friendly publisher.
This book is made from Forest Stewardship Council® certified paper.

Frontispiece: *Trafalgar (8): 5.30 pm, End of the Action* (for details see p.108)

Contents

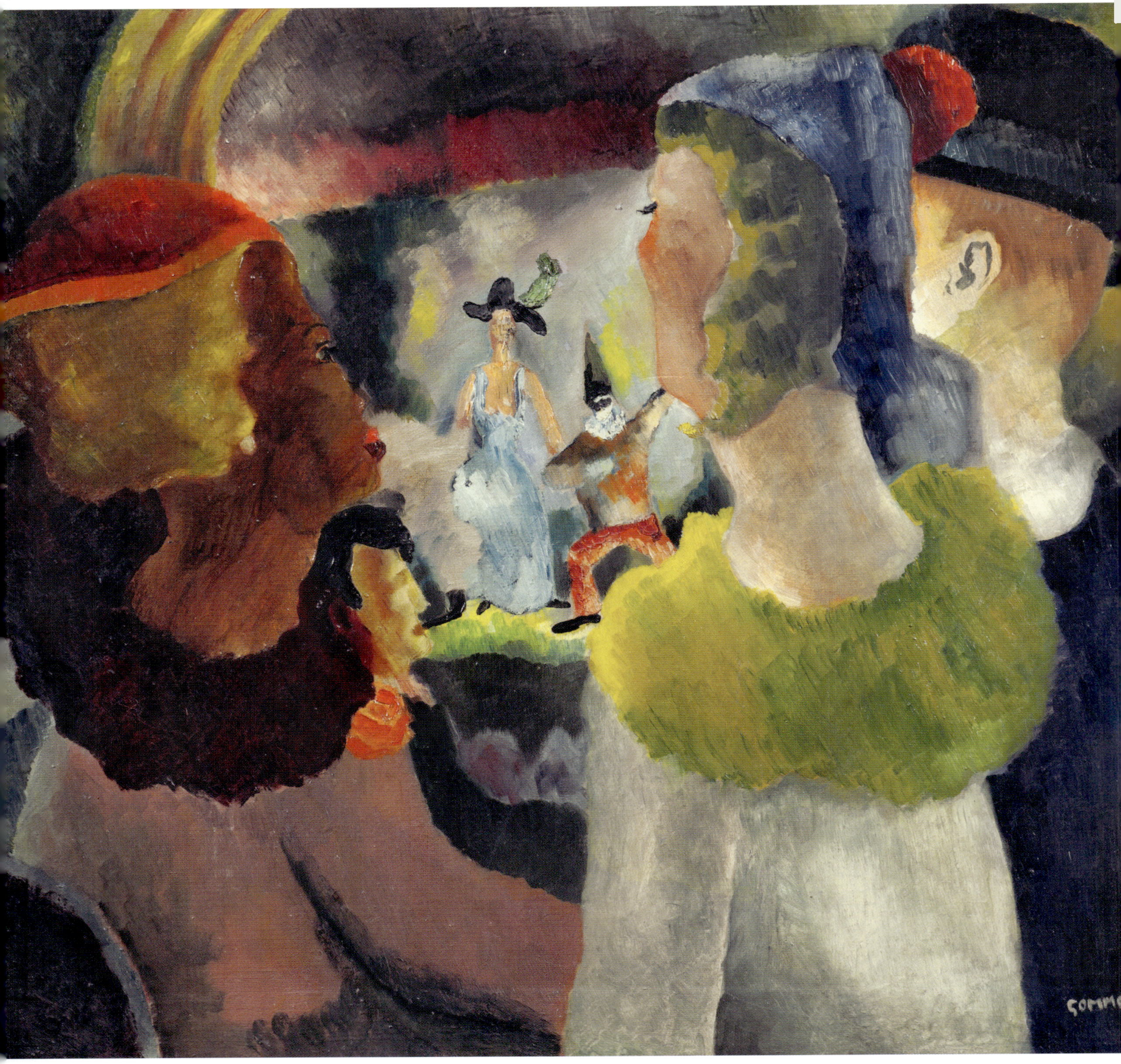

Music Hall / *c.*1934, oil on canvas, 68 x 81.5 cm / Towner Eastbourne

In modern company
the patron and the protégé

Karen Taylor

THE TOWNER COLLECTION AND GALLERY THAT WAS ONCE HOUSED IN Eastbourne Old Town now resides in a purpose-built modernist structure just a stone's throw from the seafront. In the middle of the building is the art store, home to the thousands of artworks that form the gallery's permanent collection. Rows of metal racks line the store, each stacked top to bottom with a diverse arrangement of extraordinary paintings, ordered by the decade of their making. Some are framed in ornate, gilded plaster frames; others in simple, square-profile ones: a nod to the minimal aesthetic of mid-century modern. Within this functional space, cataloguing and conservation work is undertaken; travel crates and display cases are piled high — the flotsam of temporary exhibitions. Yet it's not these things that visitors tend to note when they first enter the space. Instead, they are enthralled by the promise of the 'hidden' paintings that are likely to delight, inspire and intrigue. Amongst the many works in the collection is an oil painting by David Gommon known as *Music Hall, c.*1934 (opposite), the only work by Gommon presently held in the Towner Collection.

When I first came across Gommon's *Music Hall*, my attention was caught by its arresting colours and distinct luminescence, despite its position high up on the rack. I moved it lower to align myself with it as a viewer in a gallery would, and as the artist himself would have while painting it. And, as I stood before it, it drew me in, invoking the eager ambience of a bustling theatre, with the dimly lit auditorium highlighting the saturated vibrance of the well-lit stage.

I found myself imagining the sounds, smells and movements in the theatre and wondering who the audience members huddled in front of the artist were — the people who had arrived before him and were hampering his view. I noticed how the attire of the onlookers so delicately, and playfully, references that of the entertainers on the stage: the extravagant fur collars echoing the clown's ruffled collar, and the red pom-pom on the woman's blue hat conjuring memories of circus performers. Something about this painting's sense of dynamism and modernity for its time, the 1930s, captivated me.

As I studied the Towner Collection in my role as curator, I was instinctively drawn to similar 'modern' paintings that were spread across the many racks of the art store. My attention was focused when several paintings by Kathleen Walne were offered to the gallery in 2015 as Towner already held works by her. *Girl with Cat* (undated) and *Self-Portrait* (c.1935), both by Walne, and amongst the works I had been drawn to, including Gommon's *Music Hall*, were credited as part of 'The Lucy Wertheim Bequest' — a gift of 50 works that avid art collector and gallerist Lucy Wertheim (1883—1971) had left to the Towner on her death.

It struck me just how strongly the artistic instincts and insights of one individual in the 1930s could still be affecting those of people like myself almost a hundred years later. It seemed obvious that the next step was to reunite all the paintings from the Lucy Wertheim bequest — so that the aesthetic that drew them together through the eyes of their collector could be more fully witnessed and appreciated. Once I had gathered these paintings onto one rack from their different locations across the Towner's art store, I found assembled before me an impressive medley of artists, amongst them Frances Hodgkins, Christopher Wood, Alfred Wallis, Helmut Kolle and Phelan Gibb, as well as the already mentioned Kathleen Walne — and David Gommon. Collectively, these works exuded intensity and vitality through a combination of confident mark-marking, abstract figures, simplified forms and fluid landscapes — all aspects that I came to realise were essential to Lucy Wertheim's vision of modern art in the 1930s (the decade in which she acquired most of these pieces for her collection).

Lucy Wertheim was a formidable woman from Manchester whose family had gained some wealth as cotton merchants and who started her working life as a governess and went on, without formal art training, to open an art gallery in London's Burlington Gardens, in October 1930. A bold, discerning character, she established the Wertheim Gallery with the financial backing of her husband, a Dutch consul, Paul Wertheim. Her gallery was unusual as it resembled a drawing room with armchairs and vases of flowers rather than the standard for the time, which was to replicate a museum setting.

Driven by passion, intuition and a belief that young British artists should have the same opportunities as their European counterparts, Wertheim showed great dedication to a wide array of artists over the years. Among those who benefited from her vision and support were Victor Pasmore, Edna Ginesi, William Townsend, Roger Hilton and Kenneth Hall — to name but a few. Understanding the importance of her artists being represented in public galleries, Wertheim often generously gifted works of art to public collections, such as the Towner, in order to give artists the wider exposure, and the recognition, that she felt they deserved.

With this knowledge, each work from the 50 gifted to Towner in 1971 became part of a larger history; each bore a relationship not only to its maker but also to each other through their collector, the woman behind the gift. As such, *Music Hall* by Gommon now had a whole new context and companion works by other artists to shape the narrative around it.

The Wertheim Archive, held at the time of the bequest by Lucy Wertheim's descendants,[1] proffers an abundance of material with which to research *Music Hall* and its maker. This includes an assemblage of letters and scrap-books; the latter are full of newspaper clippings that detail events like the opening of the Wertheim Gallery, catalogues for both solo and group exhibitions there and exhibition reviews.

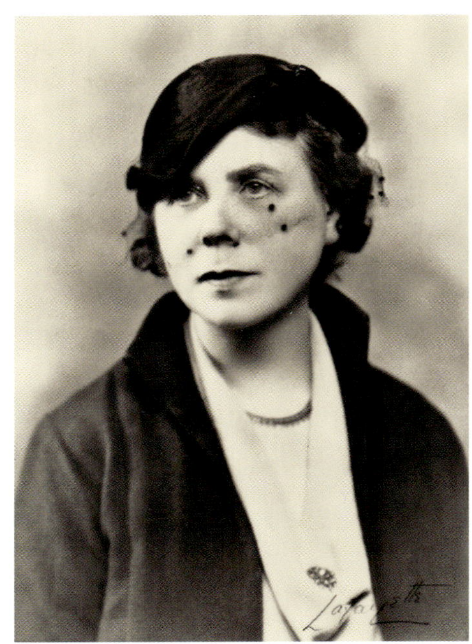

Lucy Wertheim, 1938
photo: Lafayette / The Lucy Wertheim Archive

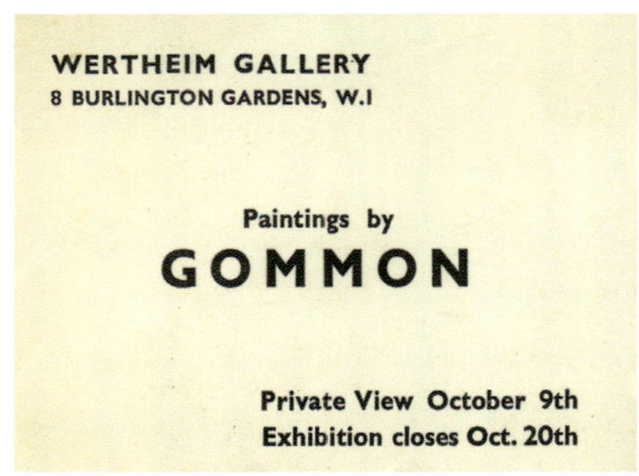

Invitation card for private view of 'Paintings by Gommon' at the Wertheim Gallery in 1934

Gommon's presence is boldly declared in a scrapbook for the 1930s, with the stark black print on the invitation to his 1934 exhibition, 'Paintings by GOMMON', demanding the readers attention.[2] Amongst the titles listed as being in this, his first solo show, were *Three Suitors*, *Crucifixion*, *Birth of Venus*, *White Horses*, several still lifes and a *Self-Portrait*.

Wertheim referred to Gommon as one of her protégés, and when — in her 1947 memoir *Adventure in Art* — she recalled her ambition to provide opportunities for the artists she chose to champion she commented on how this was often to the detriment of her financial situation:

> Pursuing my set policy, I gave many shows at this time to young and unknown artists: to Kenneth Hall and David Gommon among others. Both exhibitions were outstanding and gave me enormous pleasure personally. But both shows were disastrous as commercial propositions. I sold two pictures by Kenneth Hall and not one by Gommon.[3]

Although it was Wertheim's husband's money that had allowed her to set up her gallery, she refused to ask him for further financial help, and driven by instinct rather than financial savvy she often found herself lacking funds. On several occasions, she was forced to sell a prized painting from her personal collection to maintain her patronage and keep the doors of her gallery open.

Exactly how Wertheim and Gommon initially met is unknown; what is known is that some artists approached her unannounced, off the street, walking into her gallery with their portfolio. But it is also possible that their initial encounter was during one of her purported talent-finding visits to the London art schools.[4] Gommon had studied at the Clapham School of Art and, at the age of just 19, in 1933, was invited by Wertheim to exhibit as part of what she called her 'Twenties Group' — a group comprised, as the name would suggest, of artists mainly in their twenties whom she deemed promising.

The first Twenties Group exhibition, including work by Barbara Hepworth, had already been held by Wertheim in January 1932. So it was their second exhibition, at her gallery in February 1933, that Gommon first featured in — listed in the catalogue under the heading 'Aspirants under Twenty' (alongside other artists such as Roger Hilton, now known for his post-war abstract painting and his association with the St Ives School of artists). A painting by Gommon, entitled *Seated Man*, was on sale (for four guineas), although the listing for it included an unfortunate misprint that misnamed him 'Common'.

By the time of the third Twenties Group exhibition, in January 1934, Gommon was a bona fide member of the group in that he was now a month into his twenties. And, in October of the same year, Wertheim gave him his first solo exhibition, for which she dubbed him simply 'Gommon', a decision that did not go unnoticed by *The Times* art critic Charles Marriott, who wrote:

> Mr. David Gommon, who shows paintings and water-colours at the Wertheim Gallery ... has talent and imagination, but it is questionable if he is ready to show his work. Should he fulfil his promise, these stammering

1. Now in the Paul Mellon Centre Archive Collections.
2. Lucy Wertheim Archive, Scrapbook, vol. 4, Paul Mellon Centre.
3. L. Wertheim (1947), 'F.I. Albany' and 'The Yellow Man', *Adventure in Art* (Unicorn, 2022).
4. This is a remark extracted from a letter by the artist José Christopherson (J. Christopherson Weisbrod, letter to Salford Art Gallery curator, Judith Sanderling, December 1990, Salford Art Gallery Archive): 'Yes, I knew Mrs Wertheim very well — I was one of her "young" people!!! She came to the Art School (the Grosvenor) in London, where I was training, to "talent spot". She picked four of us to show at her beautiful gallery in Burlington Gardens — we were thrilled to have a London show! Then for many years I showed with her in both her London gallery and the one in Manchester.'

utterances will have their historical value, but they are not in themselves adequate. Mr Gommon's natural gift — apart from his intensity in conception — appears to be for a sort of baroque composition in colour values … The adoption by young artists of such signatures as 'Gommon', as one should say 'Velazquez', does not conduce to confidence in their abilities.[5]

Wertheim held six Twenties Group exhibitions between 1932 and 1937, showcasing 111 artists in total, with each exhibition featuring between 23 and 45 artists. And Gommon, who had, over the years, become a valued artist and friend of Wertheim's, exhibited in all but the first of them.

Many of the young artists she supported were straight from art school, full of expectation and enthusiasm. Generous with both her time and financial aid, Wertheim was driven by her belief in the artist's inherent need to create. She believed that with privilege came responsibility towards those less fortunate, and that it was her calling to provide them with what means she could.

She supported different artists in different ways. In Gommon's case, she provided him with a living wage ('two pounds a week plus all the paints I needed'[6]) so that he could paint unencumbered by the worry of selling his work or paying his bills. And, in return, all the work he produced — which was, in Gommon's own words 'a great deal'[7] in the 1930s — belonged to the Wertheim Gallery. In hindsight, this could be considered a problematic agreement that did not consider the potential success of an artist. However, for those who were starting out, it offered them freedom to pursue their creativity without financial hardship or pressure.

It was a risk for Wertheim as she could only recoup her investment in Gommon on selling his work. But she stood by her commitment, believing it was only a matter of time before he would be recognised. Several decades later, around 1969, when he was awarded a prize by Northampton Art Gallery, she wrote in a letter to him: 'My dear, I am _delighted_. Perhaps this time you'll get some recognition for your outstanding quality of painting.' She went on in this letter to list other artists who had achieved recent success, commenting that: 'Each one of these artists I name have made a bitter struggle to gain recognition, but in each case I was the _first_ to collect their work. I have had no case for regret.'[8]

One 'bitter struggle' that Wertheim may have been referring to was a situation that unfolded publicly in 1952. Gommon, who was viewed by many as both a skilled artist and a successful art master at Northampton Grammar School, with many of his students receiving scholarships to art schools, had never been awarded his National Diploma in Art. And this meant that he was being paid a considerable £50 a year less than his assistant. Gommon had, on several occasions, taken the exam and submitted his paintings for the diploma but had repeatedly received a verdict of 'fail' by the examiners, who declared that, in their opinion, he could not paint.

This type of narrow-minded judgement was exactly the kind of attitude that Wertheim had vehemently fought to remedy in her decision to support many

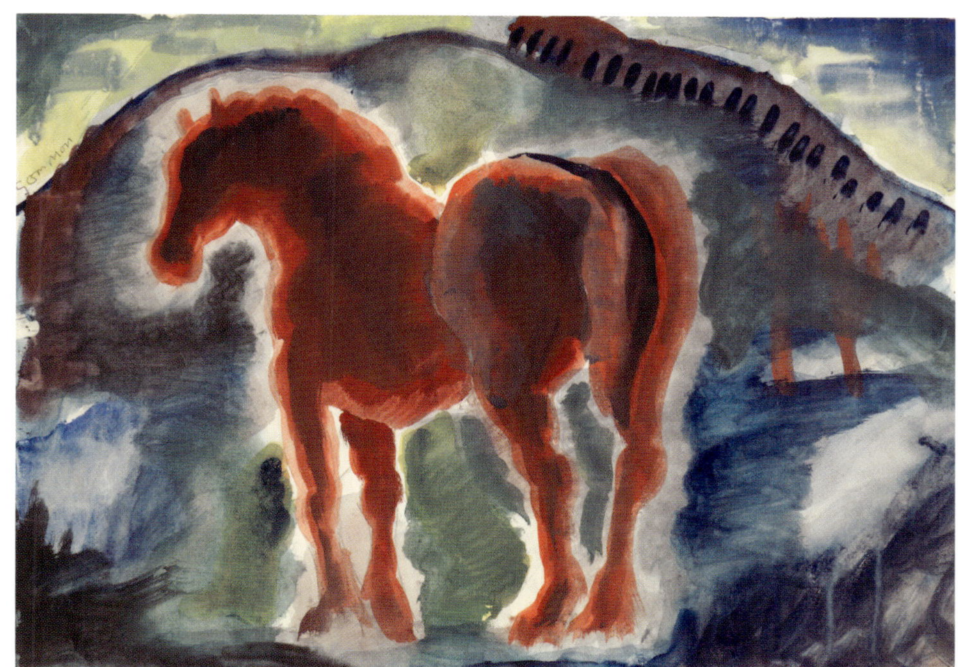

Red Horse
*c.*1934, watercolour and gouache on paper,
36 x 52.5 cm
Wertheim Estate

young, often untrained, working-class artists. As far back as 1934, she had published 'An Open Letter to City Fathers', in which she challenged the men who held most influence in the society of the time to 'wake up' and support young modern British artists, whatever their background.[9] When she met with opposition or rejection from the art establishment, she had no qualms about vigorously protesting on behalf of the artists she supported.

Gommon's struggle to be accepted by the educational establishment played out in the local newspapers over several articles. *The Birmingham Post*, for example, featured bylines like '"Brilliant" Artist Fails in Ministry Test, "Cannot Paint" Ruling Angers Headmaster'.[10] Gommon's plight was even raised by Mr Paget, the Labour MP for Northampton, in the House of Commons, where 50 of his paintings were displayed for the Minister of Education. Eventually, in August 1953, on Gommon's fifth submission, he passed his National Diploma in Art, and his salary was increased accordingly.[11]

So important was the role that Wertheim played in Gommon's life that he reflected in his unpublished memoir, written in the 1980s: 'I cannot envisage those years from 1932 until the outbreak of the war without her [Wertheim] and her financial help and interest and encouragement, and through her I was introduced to and met so many people.'[12]

It was, for example, Wertheim who introduced Gommon to London-based theatre manager and producer Lilian Baylis, one of the great creative forces behind the Old Vic theatre, as well as behind the reopening of the formerly derelict Sadler's Wells Theatre and the foundation of the companies now known as the English National Ballet and the Royal Ballet. As a South Londoner, Gommon had frequented the Old Vic from a young age. But his introduction to Baylis gave him the opportunity to meet, and draw, the performers backstage and at dress rehearsals, as shown in works such as *Study of Ballet Rehearsals*, *c.*1936.

5. C. Marriott, 'Arts Review', *The Times*, 13 October 1934.
6. David Gommon, from notes on his life taken from a hand-written account written in 1980 (and transcribed in 2020), p.5.
7. Ibid.
8. L. Wertheim (*c.*1969), letter to David Gommon, Gommon family papers.
9. L. Wertheim, *Phoebus Calling* (Wertheim, 1934).
10. *The Birmingham Post*, December 1952.
11. [Northampton] *Mercury & Herald*, August 1953.
12. D. Gommon, from notes ... 1980.

Another work by Gommon that is important to mention in connection to Wertheim is *Red Horse*, c.1934 [p.11], which was first noted in the Wertheim Archive as being exhibited in 1935 in 'Modern Watercolours at Salford City Art Gallery' (an exhibition composed entirely of artists and work from the Wertheim Gallery). Not only did Wertheim choose to include a mono-chrome plate of this painting, out of her whole wealth of material from him, in her 1947 memoir, but we also know that it is one of only a few works that she kept and that is still owned by the Wertheim Estate. This modest work on paper shows the great strength and power of the red horse amidst a landscape of broad brushstrokes washed in hues of blue and green. The simplified line of trees clinging to the edge of the hill, a motif seen in many of his early works, gives weight and grounds this watery scene.

Some of the other works produced by Gommon in the 1930s (the period during which he was funded by Wertheim) can be found in public art col-lections, such as at the Towner, of course — the lasting visual evidence of the affiliation between Gommon and Wertheim. Of the eight Gommon oil paintings currently held in UK public collections, one of which is double-sided, Wertheim was responsible for gifting six of them.

His first work to enter a public collection — a watercolour called *The Road* — was sold by Wertheim to Salford Art Gallery in 1933, when Gommon was just 19. There followed several other purchases by Salford and gifts to them from Wertheim; in total, they acquired an impressive 18 Gommon works (19 images, including the double-sided work) between 1933 and 1947.

As mentioned earlier, Wertheim had an instinctive, and important, under-standing of the need for artists to be represented in public galleries. As a result, more than 10 public institutions benefited from her generous deci-sion to share her modern art collection during her lifetime. And, in all, she gifted over 500 works to regional, national and international museums. As such, she played an important role in introducing modern art to a wider audience, with over 40 galleries, schools and libraries exhibiting works from the Wertheim Collection during her lifetime. Her international offerings to public institutions included ones in New Zealand and Australia, the most significant of which was her gift of over 150 works to Auckland Art Gallery in 1948 — 15 of which were Gommon paintings.

And, as a result of the research conducted for the 2022 Towner exhibi-tions — 'A Life in Art: Lucy Wertheim — Patron, Collector, Gallerist' and 'Reuniting the Twenties Group' — Gommon's paintings *The Storm*, 1950 (above), and *In the Wood*, 1961, are to be gifted (by private donors) to the Towner Collection. This gift will extend the Towner's representation of Gommon's artistic career, both offering the public additional insight into his practice and further illustrating the bond between him and his friend and patron.

It is remarkable to think that decisions Lucy Wertheim made almost 100 years prior to this book being written are still resonating into the present and having such a lasting impact on David Gommon's artistic legacy. And the hope, of course, is that they will continue to do so far into the future.

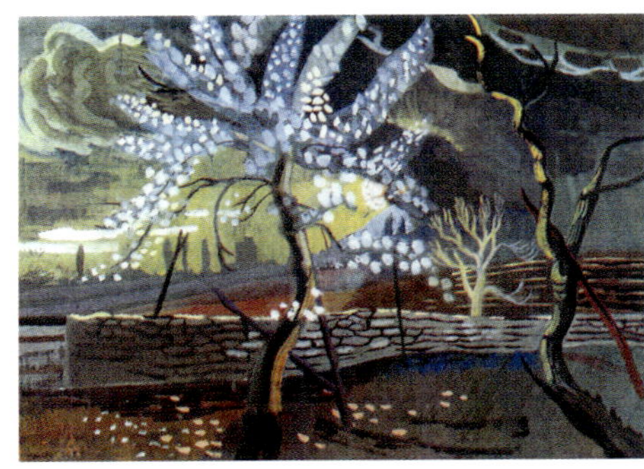

The Storm
1950, gouache on paper,
dimensions unknown
private collection

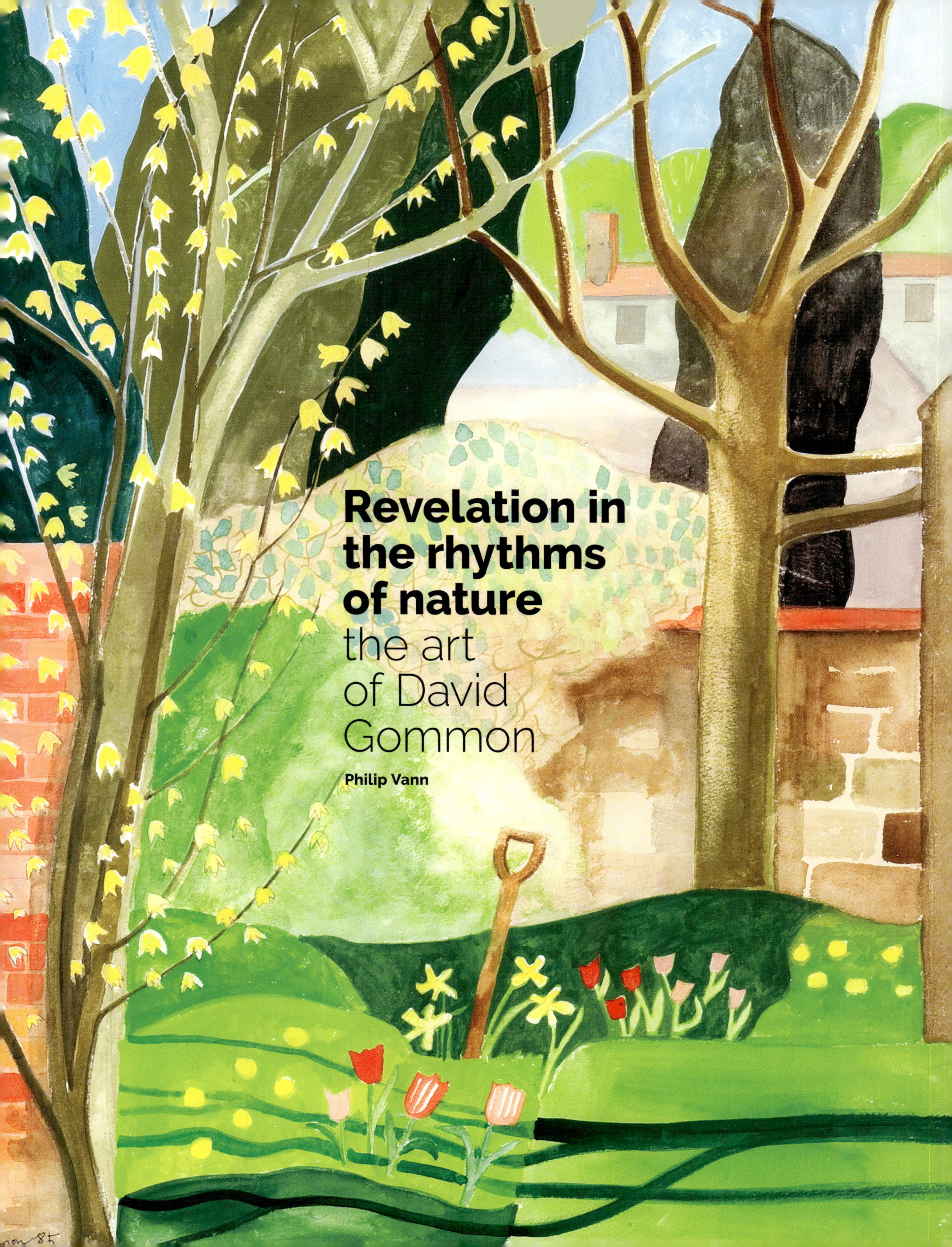
Revelation in
the rhythms
of nature
the art
of David
Gommon

Philip Vann

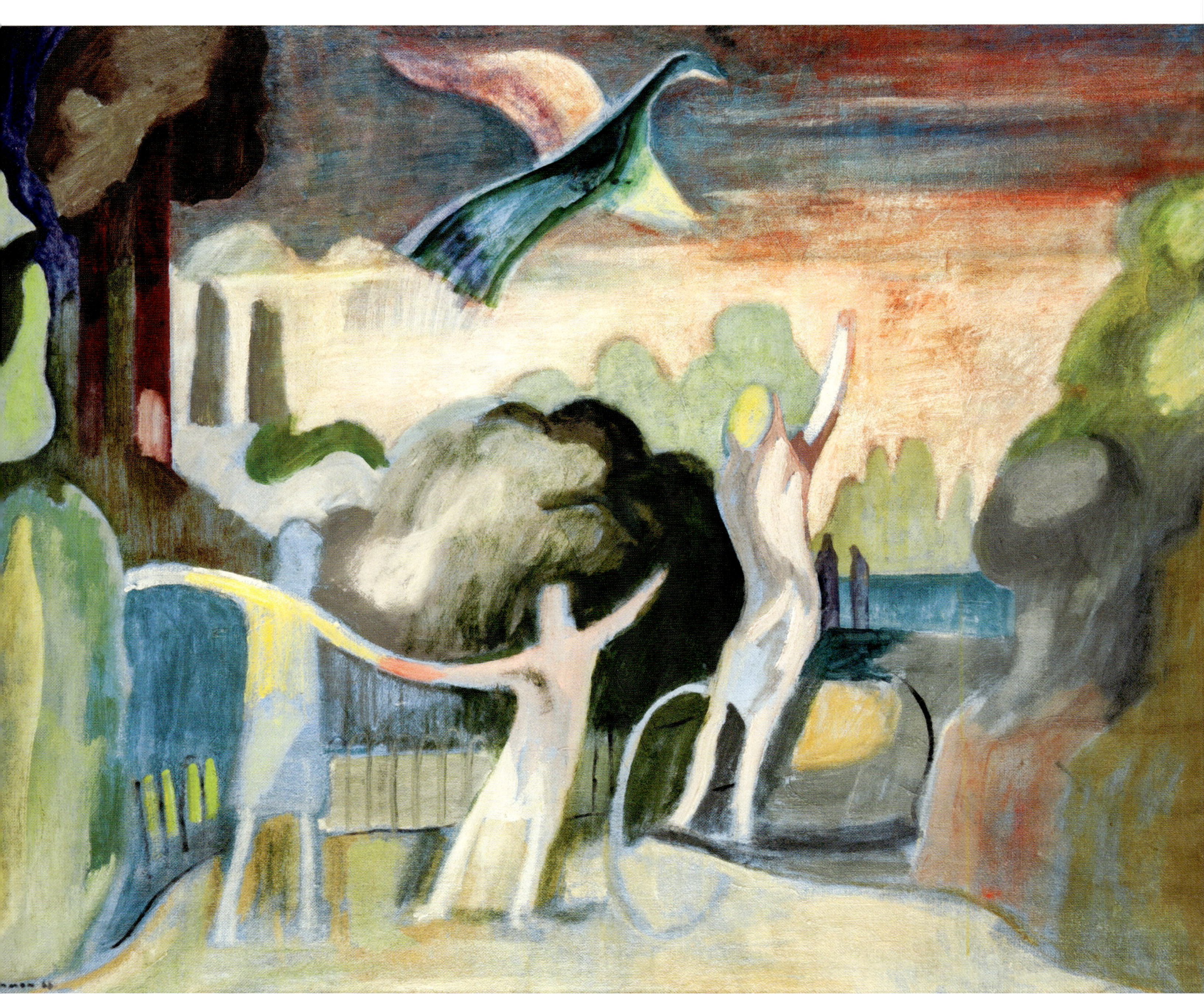

Battersea Park / 1965, oil on board, 92 x 122 cm / *private collection*

Battersea beginnings, Dorset intimations

A man's work is nothing but this slow trek to rediscover, through the detours of art, those two or three great and simple images in whose presence his heart first opened.[1]
Albert Camus

BORN IN BATTERSEA ON 12 DECEMBER 1913 — JUST SEVEN MONTHS OR so before the outbreak of the First World War — David Gommon went on to become a painter of rare visionary perceptiveness and searching philosophical acuity, an audaciously original colourist attuned to intricate and delicate as well as dynamic rhythms of nature. Many years later (in 1979) he recalled Battersea as 'a poor working-class district in London with the Thames running through it', and what he describes as 'one of my earliest memories' sets the tone for the subtle and cultivated feelings and magical tenor that distinguish much of his art: he recalled 'the Thames and its tugs and its sounds and noises, and the cry of the peacocks coming from Battersea Park, which for me is rather like one of those golden landscapes that you see in the pictures of Claude Lorrain'.[2]

Such qualities are evident early on in his artistic career. For just over eight years, after he was discovered, aged 18, by the modern art enthusiast, collector and London gallerist, Lucy Wertheim (1883—1971), he was a painter of enigmatic, phantasmagoric images that hover on the verge of Surrealism. As his patron for all that time, she paid him £2 a week for 'practically all the work I did — and I did a great deal'.[3]

The second or mid-part of Gommon's career was a relatively brief but intense one. In early-to-mid 1939 he abandoned the metier of landscape and portrait painting in favour of making an excoriatingly satirical, politically engaged artwork, *The Book of the Dead*, rooted in mixed-media drawings and collaged newspaper cuttings. He didn't resume what he considered proper painting again until 1944.

In his post-war art (lasting until his death at the age of 73), he made some highly discerning portraits of a small number of remarkably creative people whom he knew and admired. He also explored the wild, ecstatic, sometimes sinister rhythms of the British landscape in all seasons and the pulsating, scintillating fluidity of natural forms like clouds, birds and trees, as well as the archetype of the paradisical garden. The last was focused for almost thirty years mainly on his beloved walled garden in the Northamptonshire village of Hardingstone, to which he had moved around 1958 with his wife

1. From an essay, 'Between Yes and No', by Albert Camus, quoted in Harry Callahan, *Masters of Photography* (Aperture Foundation Inc, 1999), p.10.
2. 'An Interview with David Gommon, the Painter from Northamptonshire, Who Came in December of 1979 to Paint the Mural in the New Music Centre', *The Canberran* (the journal of the Canberra Grammar School, Canberra, Australia), no. 48, interviewer unknown (possibly the headmaster Paul McKeown), 1980, p.38.
3. David Gommon, from notes on his life taken from a hand-written account written in 1980 (and transcribed in 2020), p.5. (In this book, a few very minor edits — some punctuation and so on — have been made to the transcribed account.)

Jean (neé Vipond — itself probably a name with Norman origins), whom he had married in 1943, and their young son Peter, who was born in 1945. Their daughter Kate was born in 1956.

David's later garden pictures explore and celebrate such secluded spots as places where the soul can regain a state of primal innocence. These lines from Andrew Marvell's 1683 poem 'The Garden' inimitably evoke the nature of what can transcendently arise out of such 'delicious solitude' (to quote a later line from the poem):

> What wond'rous life in this I lead!
> Ripe apples drop about my head …
> Stumbling on melons as I pass,
> Ensnar'd with flow'rs, I fall on grass.
>
> Meanwhile the mind …
> creates, transcending these,
> Far other worlds, and other seas;
> Annihilating all that's made
> To a green thought in a green shade.
>
> Here at the fountain's sliding foot,
> Or at some fruit tree's mossy root,
> Casting the body's vest aside,
> My soul into the boughs does glide;
> There like a bird it sits and sings,
> Then whets, and combs its silver wings;
> And, till prepar'd for longer flight,
> Waves in its plumes the various light.[4]
>
> …

David's father, Edward John Gommon, was a journeyman carpenter, a Londoner born in Battersea, who, says Peter Gommon, 'travelled around the country to where the work was. That was how he met my grandma, Jemima [neé Brown] — it was on the Queen Mother's family estate at Glamys, where she was in service as a lady's maid. They got married at Kinglassie Parish Church in Fife on 30 September 1909 and he brought her back to London — which must have been a shock to her (even though it is known she had worked as a housemaid in Thurloe Square, Kensington in 1901 — so it is possible that they might have met before my grandpa's trip to Scotland). Her grandfather had been a ploughman and the family worked on the land. She remained Scottish to the core. I recall my grandmother with her refined Scottish accent — she spoke very clear, precise Scots.'[5] David had one older sister, Margaret.

His euphoric 1965 painting [p.14] depicting a protective mother and her two sinuously interlinked young children in Battersea Park as archetypal but faceless figures — with the colossal figure of a stork flying overhead (towards which the mother gestures in wonder) — can surely be seen as recalling happy family bonds of his own childhood. In many cultures the stork is seen as a mythic being, representing elements of rebirth and rejuvenation as well as secure nesting. The colours of the scene, imbued

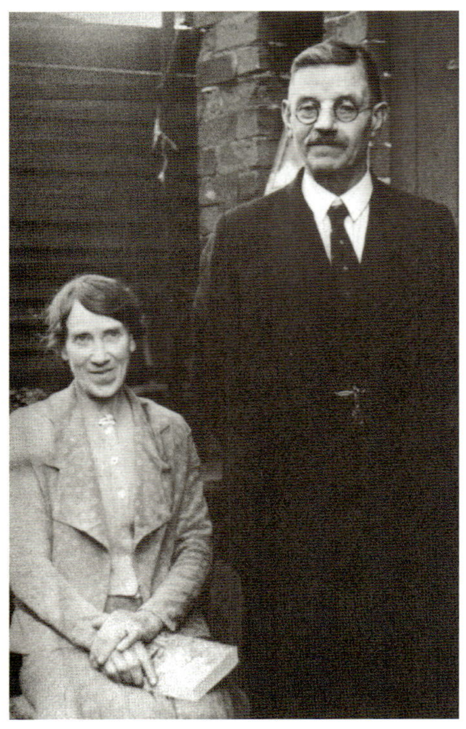

Jean Gommon in Jasmine Cottage garden, c.1984

David's parents, Jemima and Edward Gommon, date unknown

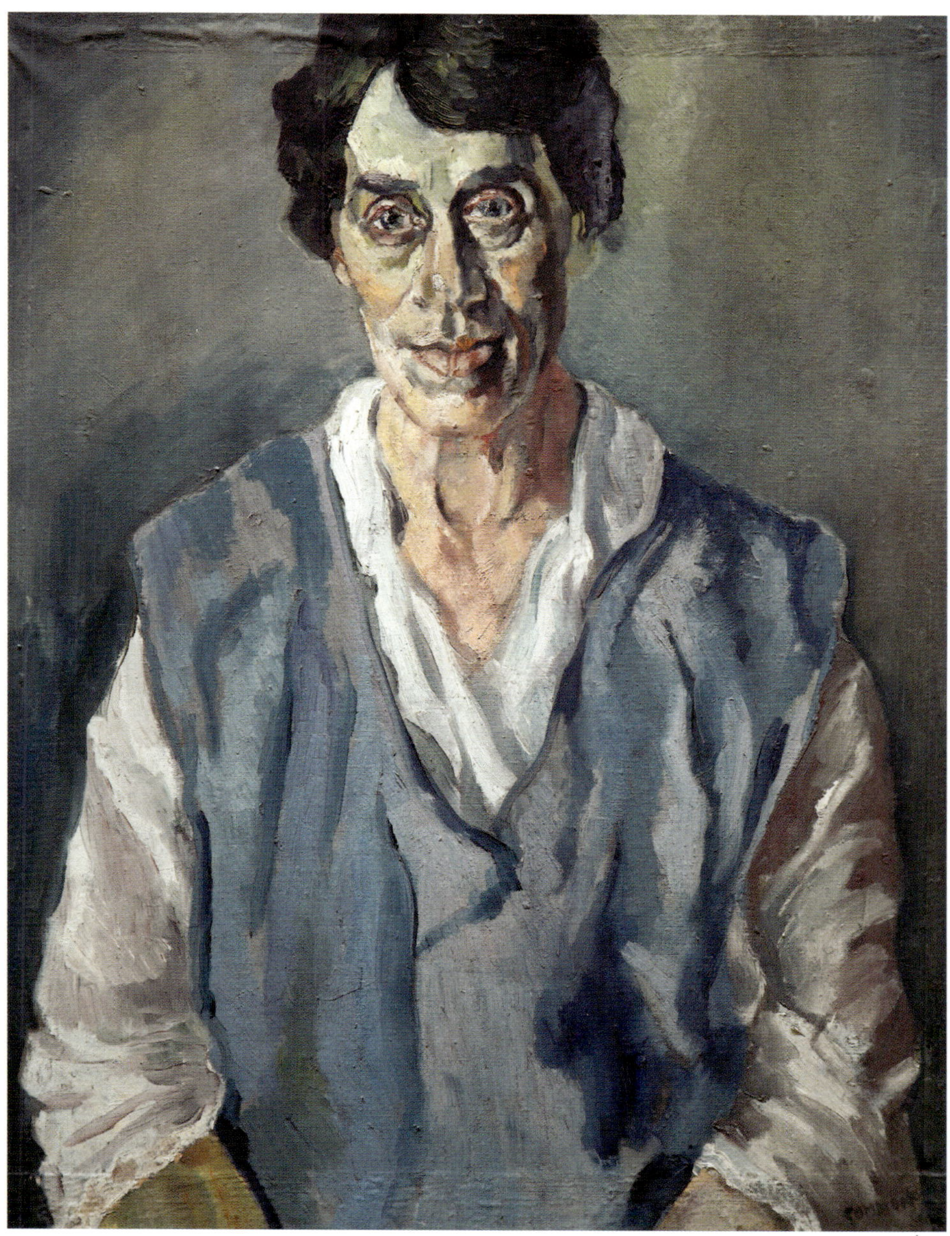

Portrait of My Mother
date unknown, oil on canvas, 89 x 71.2 cm
Auckland Art Gallery Toi o Tāmaki,
New Zealand

4. Andrew Marvell, 'The Garden', 1683, poem in George deF. Lord (ed.), *Andrew Marvell: Complete Poetry* (London: J.M. Dent & Sons, 1984), pp.48—50.
5. All quotes from Peter Gommon and Kate Currie are from two separate taped interviews with the author, the first with Peter conducted in March 2020, the second with Kate in August 2022.
6. Patrick Hayman, 'The Winter Landscape Dies', quoted in essay by Philip Vann in *Patrick Hayman: A Voyage of Discovery*, exhibition catalogue (London: Hayward Gallery, 1990) p.18.

with a quite paradisical potency, include a patch of turquoise as a glimpse of the Thames flowing beyond.

A blue hoop is seen here in dynamic play in the space between the younger child and the mother — its perfect orb seeming a harmonious emblem of balance, wholeness and the natural cycle of life. This kind of tender visionary sensibility can be seen similarly in the contemporaneous work of a fellow English artist, Patrick Hayman (1915—1988), in whose paintings and poetry the image of the 'CHILD with the Iron Hoop' is a pervasive one — as in Hayman's illustrated poem, *The Winter Landscape Dies* (1963), with its 'anxious mother' watching her child

> ... play in the mist at evening
> By the dark river port
> That delivers ships from the sea
> To slumber in its HEART.[6]

A very early memory David had was both historic and epic in character. Two of his uncles had emigrated to Australia and went on to fight in the Australian army at Gallipoli and the Somme. After the First World War had ended, and he was five or six years old, he first met these uncles at a victory parade held in London. 'I can remember the excitement of being carried through the streets of London on their shoulders. To me they seemed giants and heroes, made more splendid by their cocked hats and those very splendid badges.'[7]

David's daughter Kate Currie says,

> He used to talk about the tremendous freedom he'd had as a child. He and his friends would make home-made trolleys that they could ride on while hitching a tow on the back of a passing cart. The carters had skills in using their long whips to discourage these hangers-on, and the boys had an expression that they would call to alert each other to any potential danger.

> He was in the large choir of the local parish church. The curate there used to take these little boys to the opera and ballet sometimes, wanting really to expand their horizons. He also learnt to play the violin but he had to hide it because he got so teased and even beaten up by the other boys for it!

The childhood freedom he often enjoyed came, Kate says, because

> they used to walk everywhere; buses were expensive. There was a gang of them, safety in numbers; they would walk to Fulham to see the football matches.

> The other thing he used to describe was the Zeppelins over London. I was amazed he could remember that — he must have been three or four at the time. He said boy scouts used to run round blowing a whistle before the air raids and then he would hear the Zeppelins above, a sound he would imitate for me.

Gommon was 16 when he enrolled at Battersea Polytechnic and the Clapham School of Art. Eventually he managed to get a meagre maintenance grant of seven shillings and sixpence (7/6) a week.

He later described his art education as highly traditional, with (after a year) 'drawing from the life almost every day, [studying] architecture and the history of art, lettering and design ... On some days we worked until nine o'clock at night.'[8] But he insisted that 'the most important [artistic] influence [then] was my mother ... her mind was full of poetry, especially Scotch poetry and Border Ballads, and this is a very visual poetry.'[9]

Aged 16 he started attending the Old Vic Theatre in London — 'I could get a seat in the gallery for sixpence' — and saw many Shakespeare plays (which he would also read at home); so much so that he found he could recite long Shakespearean passages by heart. At this age he had the grand ambition of 'becoming, like Leonardo and Goethe, a kind of portmanteau man, knowledgeable in a whole range of subjects'.[10] Not being able to afford books, he borrowed them from libraries, writing out copies of lengthy passages.

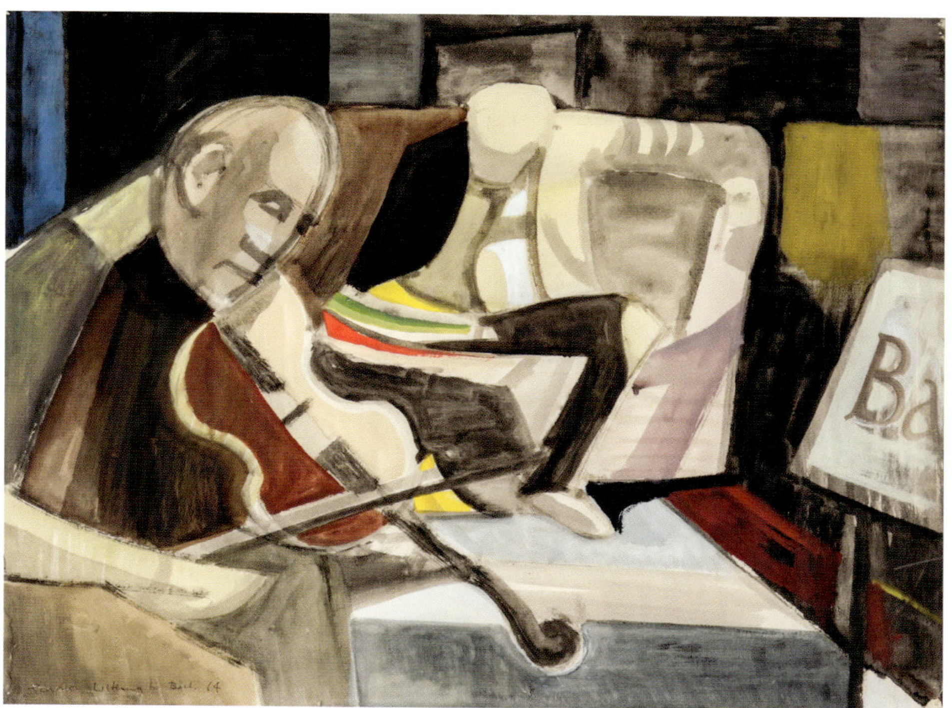

Listening to Bach
1984, watercolour and gouache on paper,
51 x 71 cm
private collection

'From all this, certain figures came into my life, and they have remained mentors ever since [he recalled in 1979] — I mean Socrates, Goethe, Tolstoy, Dostoevsky, Stendhal, Flaubert';[11] he also singled out here one contemporary figure, the iconoclastic writer and artist Wyndham Lewis (1882—1957).

Kate recalls that, later on, he always seemed to have this rich treasury within himself — a resource 'of words and music but music more than even words I think'. Her early memories of him were of his 'enormous warmth and a wonderful whistle; he could whistle like a blackbird. He would whistle around the house when there was music, especially Beethoven, being played.'

A 1984 watercolour and gouache, *Listening to Bach* [above], testifies to his love of music. A bald-headed man is pictured in an armchair playing the violin, an entranced expression on his bowed head. In this snug domestic setting a sprawling companion listens absorbedly. The latter's facial features are not evident, only the lucidity of his attention in the white of the paper shining through.

Kate says, 'There were lots of pictures in his mind's eye of places he had seen. But he was a very reticent person, very much of that war generation. He would recite poetry to you, he would sing — but it was hard to get him to say anything personal about his own experience.'

Though a reserved character in some ways, he was nevertheless an empathetic one — as a father, husband, friend and art teacher. William Mayes — the son of the journalist and editor Ian Mayes, a fellow Hardingstone resident for many years and a discerning critic of Gommon's art — recalls that when he was about 14 or 15 'David was so kind to me; I used to love disappearing through his garden gate [to his cottage]. None of my friends knew where I was or that the gate even existed. It was like having a personal

7. D. Gommon, from notes ... 1980, p.1.
8. Ibid.
9. 'An Interview with David Gommon, the Painter from Northamptonshire ...', p.38.
10. Ibid.
11. Ibid, pp.38—9.

tutor [in terms of learning about art and life].'[12] Their friendship lasted for many years.

Around the time of Gommon's eighteenth birthday, in December 1931, a series of momentous events occurred. He recalled in 1980 that he had then befriended a fellow student whose

> father, a retired sailor, lived in an old coastguard cottage near the sea and Chesil Beach in Dorset, an area famous for its wrecks … I saw that beach for the first time on a grey wintry afternoon in December. I climbed slowly out of the village of Langton Herring to the top of a very steep rise. Suddenly I was confronted — overwhelmed by the revelation of beach, the sea, the sky! It was biblical in its splendour, and that vivid sight is with me today, fifty years later. I can still hear its silence, broken only by the faraway sound of the sea.[13]

This intrepid pair of art students then decided to buy a wooden hut overlooking Chesil Beach. Such rustic retreats were affordable at the time, even for those of modest means. For example, in 1930 the writers and couple Sylvia Townsend Warner and Valentine Ackland had bought for £90 a cottage in East Chaldon, Dorset; this simple dwelling was later destroyed by a stray German bomb.[14] East Chaldon was then a poor, unobtrusive farming village but also in the 1920s and '30s a dynamic artists' and writers' colony — at one time all three of the Powys novelist brothers, John Cowper, T.F. and Llewleyn, lived there.

Before too long Gommon and his friend had found and furnished their own hut with 'the minimum of necessities', including 'a small battery wireless set'. David recalled

> another vivid memory … of lying on my camp bed at night listening to Chekhov's play *Uncle Vanya*. It was a windy night and the hut swayed and lurched, rose from the ground, squeaked and returned to the earth with a shudder. Then the rain started. Its sound intensified on our wooden roof, but the voice from the radio continued — 'and you and I, Uncle, dear Uncle Vanya shall see a life that is bright, lovely, beautiful. We shall rejoice.' The wind and the sound of the rain outside were now so loud it became difficult to hear the voice.[15]

Gommon's retreat to the sanctuary of an austere waterside hut is an experience of a kind shared by many poets, artists and composers through the ages. In a *haiku* poem, the renowned Japanese poet Yamaguchi Sodo (1642 —1716) evoked the sense of mystical expansiveness that he experienced in such a place:

> In my hut this Spring,
> There is nothing —
> There is everything![16]

Gommon shared with two other great English visionary painters of the same generation, Cecil Collins (1908—1989) and Patrick Hayman, a comparable range of epiphanic experiences, either in late adolescence or their early twenties.

In 1931 Collins and his wife, the artist Elisabeth Collins, settled in a secluded cottage in Buckinghamshire. Nourished by seventeenth-century metaphysical poetry, Cecil went on to develop his vision of the archetypal Fool — an iconic figure signifying qualities of compassion, 'a divine debonair spirit … and a careless empirical gaiety' (as he wrote in his book *The Vision of the Fool*) as well as 'the sorrow of life'.[17] In his view, 'the mechanized society of modern life … and its inhuman rejection of poetic consciousness, has defeated its own end'.[18]

In the late 1930s Hayman, living in remote New Zealand countryside, experienced what he called a sacred sense of 'a no-feeling, a feeling of nothingness'.[19] Then, nourished by the reading of poets such as Emily Dickinson and Hart Crane, and by knowledge of artists such as Munch, Chagall, Christopher Wood and the self-taught Cornish painter Alfred Wallis, he found that painting 'burst out of me with a great ease and release'.[20] Affinities between the youthful artists Gommon, Collins and Hayman are clear in this regard.

It was during the spring or summer of 1932 that Gommon went to carry out some work painting signage in a village called Iwerne Minster (about ten miles away from the birthplace of Tess in Thomas Hardy's novel *Tess of the D'Urbervilles*). During his lunch break, he went round to the village pub. 'As soon as I pushed open the door I was aware of a voice reciting … poetry I knew. It was [from *Rubáiyat* by] Omar Khayyam [1048—1131; the poem translated into English in 1859 by Edward Fitzgerald]!

> A Book of Verses underneath the Bough,
> A Jug of Wine, a Loaf of Bread—and Thou
> Beside me singing in the Wilderness—
> Oh, Wilderness were Paradise enow![21]

'Now it was not a common practice to recite poetry in country pubs in the 1930s. The reader was a very upright military-looking man. I noticed the polished shoes and the army beret worn at a very jaunty angle, the Woodbine cigarettes and the cough!' This new acquaintance explained 'that he had no time for the Church or God but the philosophy expressed [in this verse] meant everything to him'. After more conversation and ale, Gommon was invited by him to stay in his spare room. Gommon explained:

> He himself, Mr Pooley, lived in a hut at the bottom of a very long garden while his wife and three children lived in the cottage … He had tuberculosis … Certainly he slept out in that hut all through the year. The cottage stood on the slope of a hill and had quite a large garden with … fruit trees … To the south lay the long range of the Dorset heights from Bulbarrow Hill away westward to High Stoy right across the whole Blackburn Vale or in its old name the Vale of White Hart.

> I lived up on the slope of that hill all that summer and what a beautiful summer it was. I felt like one of those figures seen in a Chinese landscape painting in mystical communion with the world.

12. William Mayes, quoted from a written reminiscence about his friendship with David Gommon.
13. D. Gommon, from notes … 1980, p.1.
14. Claire Harman, *Sylvia Townsend Warner: A Biography* (London: Chatto & Windus, 1989), pp.96, 200.
15. D. Gommon, from notes … 1980, pp.1—2.
16. Yamaguchi Sodo, from *Haiku*, vol. II, 1950, translated by R.H. Blyth, quoted in Stephen Ellcock, *The Cosmic Dance* (London and New York: Thames & Hudson, 2022).
17. Cecil Collins, *The Vision of the Fool* (London, Grey Walls Press, 1947), p.19.
18. Ibid, p.25.
19. *Patrick Hayman: A Voyage of Discovery*, p.8.
20. Ibid,
21. Omar Khayyam, *Rubáiyat*, from one of four translated versions by Edward Fitzgerald made between 1859 and 1879, this excerpt is 'From "The Rubaiyat of Omar Khayyam"', published at https://poets.org/poem/rubaiyat-omar-khayyam. Gommon quoted a slightly different version in his 'notes … 1980', but it was very close to this one.

I painted landscapes, pub interiors, drew plants and insects, collected ...
wild flowers, roamed the countryside as far away as the Cerne Giant and
Maiden Castle, read Plato's Republic, Rousseau's Confessions and Darwin
and much poetry.[22]

From this time on Gommon was a keen cyclist (he did take his driving test
unsuccessfully six times but then gave up gracefully). As a young man he
often cycled vast distances — from London to Dorset (stopping on the way
to view Stonehenge) and on one epic trip (when he was 19) all the way to
Scotland (sending postcards at stages to his parents in Battersea), staying
along the way in youth hostels. He later explained that it was as a result of
a conversation with the poet Edwin Muir (*c.*1931) that 'I decided to buy a bike
and cycle, going first to Edinburgh and then on to the Isle of Skye.'[23] Peter
Gommon recalls his father's friend Teddy Pooley saying that he once took
David on a cycle ride to Cerne Abbas to show him the giant hill figure.
Ian Mayes, who knew David from about 1960 onwards, recalls that

what I remember most about those days [when they both lived in Harding-
stone] was his bicycle. You could hear him coming by the creaking chain;
I loved the sound. It was maybe a lady's bike; and as he cycled you could
see that he had a bit of a hump. I could hear his bike approaching — he
lived maybe four hundred yards away — and then came the knock on
the door. We would then talk at length. Though she was very interesting
herself, his wife Jean never participated in our discussions. Our interests
were so compatible. With his knowledge of art, literature and philosophy,
he was a very cultured man. Though I could never understand his interest
in Wyndham Lewis![24]

He and his new, verse-declaiming friend

cycled ... in the evenings ... to some of the villages he knew and called in
for the occasional drink. Our favourite village was Child Okeford, just below
Hambledon Hill, which we would climb ... and from the very top pick out
all the landmarks like Alfred's Tower in Somerset [and] then come down
to the pub, the Baker Arms ... It had a visually interesting group of regulars
who played skittles, shove halfpenny or cribbage. Some of these activities
carried on until midnight ... and to avoid the village policeman on the look-
out for lawbreakers, we all climbed out of a back window into the garden,
found our cycles, until we were safely distanced from the [pub] ...

This was often the most delightful part of the day, sometimes with moonlight or mist but always with such a range of scents, especially if the hay
meadow had been cut or the honeysuckle was flowering. And then there
were all the variety of sounds — foxes, badgers, sheep, cattle, owls. I still
have even now, fifty years later, a large reservoir of images and sounds
from that period — still as vivid as ever.[25]

He recalled that

after moving in the autumn from Chesil Beach and the hut, I lived for
a short time above a cow shed on Exmoor, some miles from Dunkery

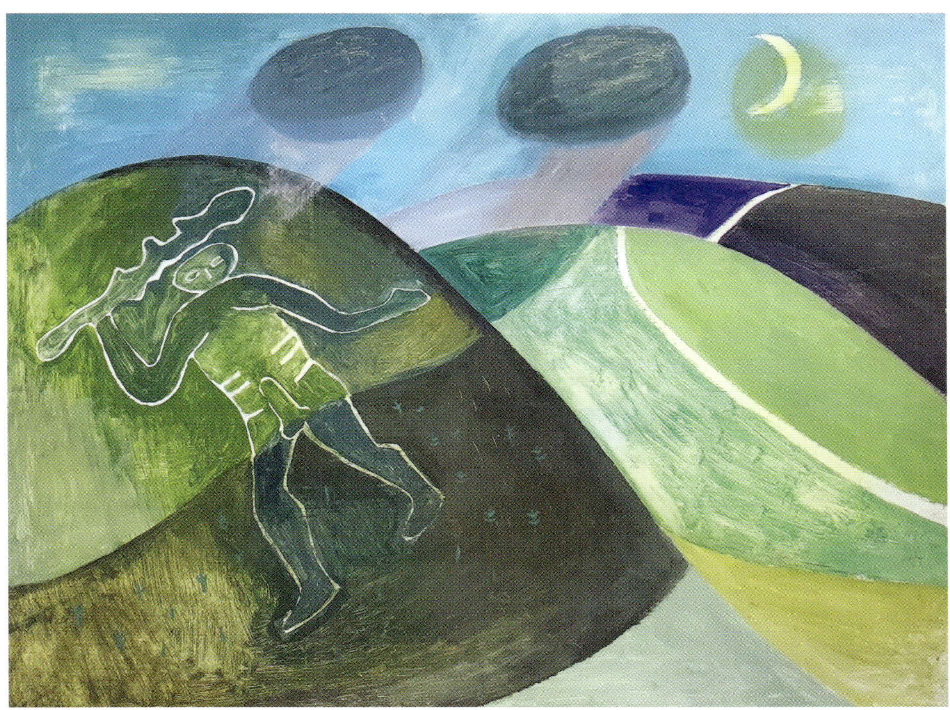

Cerne Abbas Giant
date unknown, oil on board, 92 x 122 cm
private collection

Beacon [the highest point on Exmoor and in Somerset], drawn there perhaps by its association with Coleridge and Wordsworth … the falling leaves red and gold, made continuous patterns in the sky as they fell.

I was painting prolifically at this time, especially in the evenings following a stay in the woods or on the moor, where I made notes and sketches. So many images, crystal clear … clamouring to be painted. As I worked I remember the distant sound of Minehead church bells as the ringers practised.[26]

For a fair period Gommon lived in the village of Hartgrove, where, says Peter Gommon, 'it was thanks to' the Pooley family 'that he had a roof over his head, sustenance and a critical audience'. His lifelong friendship with this family only deepened with time. Another remarkable encounter occurred around this time when 'on the Plymouth Road I met some Dutch students, two brothers and a sister, [who were] attractive with blue eyes and fair hair. Within a very short time, they had me pronouncing Van Gogh correctly …

'As a result of this meeting I was invited to Holland; the eldest brother worked in shipping and got me a very cheap passage on a cottage boat from [London's] St Katharine Docks.' He enjoyed a lengthy stay in Amsterdam,

studying the Rembrandts in the Rijksmuseum, especially *The Night Watch* and *The Jewish Bride* … The other impact came from seeing so many Van Gogh pictures together in the same gallery — and then in all the Dutch bookshops so many books by [the then best-selling contemporary British novelists] … Hugh Walpole and John Galsworthy being sold alongside unexpurgated copies of D.H. Lawrence's *Lady Chatterley's Lover* (long before this [then scandalous] novel was available in London).[27]

22. D. Gommon, from notes … 1980, pp.4—5.
23. Ibid, p.3.
24. Ian Mayes, from a conversation with the author, June 2022. On the interest in Lewis, Kate Currie wrote to the author in July 2022: 'When David tried to explain why he admired Wyndham Lewis to me when I was a child, it was very much to do with the excitement of Vorticist art in complete contrast to Impressionism' and 'I think we need to be clear that David would have abhorred Lewis's later political views; he always described the awful impact of seeing tanks parked in Battersea Park with guns aimed at workers' houses during the 1926 General Strike. He recalled also as an eleven-year-old supporting the Labour Party's first MP of colour, Shapurji Saklatvala, when he was re-elected as the Communist candidate for Battersea in 1924.'
25. D. Gommon, from notes … 1980, p.5.
26. Ibid, p.2.
27. Ibid.

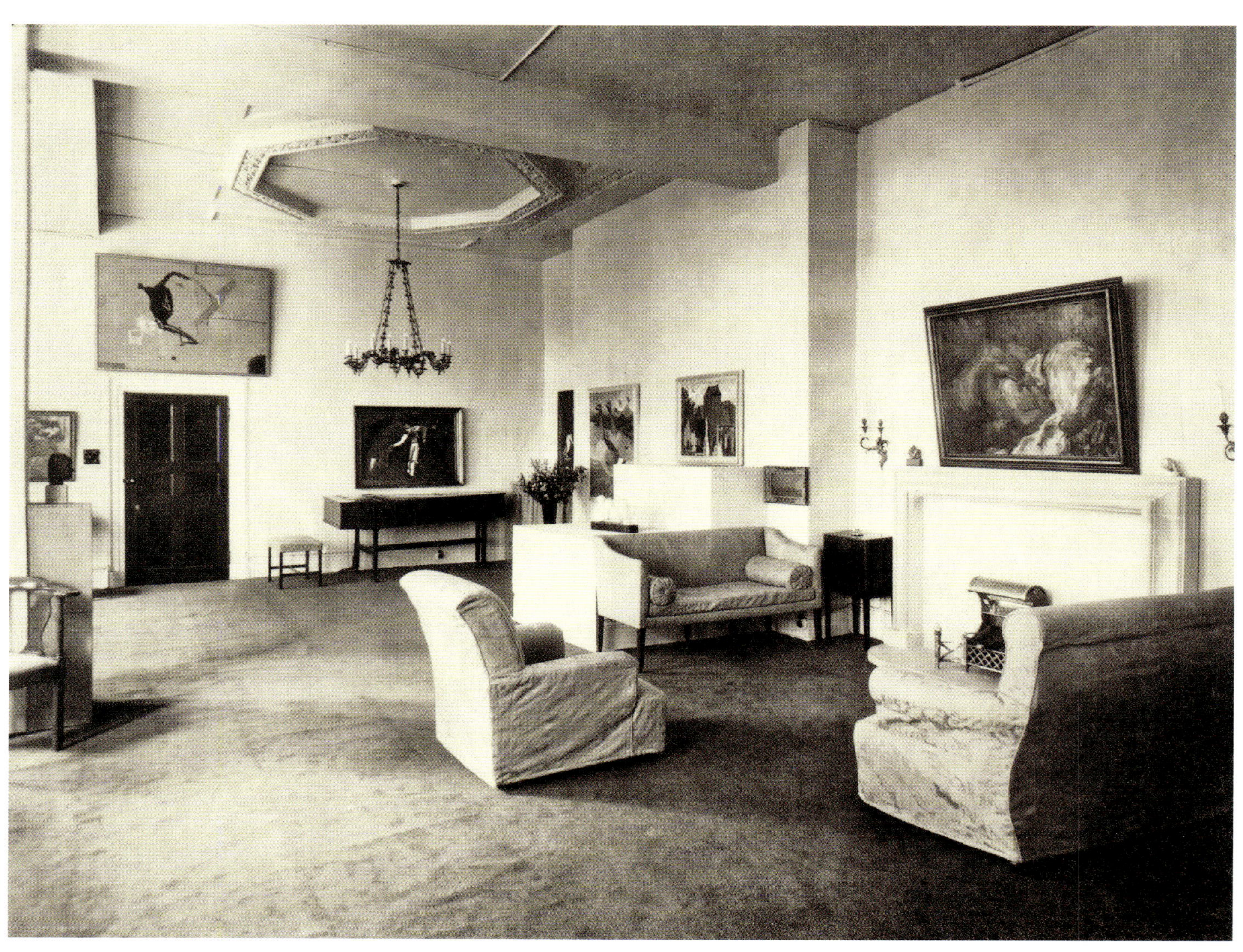

The Wertheim Gallery, exhibiting 'Modern Paintings', October 1930 / The Lucy Wertheim Archive

Lucy Wertheim
pioneering gallerist and inspiring patron

ALL THE PAINTINGS GOMMON WAS MAKING DURING THIS SEMINAL youthful period went to Lucy Wertheim — whom he had first met in 1931; that remained the state of affairs until several months into 1939.

> I was eighteen. She had a splendid gallery in London's Burlington Gardens just off Bond Street. I became a member of her Twenties Group [so-called because all her artists were under thirty] — along with Christopher Wood [who had died in August 1930], Cedric Morris, Victor Pasmore, Phelan Gibb, Frances Hodgkins, Kenneth Hall, Alfred Wallis, Rodney Gladwell. None of them in 1932 were well known. I was still an art student and to me they were simply other struggling painters.[1]

Members of the Twenties Group included Barbara Hepworth, Roger Hilton, Robert Medley, Mervyn Peake, Elizabeth Rivers and Norah McGuinness.

Lancashire-born Lucy Carrington Pearson had married Dutch-born Paul Wertheim (1878—1952) in 1906. Becoming a British citizen in 1915, he was a successful merchant who in the spring of 1931 was appointed Dutch Consul in Manchester. Initially Lucy had favoured buying what she called 'restful pictures',[2] but in the late 1920s was shaken out of her cultural complacency on encountering the Modernist art of Edward Wadsworth (her brother-in-law's cousin).

Soon after that she met the pioneering New Zealand-born painter Frances Hodgkins (1869—1947) (who had first moved to England in 1901), who introduced Wertheim to the exciting potential of modern art. Lucy was taken by her new friend's 'wit, the charm of her warm voice, her felicity of expression' — and though at first bewildered by Hodgkins' painting, she went on to buy one of the artist's pictures, which she said 'enchanted' her.[3]

In her 1947 memoir *Adventure in Art*, Wertheim described an incident which helped to spark the genesis of her gallery: 'Frances exclaimed to my husband, "Your wife should open a gallery for us poor artists: her enthusiasm would make it a success!" ... Those words[,] however[,] spoken more than half in jest, sowed a seed in my mind that was to bear fruit later.'[4]

Indeed many of the artists she showed and supported were poor and struggling at the time — certainly that was true in the case of Hodgkins herself, and it also applied to Christopher Wood (she bought a number of his paintings for her private collection and often sent him cheques when he

1. D. Gommon, from notes ... 1980, p.2.
2. Lucy Wertheim, *Adventure in Art* (Lewes: Unicorn, 2022), p.17.
3. Ibid, p.12.
4. Ibid, p.14.

was in need of funds) and Gommon himself. The modest stipend — 'two pounds a week plus all the paints I needed'[5] — that Gommon received from Wertheim over a number of years afforded him independence as a painter.

As cultural commentator Ariane Bankes has noted, the Wertheim Gallery 'was in its own way a phenomenon: the first gallery to be opened and run by a woman in London's West End'.[6] Photographs of the original gallery reveal a comfortable yet restrained setting in which a visitor would feel at home amongst pictures hung quite sparsely on whitewashed walls, able to sit on pale, capacious sofas or at a table to read, discuss and contemplate.

A *Sunday Referee* newspaper review (25 January 1931) of a Twenties Group show — including pictures by Gommon — noted: 'One of the few places in London one can see the works of *les jeunes* displayed with taste and dignity is the Wertheim Gallery ... These young people ... have, as far as I know, no market at all. But ... most of them have the potential of artistic development.'

Philippe Garner, who is married to Lucy Wertheim's granddaughter Lucilla, wrote in April 2025,

> We had for many years been custodians of Lucy's gallery archive until we recently gifted it to the Paul Mellon Centre for Studies in British Art. I have spent my career in the art world and so have a helpful frame of reference against which to situate and appreciate her 'Adventure in Art'.
>
> Lucy was a remarkable figure in her day, making her mark as a collector and a dealer in the art that touched her. She was a determined character who worked from instinct, responding with passion and commitment, notably to the work of young artists in whom she recognised creative integrity. She had no time for the slick and polished, finding charm and beauty rather in the slightly awkward, in the unpretentious yet poetic and expressive picture-making that is sometimes characterised as 'naïve' or 'outsider' art. These are labels that I fear serve inadequately to describe the particular vision of the artists she championed, among whom David Gommon, with his lyrical subjects and his simple, un-laboured graphic fluency, provides a perfect example.[7]

In the summer of 1934 Lucy Wertheim moved her gallery to ground-floor rooms at the Albany in Piccadilly. 'I saw those gracious rooms with their Adam fireplaces and harmonious proportions as the perfect setting for my pictures',[8] she wrote. Precarious finances — and the onset of the Depression — marked her time as an art dealer (there are alarming references to bailiffs in her memoir); and though she tried hard to remain independent, sometimes only her husband's economic guarantees enabled her to stay in business.

In order for the paintings she showed to become better known and more widely accessible, she created *The Wertheim Circulating Picture Society*, through which (at no charge for loans except for transport and insurance costs) artworks were regularly sent to be displayed in schools, public galleries, theatre foyers and even some restaurants around the country.

THE WERTHEIM CIRCULATING PICTURE SOCIETY
Exhibition March 19th   to   April 1st (noon)

Loaning pictures has been a feature of the Wertheim Gallery for the past few years. These loans up to the present have been confined to Public Galleries, Schools, Colleges, Hostels, Foyers of Theatres Etc. From now onwards, on payment of a subscription, private clients may also take advantage of these loans, exchanging the pictures at their pleasure. The following is the rate :—

A yearly subscription of **2** guineas entitles a member to the loan of a picture up to the value of **5** guineas

A subscription of **3** guineas to a picture up to the value of **10** guineas

A subscription of **5** guineas to a picture up to the value of **20** guineas

And upwards by special arrangement

At any time during the year the member may purchase the picture deducting the amount of his subscription

Pictures for Loan include examples by :—

Frances Hodgkins	Matthew Smith	Sickert	Christopher Wood
Phelan Gibb	Gommon	John Melville	John Banting
Cedric Morris	Dunlop	Skeaping	Henry Stockley
Alfred Wallis	Tchelitchew	Vivin	Kolle Pascin

Announcement card for the Wertheim Loan Collection
The Lucy Wertheim Archive

There was, for example, a Twenties Group loan exhibition at Worthing Art Gallery; and she noted with satisfaction that about 27,000 visitors attended an 'Exhibition of Six Modern Painters' at Salford Art Gallery.[9]

Wertheim was happy to take on artists she believed in, unswayed by any lack of artistic reputation or critical acclaim. When she first encountered Gommon, he was an unknown art student. Kathleen Walne (1915—2011) — a student at Ipswich School of Art and 'the despair of her art master' there — was given a solo show by Wertheim in 1935 after she was favourably jolted by the naïve Expressionism of what she called Walne's 'vivid and dynamic paintings'.[10] Henry Stockley (1892—1982) was a London bus driver. Having been rebuffed by many London galleries, he was on the verge of burning his enchanting paintings — ingenuous urban and park scenes on odd bits of left-over materials, with marvellously awry perspectives — before Wertheim took him on and gave him a solo show.[11]

The year after the death of the great French self-taught artist Henri Rousseau ('Le Douanier' ['the customs officer' — his profession]) in 1910, the first book on the artist was published. It was by Wilhelm Uhde, a German art critic living in Paris and also a collector and interpreter of works by Picasso, Matisse and Derain. Uhde had befriended Rousseau in his final years. In the 1920s Uhde discovered and promoted four great self-taught French artists under the title 'Painters of the Sacred Heart': these were his own maid, Séraphine Louis; a gardener, André Bauchant; a postal worker, Louis Vivin; and a circus artist, Camille Bombois. Wertheim gave Vivin (1861—1936) a solo show in February 1931 but was dispirited to find that 'neither the critics nor the public were yet attuned to the naïve vision of this artist', though 'A few enthusiasts (among them Jim Ede from the Tate Gallery) were frequent visitors to the show.'[12]

Wertheim described how, in the summer of 1930, she went to visit Uhde at his home in Chantilly.[13] She was overawed by art she saw there by the young

5. D. Gommon, from notes … 1980, p.5.
6. Ariane Bankes, 'Lucy Wertheim: A Pioneering Woman and Her Contemporaries', in *Adventure in Art*, p.165.
7. Philippe Garner writing to the author in April 2025.
8. Wertheim, *Adventure in Art*, p.117.
9. Ibid, p.106.
10. Ibid, p.194.
11. Ibid, pp.75—6.
12. Ibid, p.54.
13. Ibid, pp.48—50.

German painter Helmut Kolle (1899—1931), Uhde's long-term partner; she then met the artist, whose dark, resoundingly emotive Expressionist portraits — imbued too with a Francophile delicacy and flair — had already achieved renown in Paris. She gave Kolle a solo show in her new gallery in early 1931; but Kolle had become ill and couldn't attend. Tragically, he died later that year, aged only 32. Wertheim wrote that the 'exhibition was not liked by the public … and my feelings were jarred day after day'[14] as the critics and public received it harshly.

The longest chapter in Wertheim's memoir is devoted to Christopher Wood (1901—1930). In the spring of 1929 she had bought a small painting by the artist at a Bond Street gallery, and returning there later that day was introduced to him. 'I felt that I was in the presence of a very unusual personality, sensitive yet dynamic, and we seemed to become friends from [this] moment.'[15]

Nathaniel Hepburn has written, 'The fortuitous nature of this encounter was to some extent fictionalised for her book as it seems that Wood's introduction to Lucy Wertheim was made by [Cedric] Morris and Lett Haines. Wood writes to Lett Haines: "I have also to thank you for Mrs Wertheim who is a dear & a charming woman. She has bought one of my last pictures of Dieppe."'[16]

Soon Wertheim was helping support Wood in his itinerant life, spent between Paris, Britanny, Cornwall and London. She had intended to open her gallery with an exhibition of Wood's latest paintings. But then came the news that he had died at the age of 29 in August 1930, either by suicide or accident when, deranged by opium, he flung himself under the wheels of a train at Salisbury station.

She wrote that, at this terrible news, 'I remember a feeling of numbness overcoming me. What mattered my gallery now?'[17] It was only the patient kindness of Wood's mother that helped persuade her to continue with her gallery venture. In February 1932 she held a memorial exhibition of her own collection of Wood's paintings.

It is unlikely that David Gommon would have met Christopher Wood (who died when Gommon was 16); however, he was deeply moved and inspired by Wood's paintings — and those by the St Ives ex-fisherman artist Alfred Wallis. Kate Currie says, 'I do remember my father saying he could remember the news of Christopher Wood's death, and Lucy Wertheim going to the rescue in some way.' The magical originality of Wood's pictures impressed and inspired a whole generation of younger British artists. Wood was his own best critic, as when he wrote about his late Breton pictures of 'churches in a curious, lonely country by the sea, very restful, but very strong and determined'.[18]

By the mid-1920s the English 'Seven and Five Society' was a key exhibiting route for young Modernists such as Ben Nicholson and the painter Cedric Morris. In a letter to Jim Ede from Paris in May 1925, Nicholson wrote, 'We saw Cedric Morris — he is a charming person & … interesting work … I can see possibilities of painting beginning to "breathe" in London.'[19] (Morris claimed to have discovered Wallis even before the famed occasion when, as Nicholson wrote, he and Wood — one summer day in 1928 in St Ives — 'passed an open door in Back Road West and through it saw some paintings of ships and houses on odd bits of paper and cardboard nailed up all over the wall';[20] they knocked and met the ex-sailor working on his pictures. Wood cited Wallis's influence, referring to him as 'not a bad master' in a 1928 letter to Winifred Nicholson,[21] and Ben Nicholson intimated that in Wallis he had found the master he was looking for.

Lucy Wertheim herself visited Wallis in the summer of 1930. 'I found the old man in his little hovel (for it seemed to me no better) ... painting away ... He had a predilection for the ends and sides of Quaker Oat boxes!' She showed 20 of his works in early 1931. To her great disappointment, 'They did not cut much ice with either the public or critics.'[22]

One of the works that Wertheim acquired on her visit was *Boats at Quayside*, signed by Alfred Wallis on the reverse of the canvas. It has transpired that only the lower part of the picture — the lighthouse, harbourside and sea (as well as two seagulls on the quayside) — was painted from scratch by Wallis. Recent technical analysis has revealed that Wallis had painted over an earlier (perhaps unfinished) composition which included these elements seen in the final painting: the quayside, a number of figures as well as two fisher-men in boats, the building facades and the intermingled pink and blue sky. Although these original elements remain, Wallis overlaid a good part of the buildings with his own admixed silvery grey and white paint, adding his own tall, narrow house to the left of the portrayal of a café. Further research has established that the original composition, a view of Concarneau, was made by Christopher Wood during (and possibly still worked on after) his stay in Britanny, ending in September 1929. It is assumed that Wood gave this can-vas to Wallis in March 1930, when he was in St Ives. Wertheim visited Wallis only a few months later.

In *Adventure in Art*, Wertheim wrote:

> Now, after a number of years, Wallis is coming into his own and his
> work is frequently compared with that of Christopher Wood. Indeed,
> I have often heard it remarked that Wallis influenced the young painter ...
> As I possess a painting by Alfred Wallis done on the back of a photograph
> of one of Christopher Wood's pieces [this does not appear to be a reference
> to the Wood/Wallis painting *Boats at Quayside* that she owned], I some-
> times wonder if it was not the other way about![23]

Boats at Quayside, which was displayed in the Kettle's Yard house in Cam-bridge from 13 February to 9 June 2024, has been described by curators at the art gallery and house as 'a unique document of a dialogue between artists, who both found sustenance in the other's vision and friendship, dur-ing a period when broader critical support for modern art in England was lacking'.[24]

Wertheim and Rex Nan Kivell (1898—1977) — the New Zealand-born art dealer and collector who joined London's Redfern Gallery in 1925, becoming

14. Wertheim, *Adventure in Art*, pp.50–52.
15. Ibid, p.23.
16. Nathaniel Hepburn, *Cedric Morris and Christopher Wood: A Forgotten Friendship* (London: Unicorn Press, 2012), p.84.
17. Wertheim, *Adventure in Art*, p.41.
18. Christopher Wood, from a 1930 letter to Lucy Wertheim, quoted on the website of the Robert Upstone gallery, London, www.robertupstone.com/wood-church-at-treboul.html.
19. Quoted from Ben Nicholson, letter to Jim Ede, in Hepburn, *Cedric Morris and Christopher Wood*, p.45.
20. Hepburn, *Cedric Morris and Christopher Wood*, p.77.
21. Letter from Christopher Wood to Winifred Nicholson, 31 October 1928, Tate Archive.
22. Wertheim, *Adventure in Art*, pp.150–51.
23. Ibid, p.151.
24. 'Alfred Wallis and Christopher Wood: A Meeting on Canvas', article on Kettle's Yard website, 12 February 2024, www.kettlesyard.cam.ac.uk/stories/alfred-wallis-and-christopher-wood-a-meeting-on-canvas.

its Director in 1931 — were two rare London gallerists then responsive
to the quality of Wood's art and that of first-rate self-taught painters such
as Wallis and the ex-mining artist George Bissill (1896—1973). Raised in a
Derbyshire mining village, Bissill had become a miner somewhere between
the ages of 11 and 13; he then gladly escaped the mines by joining the war
effort in 1915. Invalided out of the army in 1918, after being trapped for three
excruciating hours in a tunnel he was digging after its roof collapsed (it was
with a cruel irony that his mining expertise was utilised in his duties as a
Sapper, one of these former coal miners drafted in mainly from the pits) —
and then later gassed in the trenches — he began studying at Nottingham
School of Art in 1920. He explained, however, that 'The mine is in short the
only art school I ever had.'[25] In 1922 Bissell 'came to London and worked
as a pavement artist outside Bush House [in the Aldwych], which was then
being built. I rarely took more than 3 shillings a day. My existence was very
precarious.'[26]

Soon Bissill's distinctive talent started to be recognised. Nan Kivell gave
him his first solo exhibition at the Redfern Gallery in April 1925; his work
sold well and the former miner, described at the time as 'a quiet dark
youth of 28',[27] found himself famous; he had further critically acclaimed
shows there in 1926 and 1927.

Wertheim showed his paintings at her gallery, also including them in her
Loan Collection alongside works by Gommon, Wallis, Wood, Hodgkins,
Vivin, Wadsworth, Walne, Sickert and Matthew Smith. Bissill's abstracted
renditions of arduous, claustrophobic coal-mining existence have a
poignancy and sensuous muscular immediacy about them perhaps
not even rivalled in fine comparable pictures by Moore and Sutherland.

Gommon wrote:

> Rex Nan Kivell encouraged me by buying some of my work. It was
> some time after my first meeting with Wertheim that she suggested
> that perhaps we might come to some financial working arrangement.
> She would give me two pounds a week plus all the paints I needed and
> she would have all the work I did; this arrangement lasted until several
> months before the war. This meant she had practically all the work I did
> between 1931 and 1939; and I did a great deal. Some of this work she still
> had in London when the bombing started, and some of it was destroyed
> in the great fire raids.
>
> It was Mrs Wertheim who gave me an exhibition in London [in 1934] …
> I cannot envisage those years from 1932 until the outbreak of the war
> without her and her financial help and interest and encouragement,
> and through her I was introduced to and met so many people.[28]

Writing in *The Observer* (article date unknown), the art critic and artist Jan
Raven was impressed by this 1934 show, saying that, despite his young age,
'he almost displays the power and authority of a painter of 20 years standing.
Such virtuosity at so early an age tempts one to wait and see what direction
Gommon's strange imaginative gift will take.'

Pages from the Wertheim Gallery Visitors Book give an insight into its unique allure: visitors in 1930—1 included painters such as Eileen Agar, Vanessa Bell, Harold Harvey, John Piper and Paul Nash and the linocut artist Claude Flight; the photographer Cecil Beaton; the writer and literary editor John Lehmann; and the Bloomsbury hostess Ottoline Morrell. They came to see exhibitions which included works by Wood, Wallis, Gommon, Walne, Kolle and other members of the Twenties Group. From 14 to 24 December 1931, an 'Exhibition of Pictures by Children — Arranged by [the painter] Nan Youngman' was held at the gallery; these were pictures by children between the ages of seven and seventeen, from all around the country. Children's art was then increasingly appreciated for its expressive immediacy and candid truth-telling. In the catalogue Youngman wrote: 'the aim of this exhibition is to show that there is a kind of picture which is characteristic of childhood, and which children produce wherever they are given sympathetic direction, with the opportunity of working in their own way'.

During his time as an assistant curator at the Tate Gallery, from 1921 to 1936, Jim Ede (1895—1990) collected works by artists such as Brâncuşi, Ben and Winifred Nicholson, Henri Gaudier-Brzeska, David Jones, Wood and Wallis; his collection was later displayed in the four cottages he converted in Cambridge, a space where pictures and *objets d'art* were arranged by him with artful ease, and where he lived and welcomed student visitors. In 1966, Ede gave the house and collection to the University, creating the Kettle's Yard art gallery. Ede and Wertheim's artistic sensibilities were clearly akin, indicated by these words by Ede: 'From Kit [Wood] I learnt a clarity of perspective in regard to contemporary painters, a direct enjoyment ... which became a touchstone in the world of what has been called naïve painting, and so came Douanier Rousseau and with him no doubt many works now held by Kettle's Yard ... David Jones was different: he brought shape to the ephemeral in me, his profound vision of essential truth supported me. He had tolerance not usual in artists and this enlarged my vision ... I think it was in 1926 I first began to get paintings by Alfred Wallis. They would come by post, perhaps 60 at a time, and the price fixed at 1/-, 2/-, 3/-, according to size ... I never met him but he wrote me many interesting letters and I was grateful for the unsophisticated beauty of his work.'[29]

Two paintings displayed in Kettle's Yard have an especial affinity to pictures Gommon was producing as a young man: *The Glen*, by a boy of 12 called Winston McQuoid (1909—1984), an intuitively sophisticated work with what Ede called 'a total innocence of all endeavour or contriving';[30] and *Skye*, a land-and-seascape by Kate Nicholson (1929—2019), which Ede wrote was 'so vibrant in its sweeping width of outlook, even at the age of seventeen ... totally disregarded as children's nonsense — the animals are a little queer ... but they are individuals, and all is so open and full of air'.[31]

The gouaches that Gommon painted for Lucy Wertheim in the 1930s are notable for their luminous intelligence and radical ingenuity but also for their blissful childlike immediacy — 'a certain quality' (adapting here Cecil Collins' words evoking the 'inviolate eternal innocence' of his own Fool figure) of 'continuous wisdom and compassion that heals with fun and magic. It is the joy of the original Adam in men.'[32]

25. Frances Wilson. 'George Bissill Mines Hell for a New Depiction of Civilisation', *Apollo*, February 2022, p.2.
26. Peter Seddon, 'George Bissill — Derbyshire's Forgotten "Pitman Painter"', Derbyshire Life, 19 October 2015, https://www.greatbritishlife.co.uk/magazines/derbyshire/22631998.george-bissill---derbyshires-forgotten-pitman-painter.
27. Ibid.
28. D. Gommon, from notes ... 1980, p.5.
29. Jim Ede, *A Way of Life: Kettle's Yard* (Cambridge University Press, 1984), pp.15—16.
30. Ibid, pp.188—9.
31. Ibid, p.195.
32. Cecil Collins, *The Vision of the Fool* (London: Grey Walls Press, London, 1947), pp.21—2.

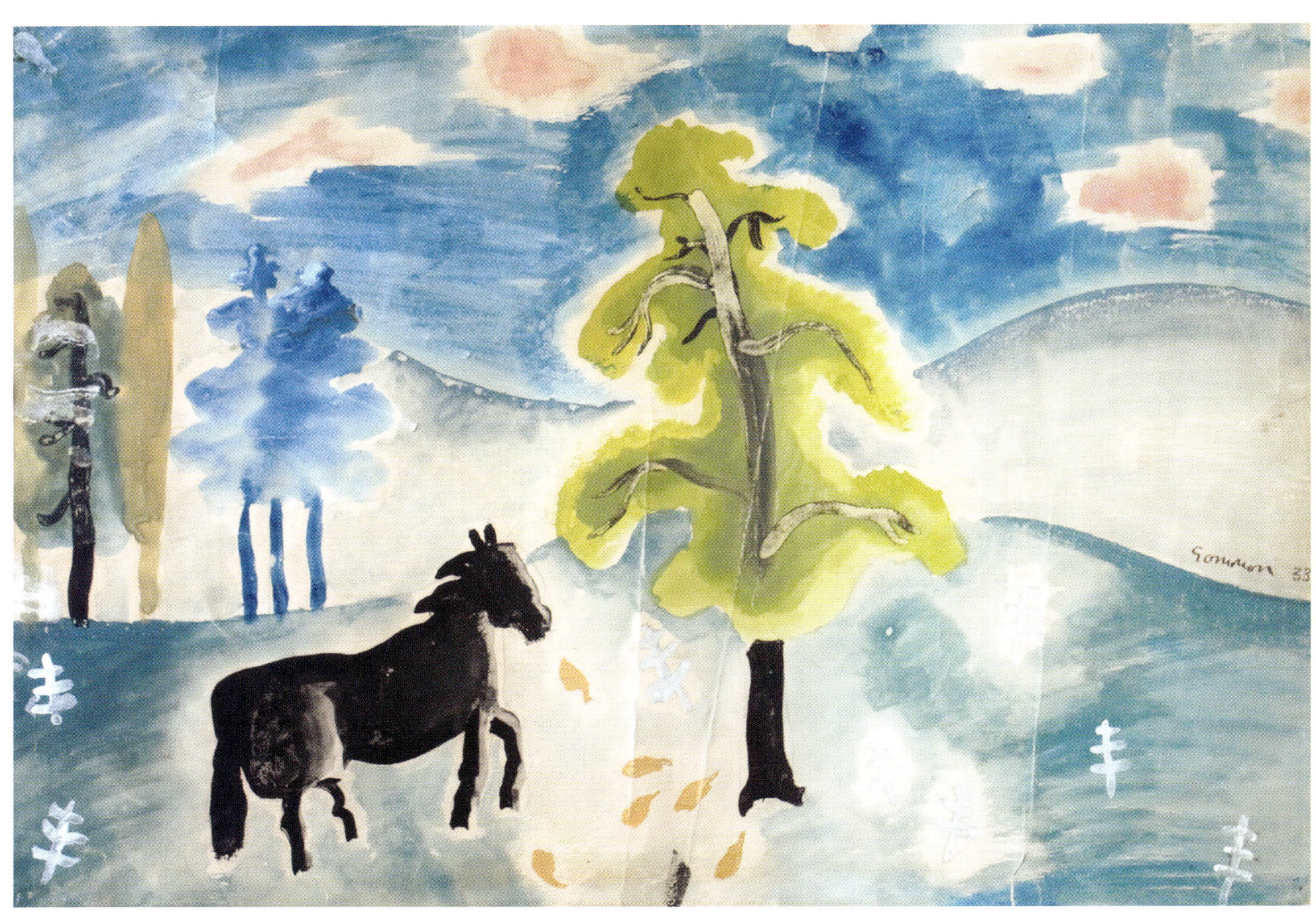

Untitled (The Black Horse) / 1933, watercolour and gouache on paper, 37 x 54 cm / private collection

Equine and balletic images of freedom

HORSES FEATURE IN A NUMBER OF GOMMON'S 1930S PAINTINGS. IN two versions of a *Red Horse* theme (*c.*1934), the animal assumes majestic proportions, with a muscular, dark red body and an impressive tail. Its overall outline is charged with a fiery glow, which in one of the versions [p.11] is the same colour as that of two distant tree trunks, their forms half obliterated by swathes of opaque landscape green. In the other version [below], the horse is attended by a mysterious figure of equal monumentality, whose colours echo the background landscape.

In such works the horse appears as both earthbound and as a symbol of primordial freedom (wild equine portrayals go back to Palaeolithic times). Gommon evokes the creature's slow-breathing peacefulness as well as its galloping vigour in images imbued with a mysterious, playful gaiety. There are resonances here of wild Expressionistic horses painted in blue, pink, red, ochre and ivory tones by Franz Marc and Wassily Kandinsky — in the years before the First World War — as members of *Der Blaue Reiter* (*The Blue Rider*), a group inspired by central and eastern European folk art and children's art.

A parallel closer to home can be made with paintings Ben Nicholson had been making in the late 1920s, such as *Cumbrian Landscape* (*c.*1928; Kettle's

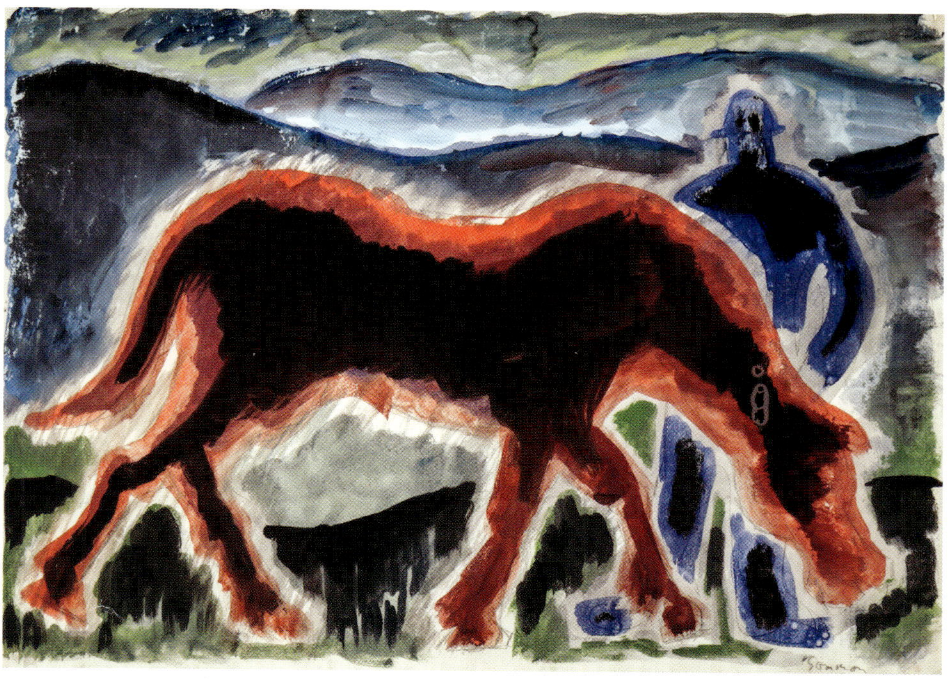

Untitled (Red Horse)
*c.*1934, gouache on paper, 38 x 56 cm
Wertheim Estate

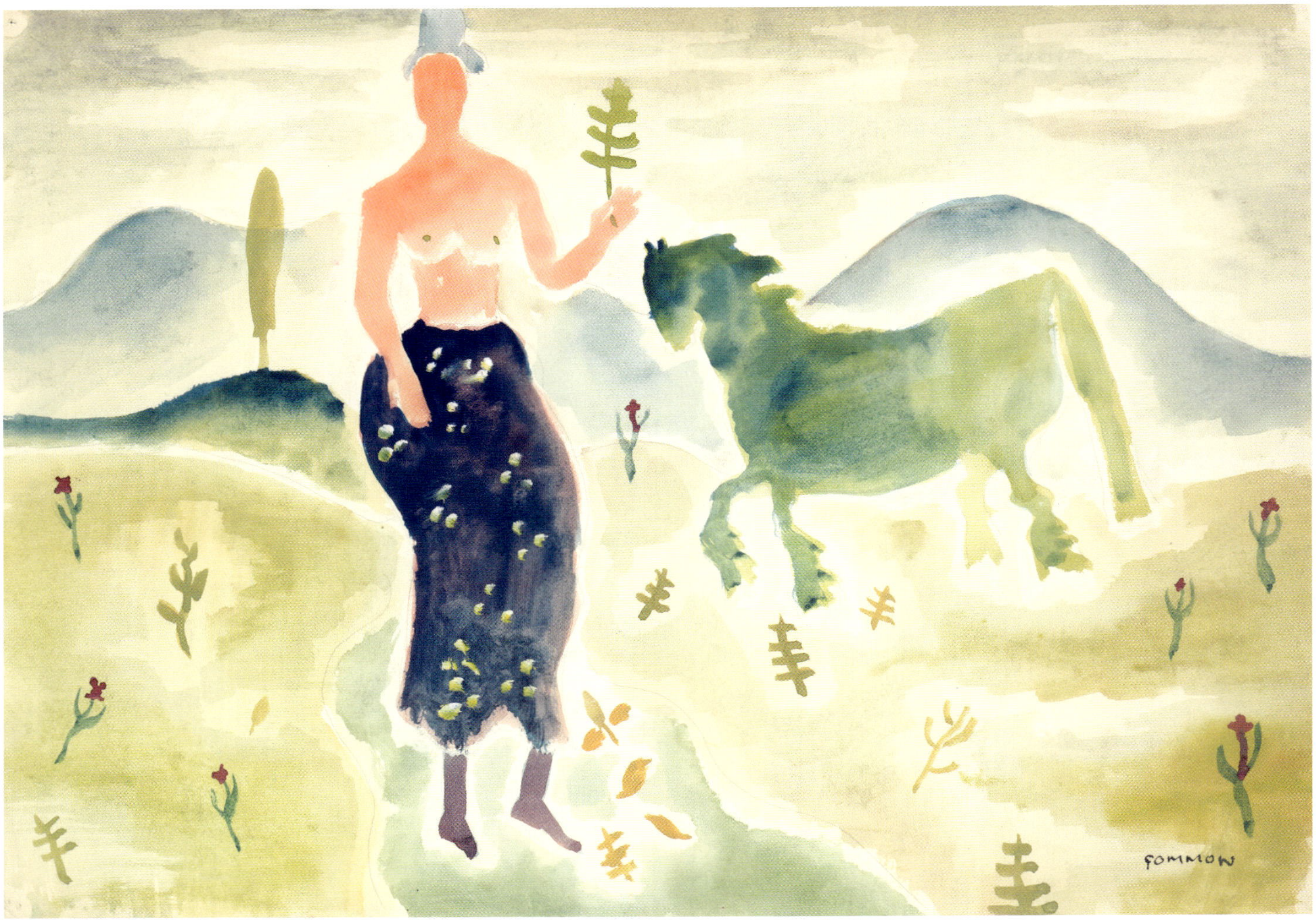

Untitled (Semi-Nude Woman Holding Flower — with Galloping Horse)
*c.*1931—9, watercolour and gouache on paper, 38.2 x 56 cm / Wertheim Estate

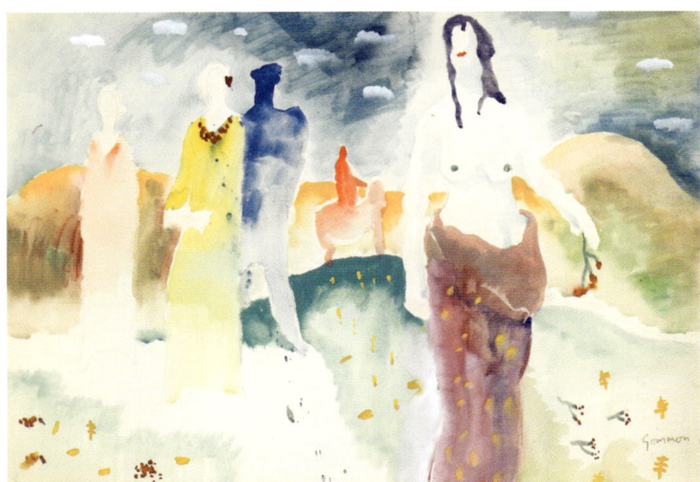

Untitled (Woman with Three Figures)
*c.*1931—9, watercolour and gouache on paper, 38.2 x 56 cm
Wertheim Estate

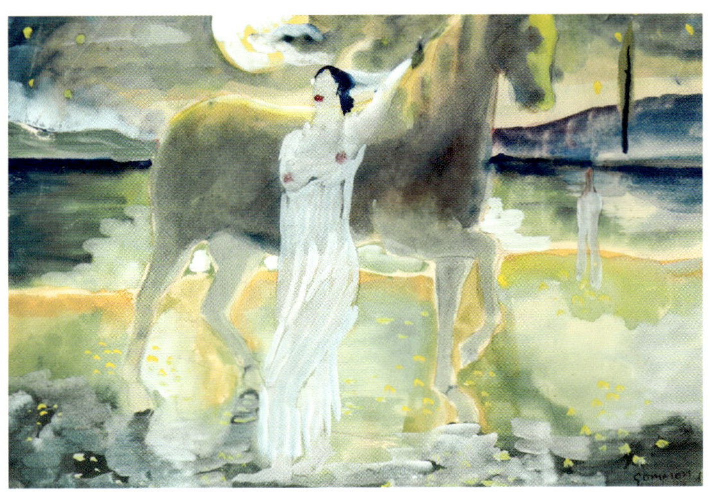

Tess
1934, watercolour and gouache on paper, 37 x 54 cm
private collection

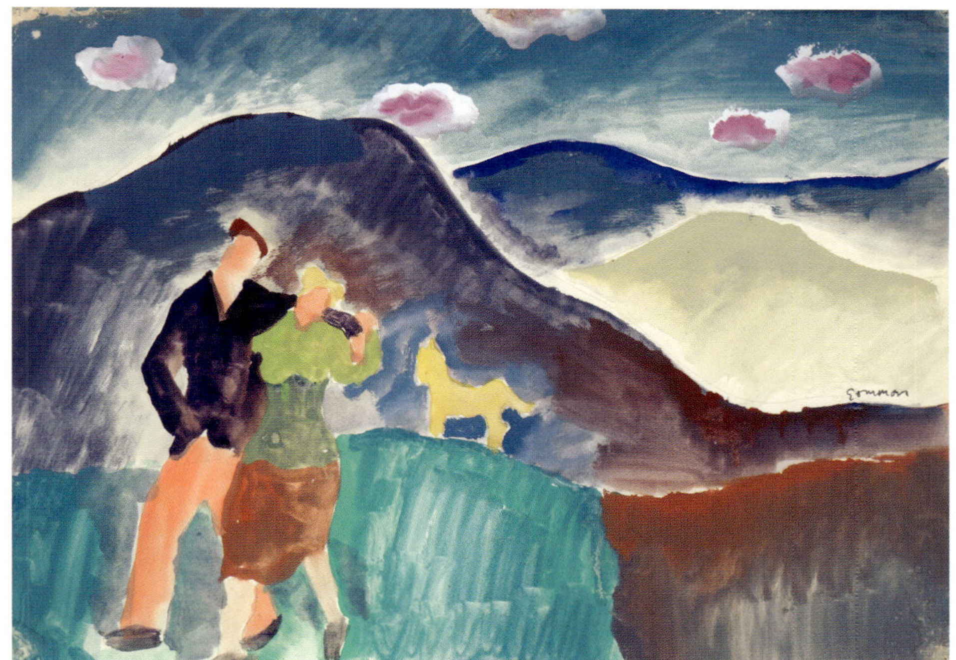

**Untitled
(Couple Arm in Arm — with Yellow Horse)**
*c.*1931—9, watercolour and gouache on paper,
38.2 x 55 cm
Wertheim Estate

Yard), in which two gently animated horses are portrayed with a deceptive childlike simplicity in silver-grey silhouette against a washed-out turquoise field — lines of trees above in similar tones, balletically beckoning.

The poet Kathleen Raine, a perceptive writer on Blake, W.B. Yeats and Cecil Collins, observed: 'when he [Ben], Winifred [Nicholson] and Christopher Wood were working together [in Cumbria around 1928], there was a quality of feeling in Ben's work which, for all his later mastery, it perhaps later lost.'[1]

In Gommon's watercolour and gouache *Untitled (Semi-Nude Woman Holding Flower — with Galloping Horse)* [facing page], a tall, featureless, bare-breasted young woman — quite likely an imaginative portrayal of Hardy's Tess — stands upright in a pose of hieratic stillness, holding aloft an abstracted flower form like some esoteric talismanic object. Vigorously inclining towards her is a horse of translucent mixed green, yellow and blue hues, its bluish eye just visible. The atmosphere here is of transcendental happiness.

The ecstasy of young love is evoked in his idiosyncratically colourist picture — *Untitled (Couple Arm in Arm — with Yellow Horse)* [above], in which a blank-countenanced couple walk jauntily together on a turquoise ground; they are counterpointed by the miniscule silhouetted figure of a yellow horse (against a blue and russet hillock) reaching towards them.

Blank (or nearly featureless) faces — portrayals in which only (or mainly) the white of the paper is seen — are typical of Gommon's works on paper at this time. There are echoes here of Christoper Wood's paintings from 1930 — such as *The Yellow Horse* (a picture acquired by Wertheim), in which, against a bleak wintry landscape, a horse in pale ochre is set as an iconic still presence against the snow, and the two melancholy male figures to the left have faces distressed to oblivion. There are resonances here too of archaic Cycladic head sculptures in white marble, whose stark minimalism

1. Kathleen Raine, *The Land Unknown* (London: Hamish Hamilton, 1975), p.138.

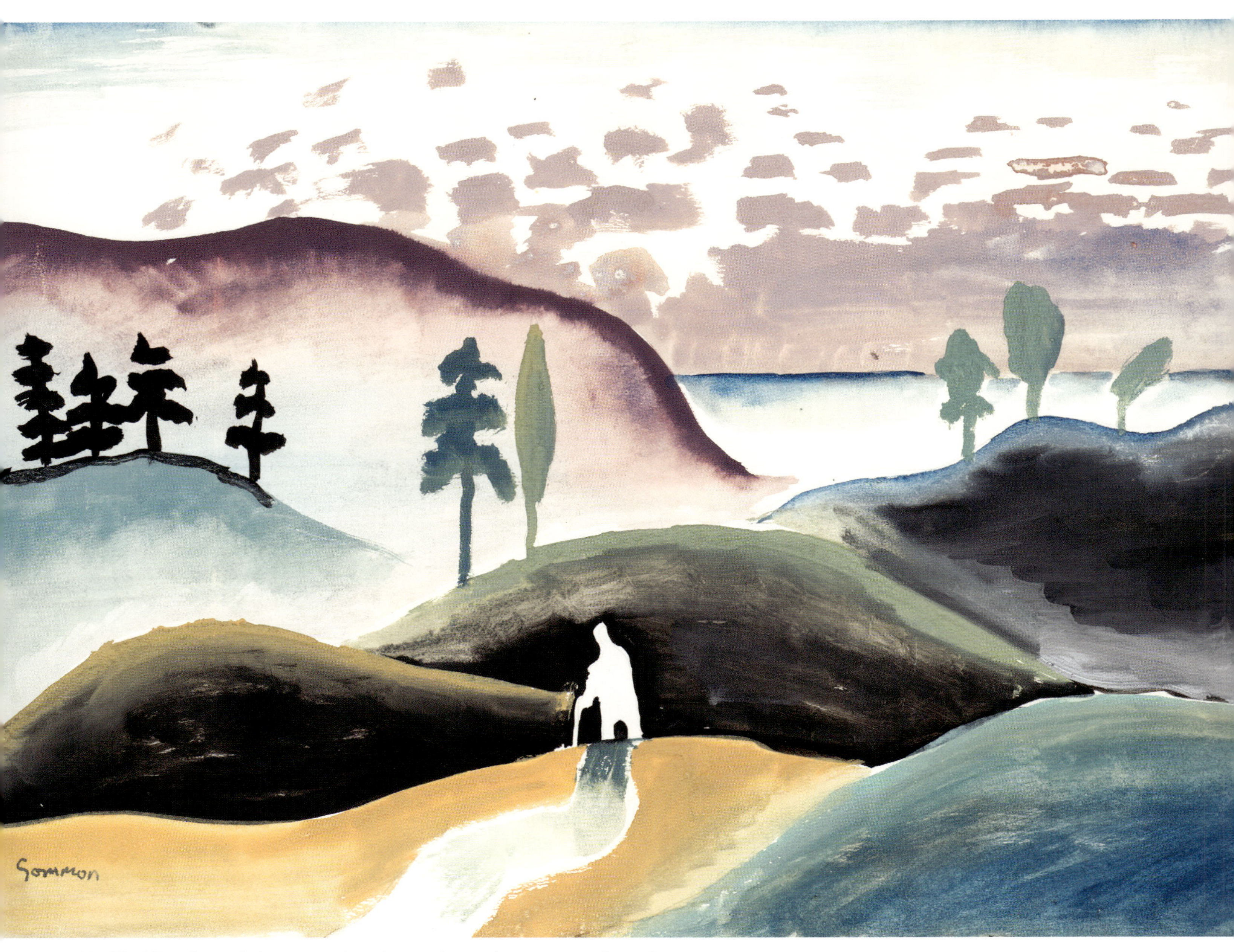

Untitled (Landscape) / *c.*1934, watercolour and gouache on paper, 38.3 x 56 cm
Auckland Art Gallery Toi o Tāmaki, New Zealand

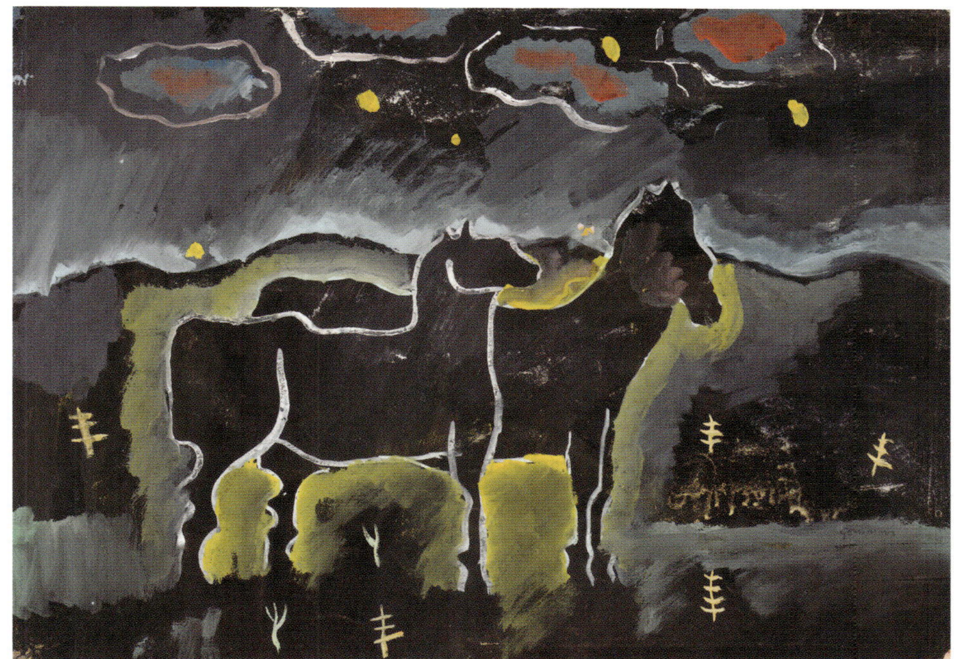

Horses
*c.*1931—9, gouache on black card,
38.4 x 56 cm
Queensland Art Gallery (Qagoma),
Brisbane, Australia

helped inspire mysterious, mask-like faces in art by Modigliani, Picasso and Brâncuşi [for example, see left].

In Gommon's *Horses* gouache [above], the unadorned black card is itself eloquently expressive — evoking not only much of the night sky (with its outrageously swollen stars) but also the ground (strewn with the repeated motif of simple linear, starlit flowers) and the blackened, monumental bodies of the two horses themselves, outlined in chalky white. This is a painting imbued with (using the eighteenth-century poet Henry Vaughan's metaphysical term) 'A deep, but dazzling darkness'.[2]

It was around 1931 that Gommon was introduced by his new Dorset friend and host Mr Pooley to the Orkney-born poet Edwin Muir (1887—1959), whom he then visited at his home in Hampstead. In their wide-ranging discussions there was clearly a meeting of minds. Muir was, all his life, himself enchanted by the reality and symbolism of horses — writing about them as golden, seraphic creatures which, as a boy, he had first seen coming in from his father's fields,[3] their gigantic forms 'filling me with a stationary terror and delight from which I could get no relief'.[4]

Some early pictures — like *Untitled (Woman in Red with Dog)* and *Untitled (Woman Walking Her Dog — with Yellow Horse)* [both overleaf] — not only depict young female figures as delicately silhouetted bodies of coloured light but also illuminate their dogs in similar fashion, devoid of any detailed features; these appear as gentle, sprightly, companionable creatures, enjoying the air as much as their 'owners'.

Gommon's *Untitled (Landscape with Object or Seated Figure)* [p. 39] appears like a theatre set of indecipherable strangeness: a sexless figure in grey (with broad-brimmed hat) is depicted sitting on a grey chair or stool in the middle of nowhere, so to speak — an enigmatic spectator of a landscape of trees and

2. Henry Vaughan, 'The Night', in Alan Rudrum (ed.), *Henry Vaughan: The Complete Poems* (Harmondsworth: Penguin Books, 1976), p.290.
3. Edwin Muir, 'Horses', *Edwin Muir: Collected Poems 1921—1958* (London: Faber & Faber, 1960), pp.19—20.
4. Edwin Muir, *An Autobiography*, (Edinburgh: Canongate Books, 2000), p.12.

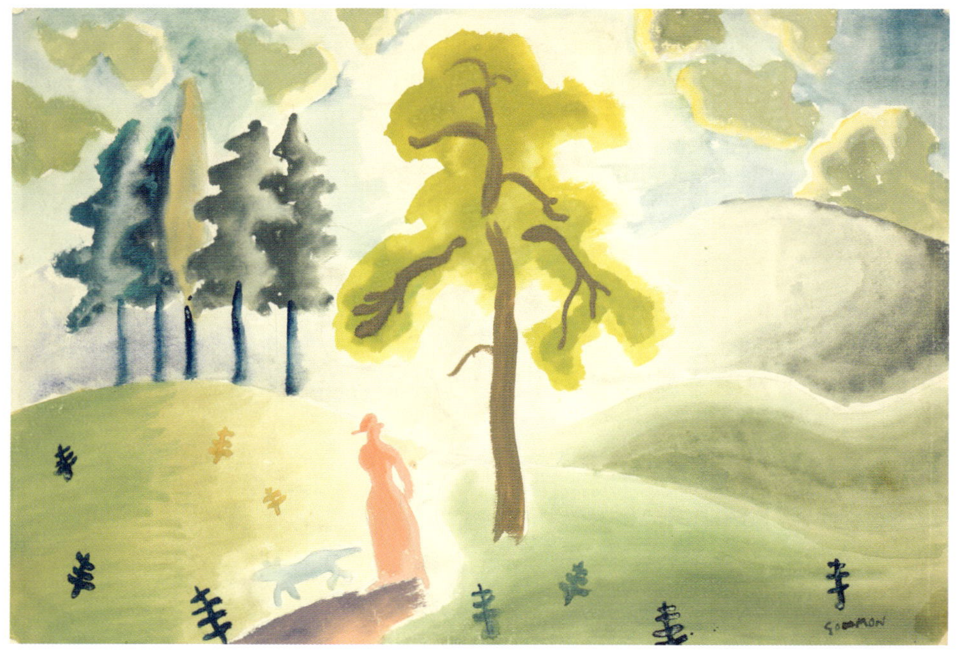

Untitled (Woman in Red with Dog)
*c.*1931—9, watercolour and gouache on paper,
38.2 x 56 cm
Wertheim Estate

undulating hills. Or it may be that the supposed seated figure is actually some imponderable surrealistic object (with maybe an ambiguous suggestion too of a human element).

Other pictures of this period by Gommon appear less hallucinatory in atmosphere, and as such look forward to some of the landscape pictures he produced after 1945. The former include the scenes *Untitled (Cart and Yellow Horse)* [p.40], showing two harvesters loading hay into a cart; the dynamic *Ploughing* [p.40]; a panoramic wintry *Landscape* with birds as bold, black shapes swooping and swirling [unillustrated]; and *Untitled (Landscape with Two Birds)*, its fields, copses and hedges depicted in a Fauvist-like palette [p.41].

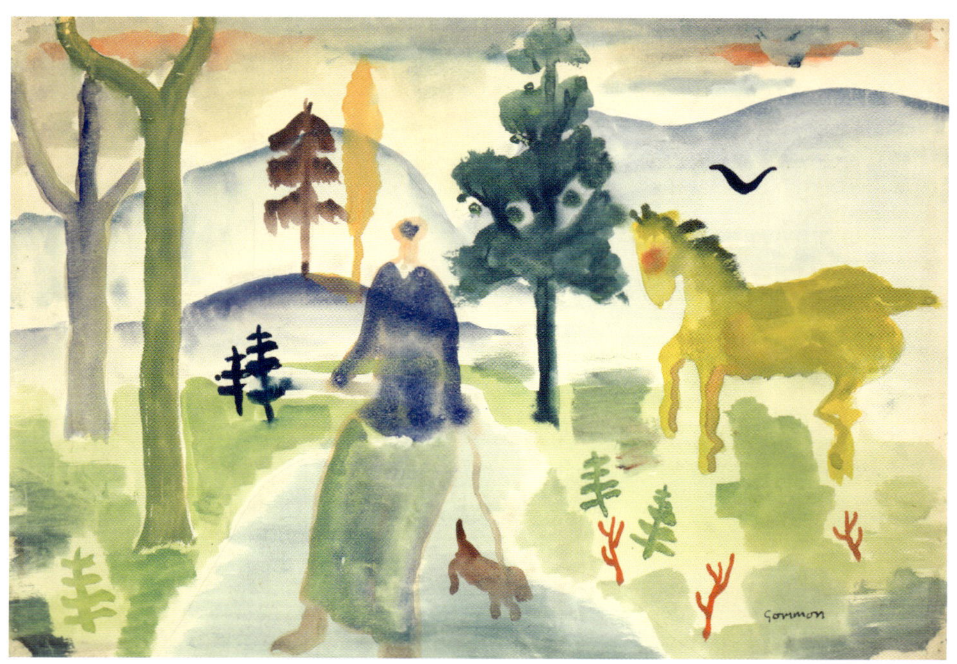

**Untitled (Woman Walking Her Dog
— with Yellow Horse)**
*c.*1931—9, watercolour and gouache on paper,
38.2 x 56 cm
Wertheim Estate

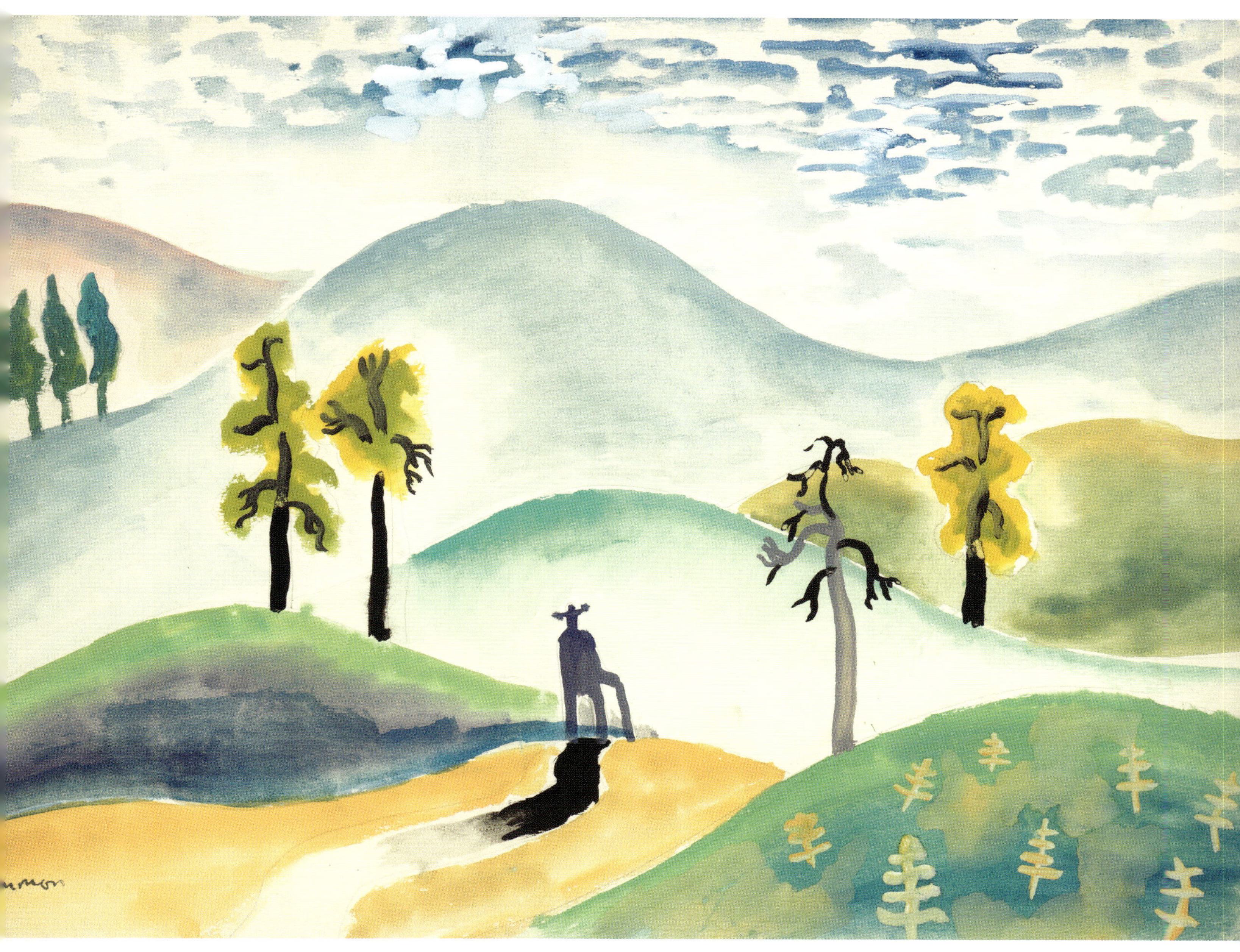

Untitled (Landscape with Object or Seated Figure) / *c.*1931—9, watercolour and gouache on paper, 38.2 x 56 cm / Wertheim Estate

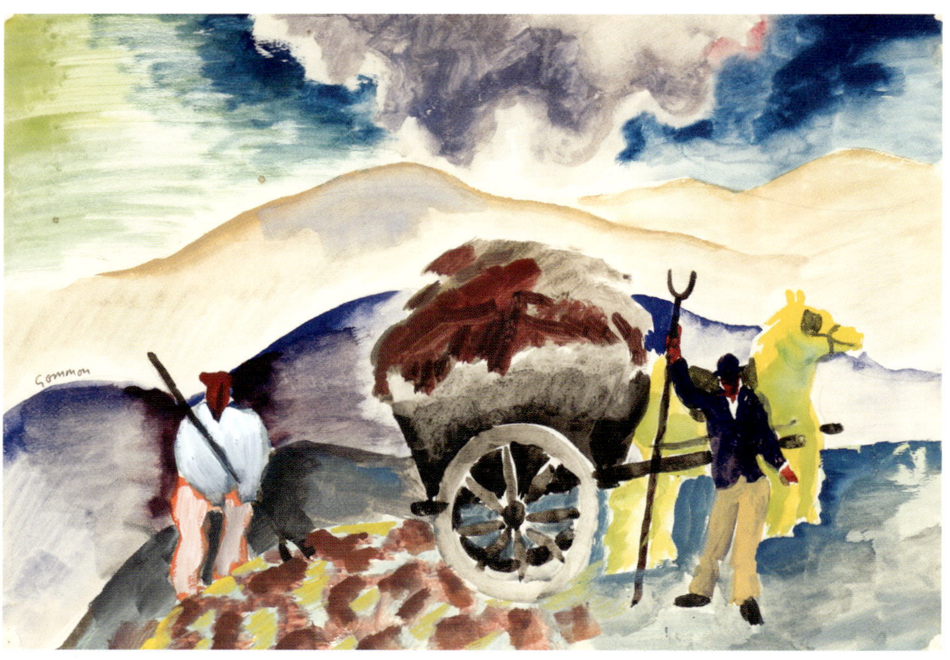

Untitled (Cart and Yellow Horse)
*c.*1931—9, watercolour and gouache on paper,
38.5 x 55.9 cm
Auckland Art Gallery Toi o Tāmaki, New Zealand

The last painting conjures up something of the terrain described by Thomas Hardy in *Tess of the D'Urbervilles* (1891):

> An up-hill and down-dale ride of twenty-odd miles ... brought [Clare] ...
> to a detached knoll ... whence he again looked into that green trough
> of sappiness and humidity, the valley of the Var or Froom. Immediately
> he began to descend from the upland to the far alluvial soil below, the
> atmosphere grew heavier; the languid perfume of the summer fruits,
> the mists, the hay, the flowers, formed therein a vast pool of odour
> which at this hour seemed to make the animals, the very bees and
> butterflies, drowsy.[5]

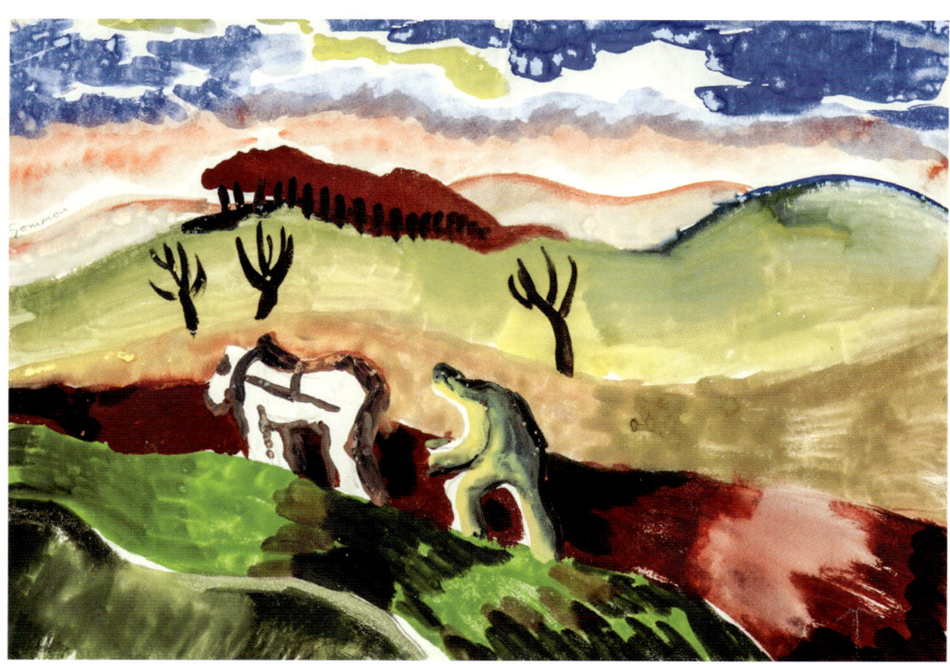

Ploughing
*c.*1931—9, watercolour and gouache on paper,
38 x 56 cm
whereabouts unknown

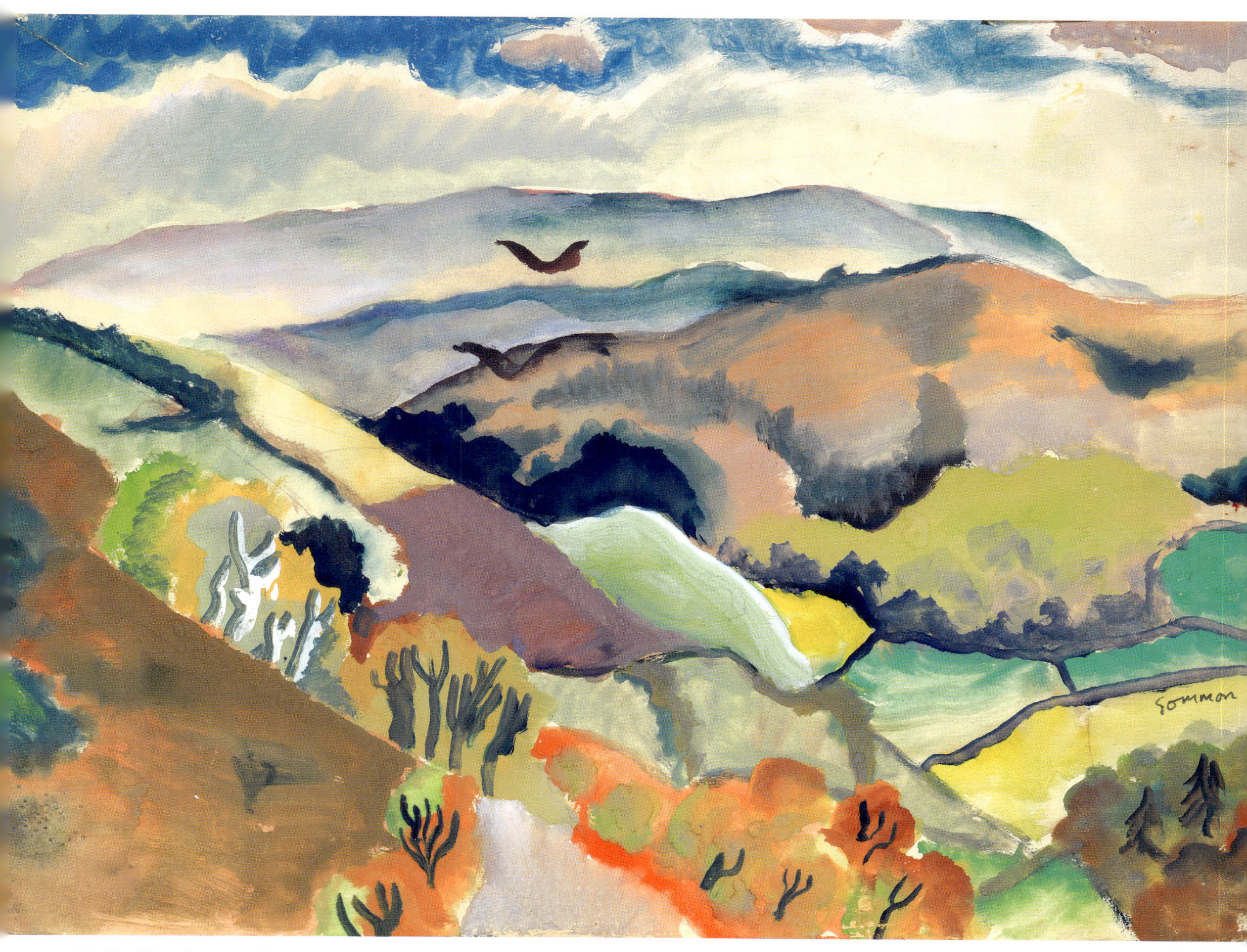

Untitled (Landscape with Two Birds) / *c.*1931—9, oil on cardboard, 38 x 51.3 cm / Wertheim Estate

5. Thomas Hardy, *Tess of the D'Urbervilles*.
(Oxford University Press, 2008), p.186.

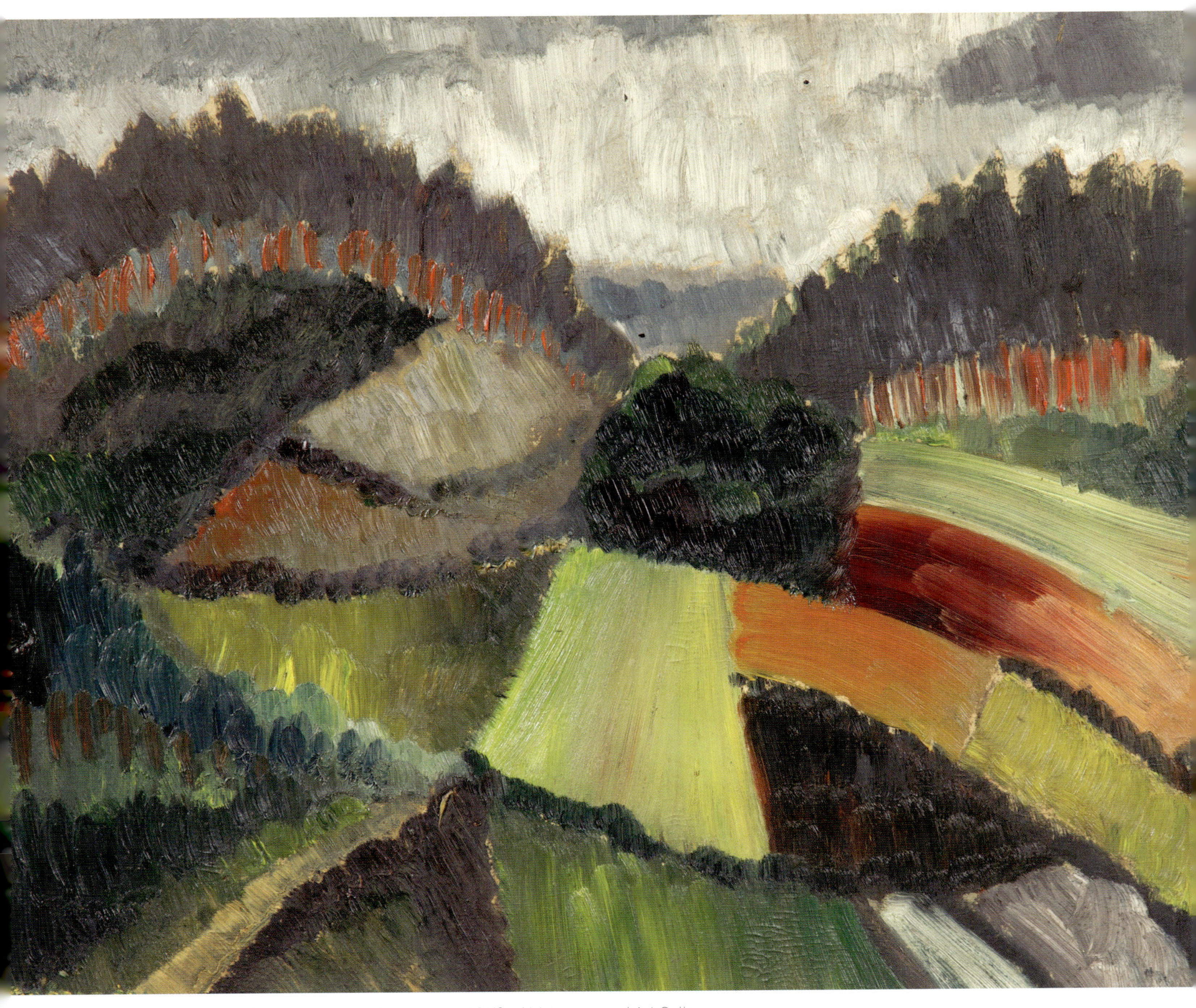

Landscape / *c.*1933, oil on cardboard, 38 x 51.3 cm / Salford Museums and Art Gallery

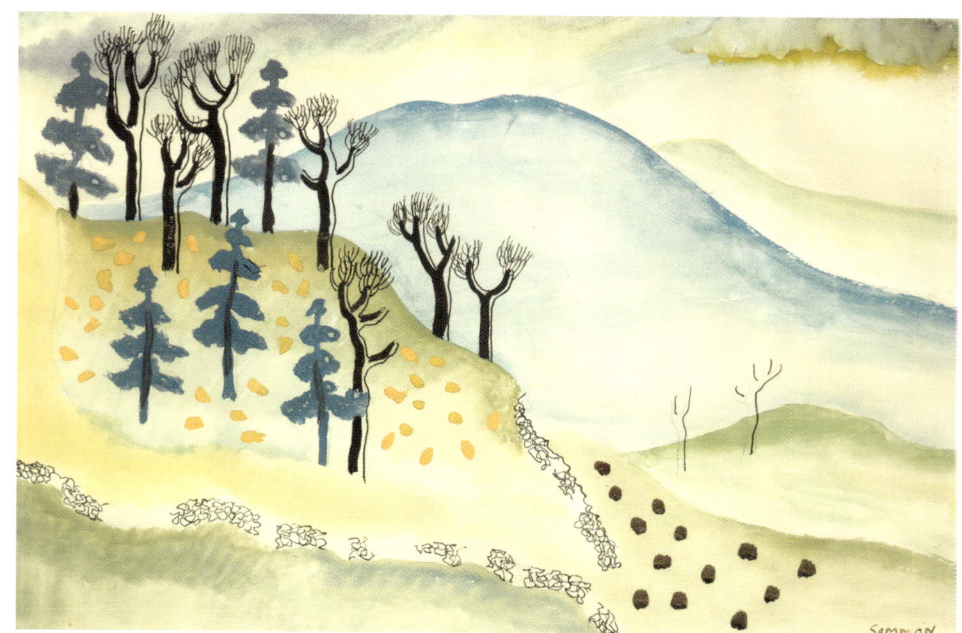

Trees in a Landscape
*c.*1931—9, pen and ink and watercolour,
38 x 56 cm
private collection

The relatively unspoilt 1930s rural Dorset Gommon knew was in some respects still close in nature to that known by the nineteenth-century poet and priest William Barnes (1801—1886) — although in both periods there was a good deal of poverty and deprivation, as well as embittered class relations, in the county. As John Betjeman wrote in an essay on Barnes, Barnes's poems in local dialect recall the days 'when Dorset villages really were remote and white lines went up chalk hills from thatched village hamlets. No aeroplanes, no poles, no tarmac — just bells and footpaths. On weekdays the rumble of wagons and on Sundays the sound of bells and always the rustle of leaves and singing of birds and the sight of the clouds travelling over the parish. Real deep country.'[6] Gommon was fortunate himself to have experienced this kind of 'real deep country' (even though increasingly there was the noise and fumes of motor cars and buses on tarmac roads along with the thick acrid smoke from speeding trains) — in perhaps the last days when thousands of miles of footpaths and bridleways around Britain were still open to horses.

Street Corner, Battersea, Saturday Night [p.45] is a rare surviving 1930s picture by Gommon of urban life. It depicts a young couple (the young man with a bowler hat and a Prussian blue tie or neckerchief, the young woman with rouged cheeks and a jet bead necklace) seen in profile walking on a pavement. The shoulder of her pale, filmy dress half obscures a figure in high heels behind, wheeling a black pram under a street lamp. In the background two shadowy male figures look into the pale blue void of a shop window. This is a quotidian scene in which an ordinary Cockney couple in their dapper prime are seen as archetypal lovers, the passing pram an allusion perhaps to their procreative powers.

Two 1934 oil paintings evoke the daredevilish atmosphere of the Baker Arms pub in Child Okeford — with its 'visually interesting group of regulars who played skittles, shove halfpenny or cribbage. Some of these activities carried on [illicitly] until midnight ...'[7] In one of these paintings, *The Card Players (The Baker Arms)* [overleaf], the faces of two pipe-smoking regulars

6. John Betjeman, *Trains and Buttered Toast* (London: John Murray, 2006), p.209.
7. D. Gommon, from notes ... 1980, p.5.

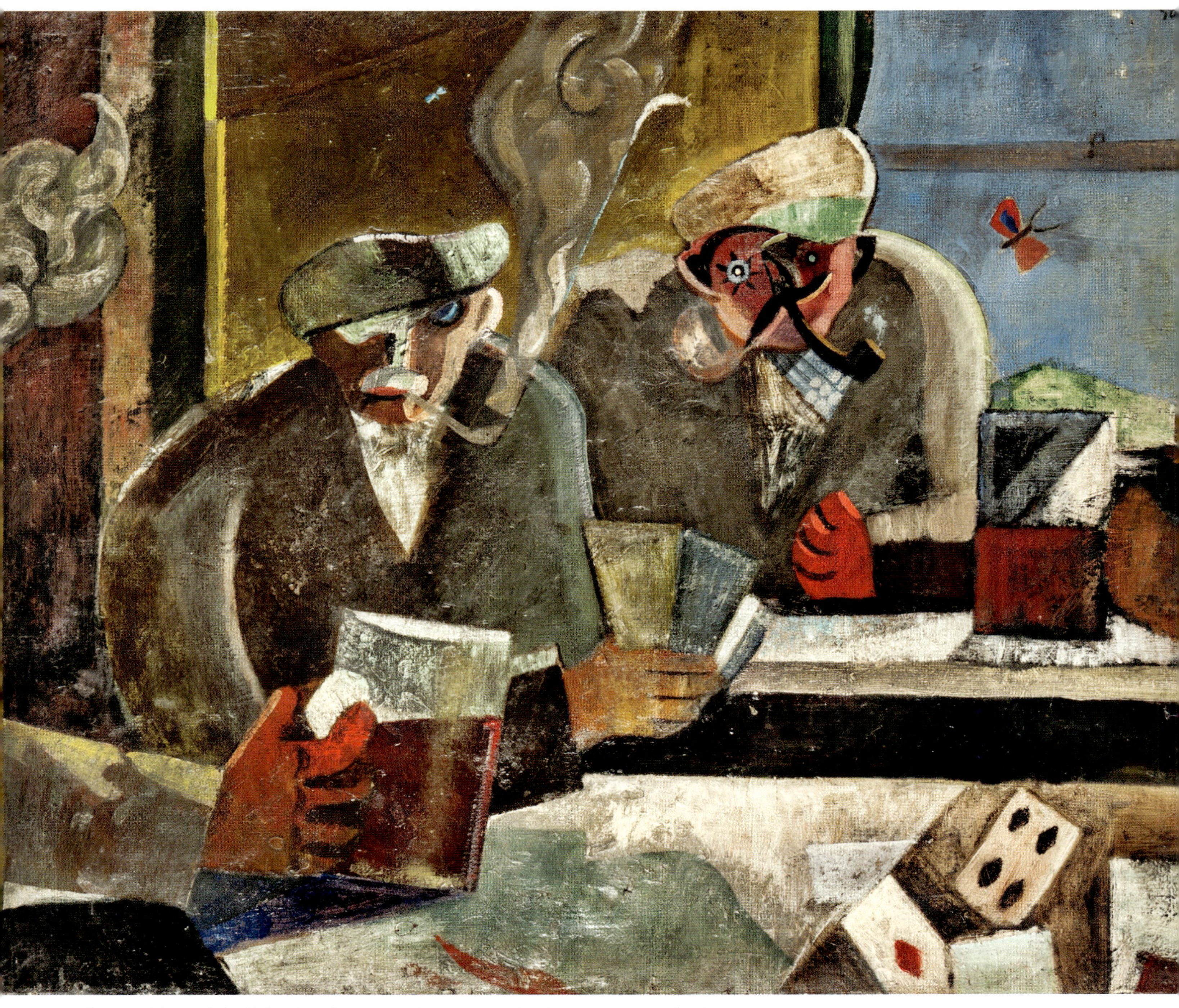

The Card Players (The Baker Arms) / *c.*1933, oil on canvas, 68 x 81 cm / private collection

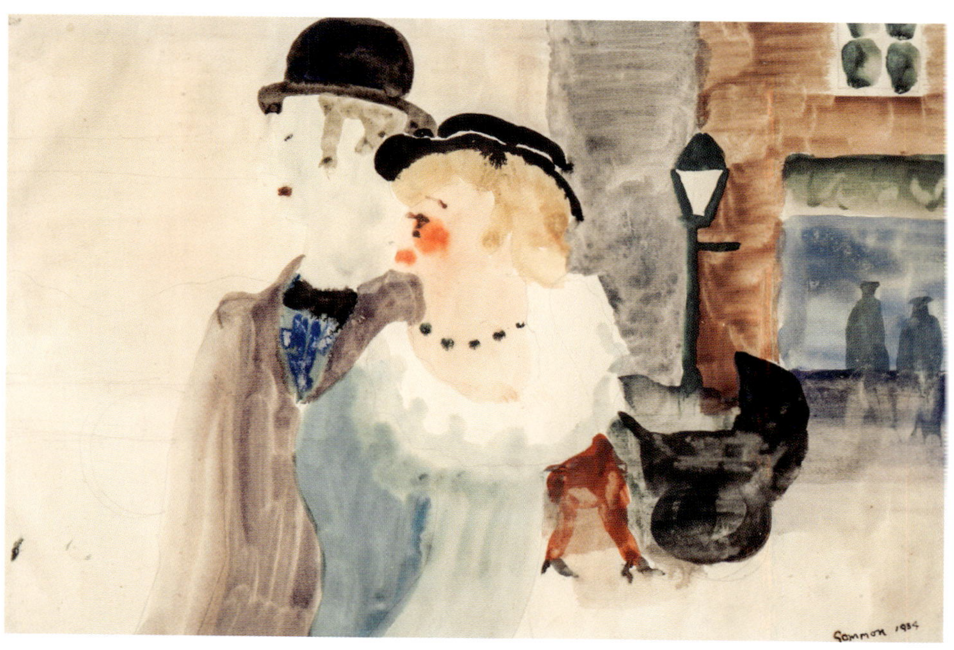

Street Corner, Battersea, Saturday Night
1934, watercolour and gouache on paper,
36 x 53 cm
private collection

are an admixture of oddly askew moustaches and eyes both concealed and staring intimidatingly (one eye perhaps a glass eye). A third, largely hidden, regular is represented by a vast, blood-red fist proffering a huge, cuboid tankard of beer. Pipe-smoke swirls have here taken on an almost rococo flourish, like ornate plasterwork. Scattered playing cards appear in some later paintings by Christopher Wood; and card and dice players recur in the artist Edward Burra's contemporaneous visions of louche nightclubs and bars. In Gommon's picture, the cards surely allude to the raw, precarious state of existence endured by these labouring men. However, the regulars are not grotesques but viewed with a certain admiration and compassion — and the vivid butterfly at the window endows the picture with an accent of hopeful metaphysical release.

In 2013 (in an unpublished note on the Baker Arms picture) David's son Peter wrote:

> *The Card Players* is very much of its time, with its sombre earth colours and characteristic details as in works by Braque and Picasso. For me it embodies a mystery … I knew my father as a middle-aged man, and while he cycled everywhere, I can't ever remember going into a pub with him; he rarely if ever drank anything, and he certainly didn't hang out with farm labourers, something that I did a lot, as well as drinking, in my youth.

> So I find a window onto my dad in his youth, adventurous, free-spirited, an ale drinker, on the road, falling in love with new places and people, and trying out a new identity which was developing in Dorset.

Even more scrupulously stylised than *The Card Players* is the 1937 painting *Interior of the White Hart, Men Drinking* [p.47]. Here, in a plain setting with nicotine-hued walls and a long table, one pub-goer appears fairly refined in a trilby and jacket and tie, amiably aloof as he smokes his pipe; to his left, a gruff, curmudgeonly looking figure with a cloth cap rests his curved forearm on the table. The man dominating the right-hand section — black-moustachioed, rubicund-faced, drawing a gargantuan beer glass to his lips — takes on the proportions of a mythic figure, larger than life.

Set in a small Dorset town. T.F. Powys's 1927 allegorical novel *Mr Weston's Good Wine* evokes the atmosphere of the Angel Inn — a pub in a small Dorset town with a farcically benign landlord, Mr Bunce, where time literally stops when Mr Weston, who is apparently a wine merchant but is in actual fact God, visits. It is interesting to set Gommon's pictorial pub regulars alongside Powys' evocation of one of 'Mr Bunce's parlour folk':

> The drugged, solid air of the Angel Inn parlour became more and more human as the evening progressed ... even Mr Grunter's old boots took a new hue to them, and the caked mud upon them became humanised ... The hand that held the mug to the gross lips was changed. It was no more the work-ridden hand that had delved with the spade all the hours of the day; the hand had a higher calling now, it served as a festival.[8]

Peter Gommon's reference to Braque in this context can be related also to later comments by David, where he stated that, when he first started showing at the Wertheim Gallery, 'Apart from Van Gogh and Gauguin, there were obviously other influences like Matisse, Picasso and Braque. Braque has always been a great influence on me ... [it was] the added element that Braque is always expressing. Braque said that you really couldn't define this mysterious poetry.'[9]

Since the age of 14, Gommon had regularly attended Shakespeare plays at London's Old Vic (paying sixpence a time to sit in the gallery); these were produced by Lilian Baylis (1874—1937). It was around 1932 that Lucy Wertheim introduced Gommon to Baylis herself, who

> gave me permission to draw and paint backstage at both the Old Vic and Sadler's Wells; at the latter Baylis was now producing opera and ballet.
>
> I remember my first attendance at a Sadler's Wells ballet rehearsal — sidling nervously into a large room hung with very large mirrors with a bar at waist height on each wall; in the corner an upright piano, being played very vigorously ... The corps de ballet were going through their exercise routines under the supervision of a severe lady with a commanding voice. Later I learnt it was Ninette de Valois.
>
> All the dancers wore black tights, black leotards. [The dancers] Alicia Markova and Anton Dolin came in with [the composer] Constant Lambert, and a break for coffee began. Then came a rehearsal of bits from Lambert's *Rio Grande* [1927; a jazzy secular cantata based on a setting of a poem by Sacheverell Sitwell].
>
> I was drawing the moving figure for some weeks — filling pages as the dancers whirled and danced around me. Gradually I began to learn their names. One I remember as a particularly thin girl, Margot Fonteyn, [and] a male dancer Robert Helpmann — at that time just beginning their life's

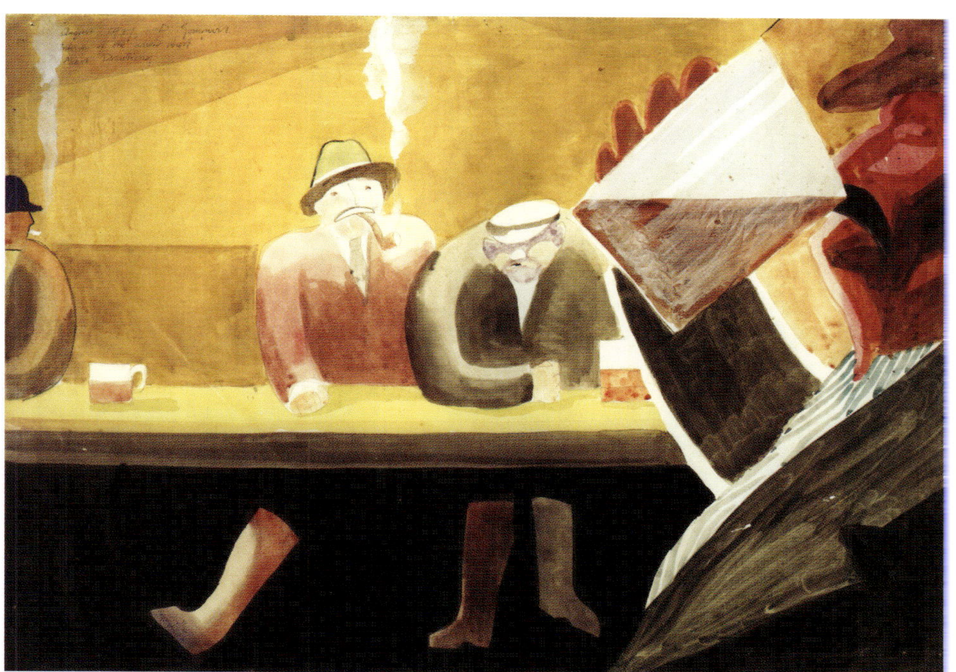

Interior of the White Hart, Men Drinking
1937, watercolour and gouache on paper,
38 x 55 cm
private collection

work, and unknown to the world. I did a series of ballet paintings, one of which was presented to Lilian Baylis, and Robert Helpmann promised to come and sit for his portrait.[10]

Gommon also said: 'The drawing of figures in movement is a splendid training of hand and eye. Rodin always drew his models as they moved and danced around his studio.'[11]

Gommon's timing in meeting Baylis turned out to be fortuitous — and in fact impeccable. In 1931, the Vic-Wells Ballet had opened (later to be named the Sadler's Wells Ballet), with Ninette de Valois as leading dancer and choreographer. Initially there were just six dancers, including de Valois, Markova, Fonteyn and Lydia Lopokova. Lambert became Musical Director.

Gommon's *At the Ballet* [overleaf] — which appears to depict Fonteyn in the principal role in Tchaikovsky's *Swan Lake* — is a painting with a quite synaesthetic merging of music, movement and landscape backdrop. 'Backdrop', though, is not quite the right expression because what is represented here is an actual-looking landscape of hills, fir tree, clouds and sky (their coalescing shapes reflected in the realistic-looking 'lake' on which the dancers perform).

The prima ballerina — as Odette the White Swan, redemptive symbol of the power of love, a human in swan form — is in *Écarté derrière* position, her outstretched arms indicating the power of a swan's wings. Two simple lines — a black stroke for her eyes, an upturned reddened one for her mouth — conjure up a beatific mien. Her fellow dancers are portrayed as a mass of oscillating white tones, their faces non-individuated. To the bottom of the picture the lone figure of the conductor in seen in back view, his head of red hair and an aspect of his face luminously present. His upraised right arm and fist hold the baton line assertively aloft, its slender shape piercing the fictive world above.

8. T.F. Powys, *Mr Weston's Good Wine* (London: Vintage Books, 2006), p.93.
9. 'An Interview with David Gommon, the Painter from Northamptonshire ...', pp.39—40.
10. D. Gommon, from notes ... 1980, p.6.
11. 'An Interview with David Gommon, the Painter from Northamptonshire ...', p.39.

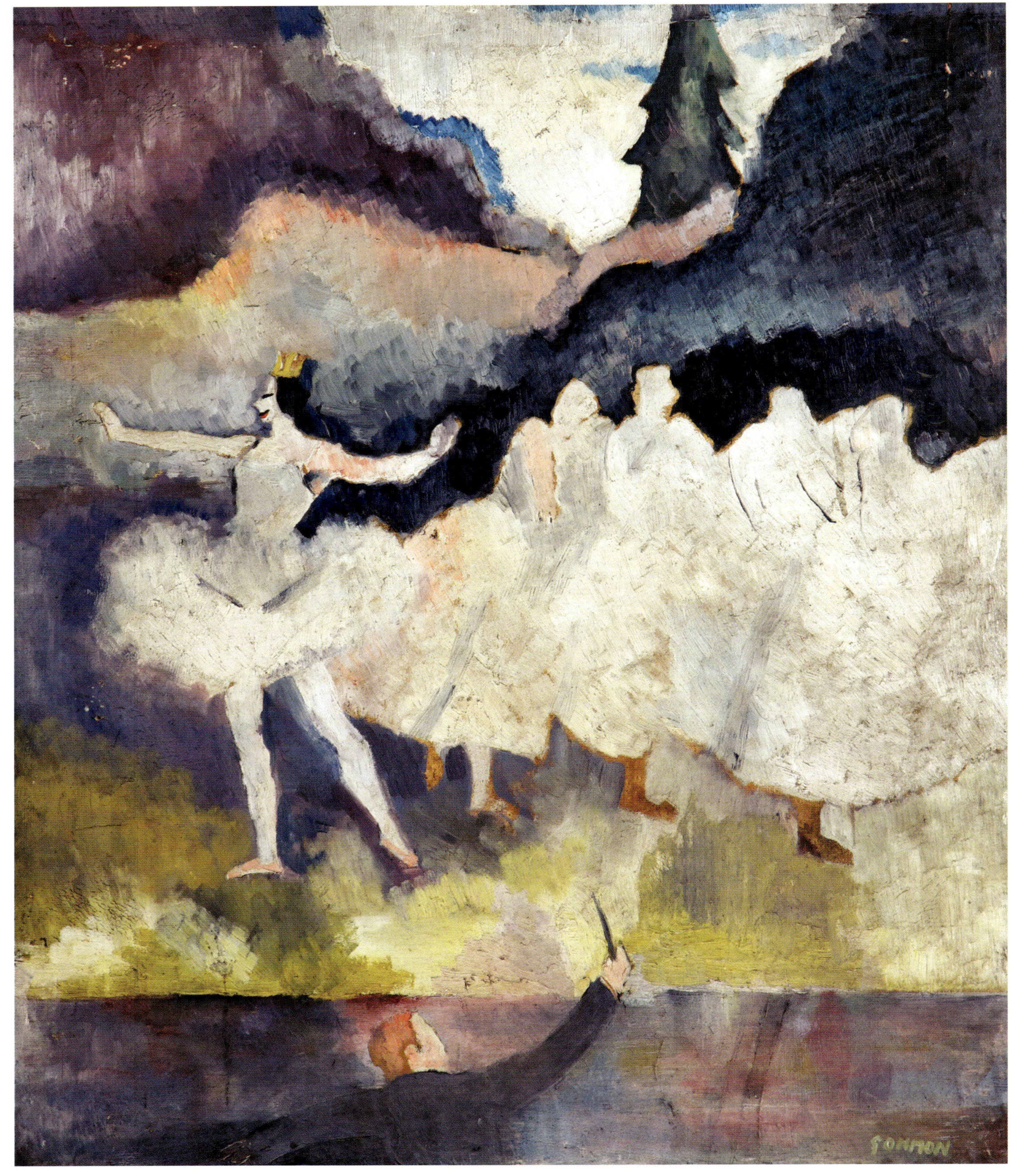

At the Ballet / *c.*1933, oil on canvas, 81 x 68 cm / Salford Museums and Art Gallery

An early 1930s catalogue for the Twenties Group at the Wertheim
Gallery shows two of Gommon's paintings entitled *At the Ballet* on sale
for 25 guineas each — a sizeable sum at the time (annual wages for many
in the cities were then around £130).

Only a few of Gommon's 1930s pictures depicting theatrical settings survive.
One such image — a watercolour *Theatre Study* — is entirely angled, Sickert-
like, on a shadowy crew of diverse characters sitting attentively but spectral-
faced in the dress circle. Gommon would have seen Sickert's paintings
exhibited at the Wertheim Gallery.

In another painting, the vibrant *Music Hall* (*c.*1934) [p.6], the view is apparently
that of a spectator in the stalls from a few rows back. The subject is thus as
much audience members directly in front (a woman, possibly black and with
dyed blonde hair, in profile, and an equally stylishly attired man and woman
in semi-profile, all inscrutably attentive) as the figures on stage. The latter,
diminutively seen, are a voluptuous young woman in a low-cut evening dress
and the droll figure of Pierrot, gesturing plaintively. (Pierrot, a stock clownish
character in *commedia dell'arte* and pantomime, appears in Watteau's paintings, and was later reimagined by artists such as Ensor, Picasso, Gris and
Macke.) This curious pairing of characters on stage is surely a wry satirical
allusion to mercurial relations between the sexes.

In London, around 1934, Gommon was invited to meet Jack Beddington
(1893—1959), pioneering Director of combined publicity for Shell-Mex and
BP, the two oil companies. He recalled in 1980, 'Colonel Jack Beddington,
a tall military-looking gentleman ... had a palatial office in Shell Mex House
[an Art Deco building opened in 1932] on the north bank of the Thames.'
Gommon turned down Beddington's offer of commissioning paintings
for use on Shell posters — to his eternal regret.

> He was giving similar commissions to Graham Sutherland and to
> Paul and John Nash ... and was responsible for the now very lively
> and famous Shell Mex advertising [which also included work by Ben
> Nicholson, Cedric Morris and Edward McKnight Kauffer]. Shame fills
> me now when I think of him and his great kindness and of all the help
> he offered. Oh the stupidity of youth! I felt that as an artist, posters and
> commercial art were not for me![12]

12. D. Gommon, from notes ... 1980, p.3.

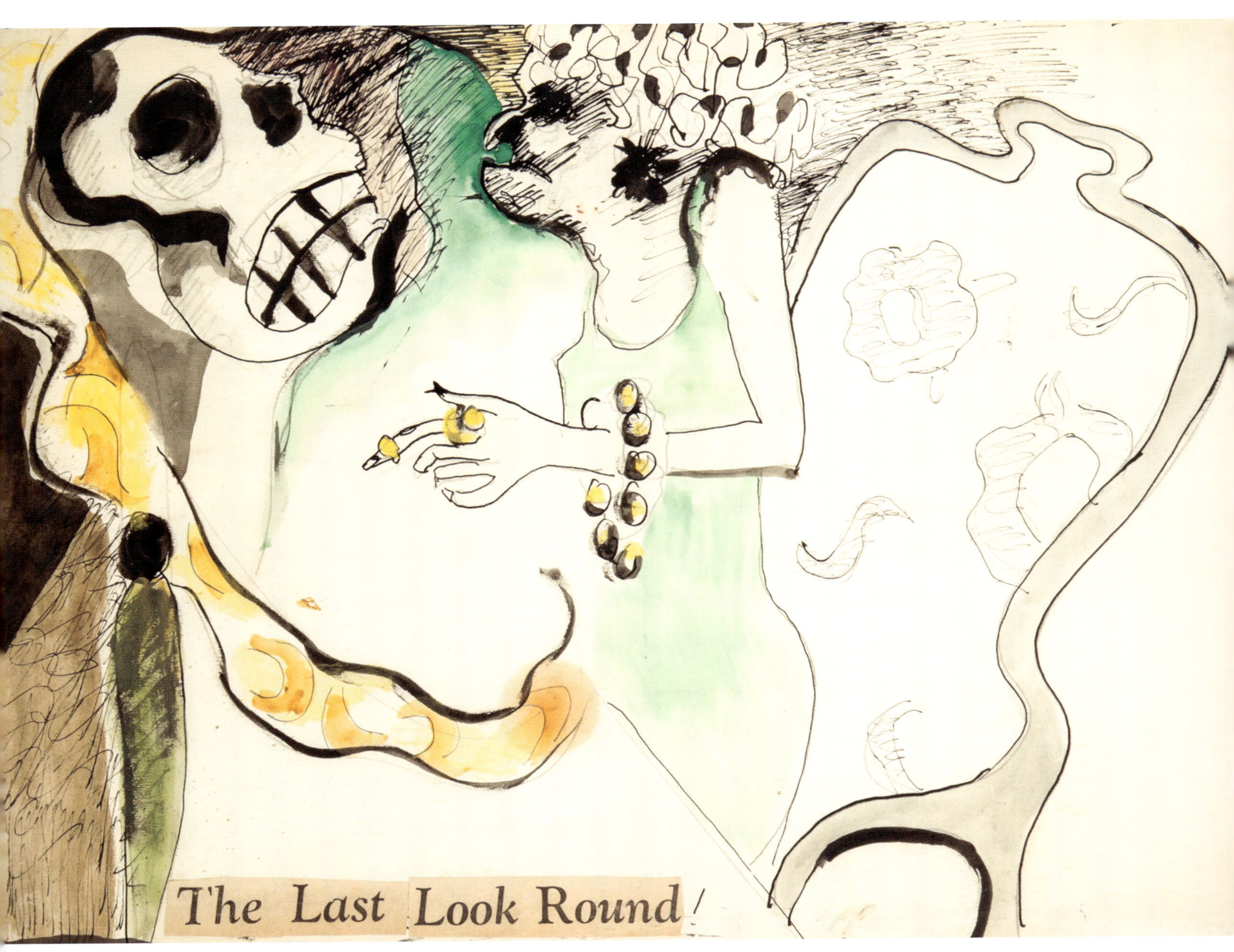

The Last Look Round from **The Book of the Dead, a 'Comédie humaine'**
1939—44, pen and ink, watercolour, gouache and collage on paper, 38 x 56 cm / private collection

The Book of the Dead and paintings of the 'pity of war'

DURING THE EARLY 1930S, WHILST PORTRAYING BALLET DANCERS, Gommon was also spending time in the British Museum studying mainly Egyptian and Chinese art, and also making drawings at the Natural History Museum. From May 1938 until an unspecified time in 1941 he created *Man, a Splendid Animal*, an extensive series of works on paper — making sensitive copies of works of art, anthropology and popular media from diverse cultures and historical periods. These include a version in pen and black-and-white wash of Piero di Cosimo's *c.*1484 *Portrait of Simonetta Vespucci*; an elegant watercolour adaptation of a seventeenth-century Moghul miniature of an archer in profile; a brooding *Portrait of a Man after Gerard Ter Borch 1642*; and meticulous representations of African and Oceanic figures in tribal costumes.

For the cover of the volume *Man* [overleaf], Gommon inserted cut-out magazine images of two males in grey flannel attire, superimposing on one of them his own drawing of an eerily gleeful human skeleton. He has drawn the other's grimacing face as a caricature, rather resembling one of the painter Wyndham Lewis's Tyro heads (Lewis described the Tyro figure — intended as a critique of modern dilettante culture — as 'raw and undeveloped; his vitality is immense, but purposeless, and hence sometimes malignant'[1]).

Gommon later wrote that it was in the mid-to-late 1930s he found himself

> emerging from my age of innocence. I became more aware politically of the peculiar world we lived in. Influenced primarily by Shakespeare, Tolstoy, Wyndham Lewis and Schopenhauer.

> Worlds other than art began to impinge on my life … Unemployment was now a national problem… The London streets were invaded by out-of-work coal miners from the North and from Wales. I remember their singing. [Around two hundred unemployed workers marched down from Jarrow in the north-east in October 1936 to present a petition to Parliament protesting against poverty and demanding jobs in their town.] I decided to give up painting! What relevance had art in such a society?

> So came Chamberlain — Munich [the British PM Neville Chamberlain went to Germany in late September 1938, signing the Munich Agreement with Germany, France and Italy in the hope of achieving a peaceful political outcome; this is now widely regarded as a failed act of appeasement] — art had indeed lost its relevance. It was now War's turn!

1. Wyndham Lewis, from an interview with the *Daily Express*, 11 April 1921, reprinted in Bernard Lafourcade (ed.), *The Complete Wild Body: Wyndham Lewis* (Santa Barbara, CA, Black Sparrow Press, 1982), p.359.

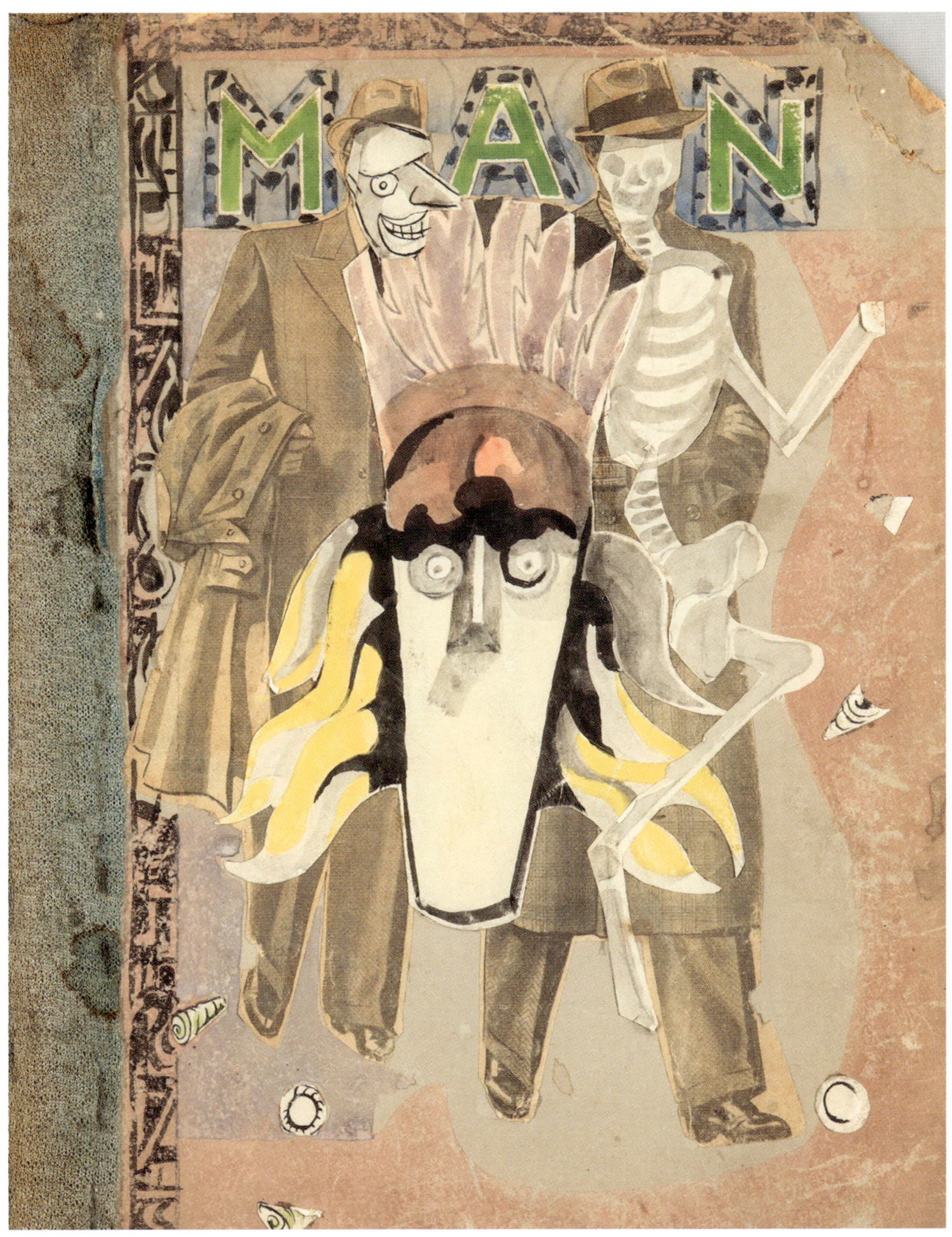

Cover of the volume
Man, a Splendid Animal
1938-41, pencil, pen and ink, watercolour
and collage on card, 38 x 28 cm
private collection

I set myself to create a modern pictorial equivalent of Balzac's *Comédie humaine*. Mine would have a visual impact and … be called the 'Book of the Dead'. Images of a dying society! With the outbreak of war all was changed. I became involved with civil defence in the city of London, and with the fire service … My life as an aspiring painter was over. It was back to Shakespeare with his 'wars and lechery, nothing else holds good' [Gommon's adapted version of some searing lines from *Troilus and Cressida*] and for six years that is how it was.[2]

During the Second World War Gommon was designated as unfit for military service because of his spinal curvature (a feature which his son Peter has recalled 'we were tacitly forbidden to mention in any way'). So he became a member of the Civil Defence Fire Service in London; he was on the site of St Paul's on the night of 29 December 1940, witnessing apocalyptic scenes of heavy German bombing all around. Efforts of the St Paul's Watch helped keep the cathedral safe at the height of the Blitz.

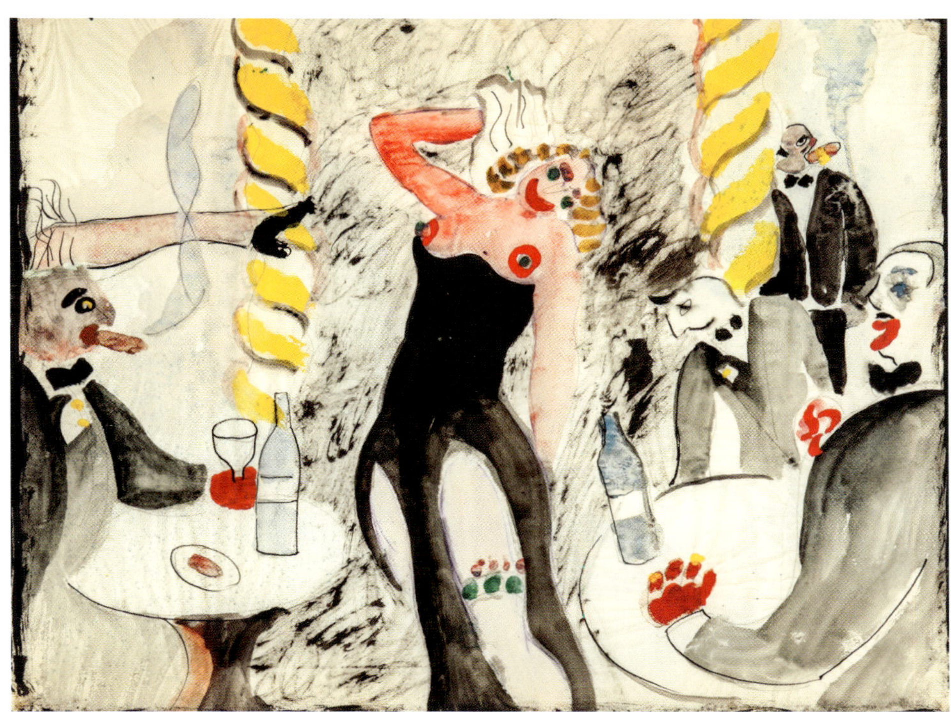

Thus, from early-to-mid 1939 to 1944, Gommon self-consciously abandoned making paintings in favour of working on this new 'Book of the Dead' project, a mordant critique of what he considered a decadent, class-conflicted society heading towards destruction. The sense of unease, at times visceral disgust, pervading this ambitious work is the antithesis of the tone characteristic of his earlier 1930s art. He used his painterly gifts now for different ends. For example, Gommon's picture *Cabaret* [above] — which has resonances of the German Expressionist George Grosz's paintings of Weimar cabaret (as for example in the latter's 1927 image of a man with nauseating porcine features kissing a naked young woman) — depicts the kind of bare-breasted, heavily lipsticked, cavorting young woman he had innocently portrayed only quite recently. But in this wartime work the woman appears quite bestial in her tight, black, revealing outfit, which may include a devilish tail — as she is leered at by capitalist cronies in black tie.

A work in this series, *Sausages; into the Whale's Belly* [overleaf], shows a middle-aged couple of monstrous proportions in grossly opulent evening dress spearing up fragments of food on their forks, looking quite delirious with greed. On a platter on the table is another dish, that of a fish whose stupefied expression could be seen as a deadpan comment on the whole appalling scene. Such a work is closely allied to a British tradition of edgy graphic political satire as practised by the great caricaturist James Gillray (1756—1815), in whose cartoons illustrious contemporaries are often represented as voluptuaries bloated and deformed by unrestrained social and political ambition and appetite.

In his rendition of the *Great Image of Authority* [p.55], Gommon mocked what he saw as the danger of reactionary collusion between the Church and military authorities on all sides. The central figure is a jackbooted, bemedalled officer, all puffed up Mussolini-style; the figure to the right is a

2. D. Gommon, from notes ... 1980, p.6.

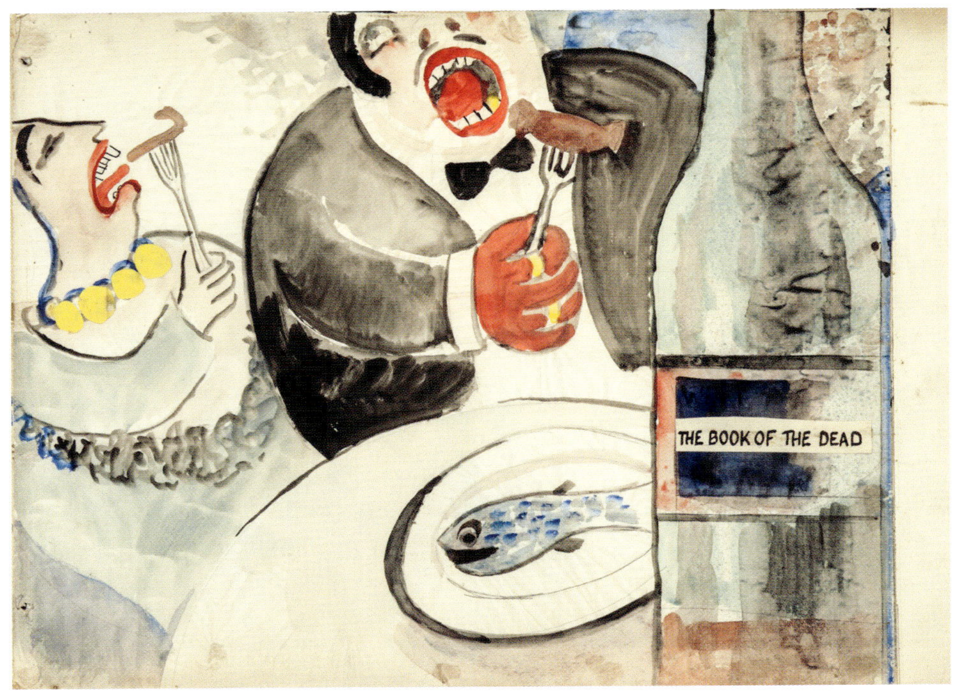

Sausages; into the Whale's Belly from
The Book of the Dead, a 'Comédie humaine'
1939—44, pen and ink, watercolour, gouache
and collage on paper, 38 x 56 cm
private collection

moustachioed, bearskin-capped British soldier of the King's Guard, wielding
a fearsome-looking sword. To their left, facing them, is a bishop imposingly
attired in liturgical garments, a mitre and a sombre crucifix hanging heavily
from his neck. Disturbingly, the bishop appears to be giving them both his
blessing.

Onto some of these pictures Gommon has collaged headlines and adver-
tising snippets from newspapers and magazines — in the manner of John
Heartfield (1891—1968), the German artist (who fled Nazism, coming to
Britain in 1938, only to be interned for a while as an enemy alien following

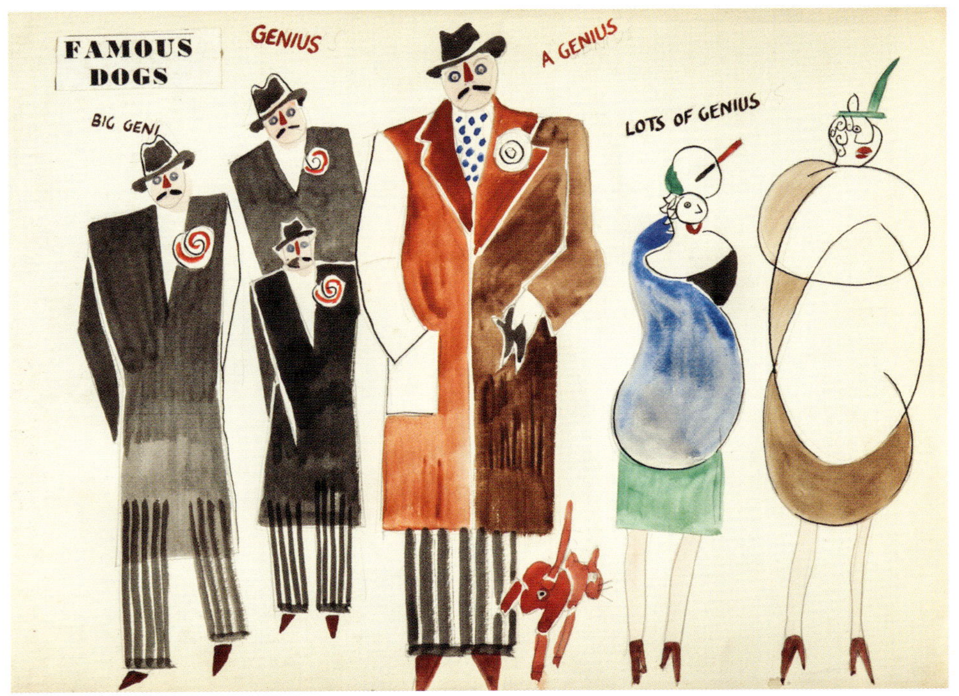

Famous Dogs – Genius from
The Book of the Dead, a 'Comédie humaine'
1939—44, pen and ink, watercolour, gouache
and collage on paper, 38 x 56 cm
private collection

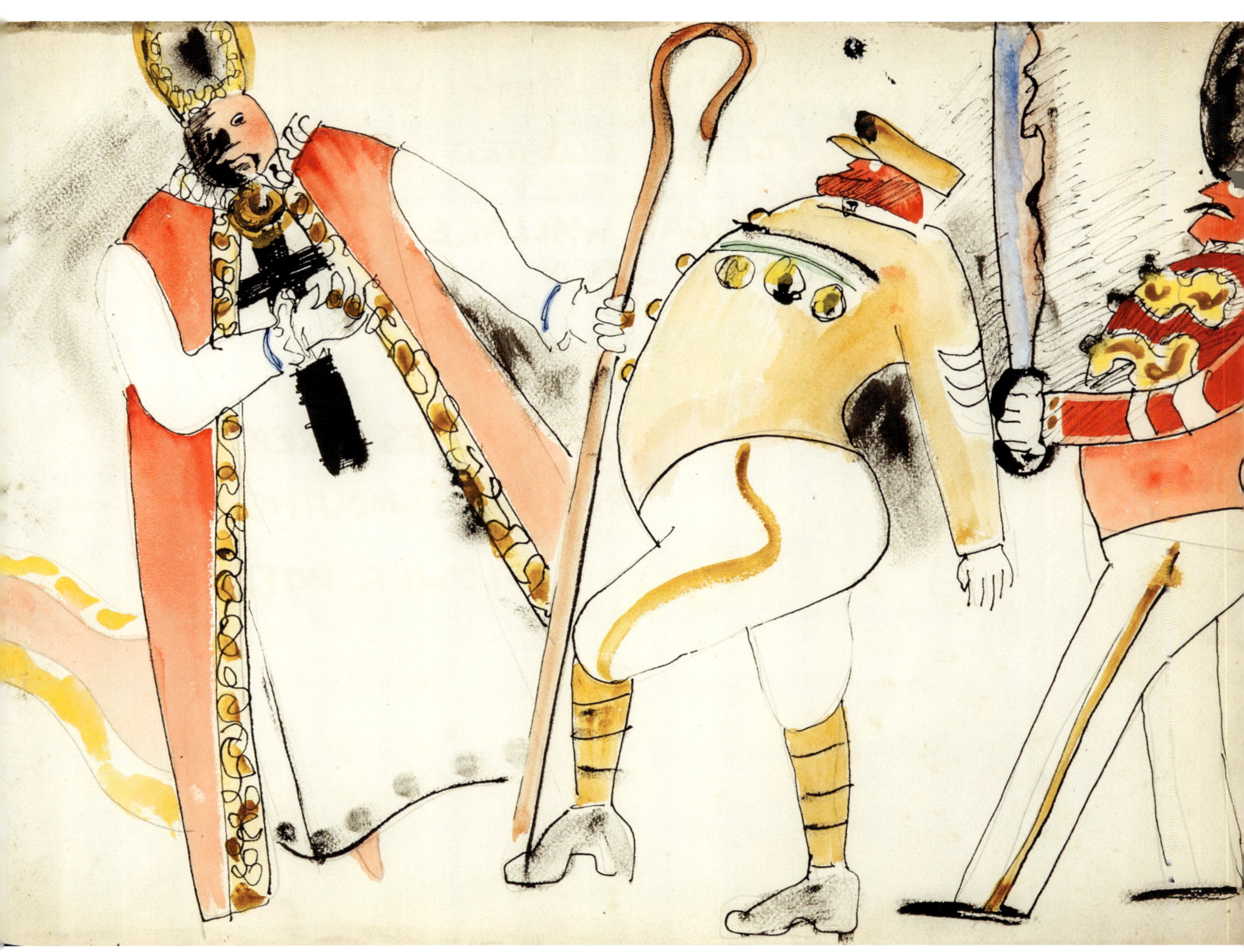

Great Image of Authority from **The Book of the Dead, a 'Comédie humaine'**
1939—44, pen and ink, watercolour and gouache on paper, 38 x 56 cm / private collection

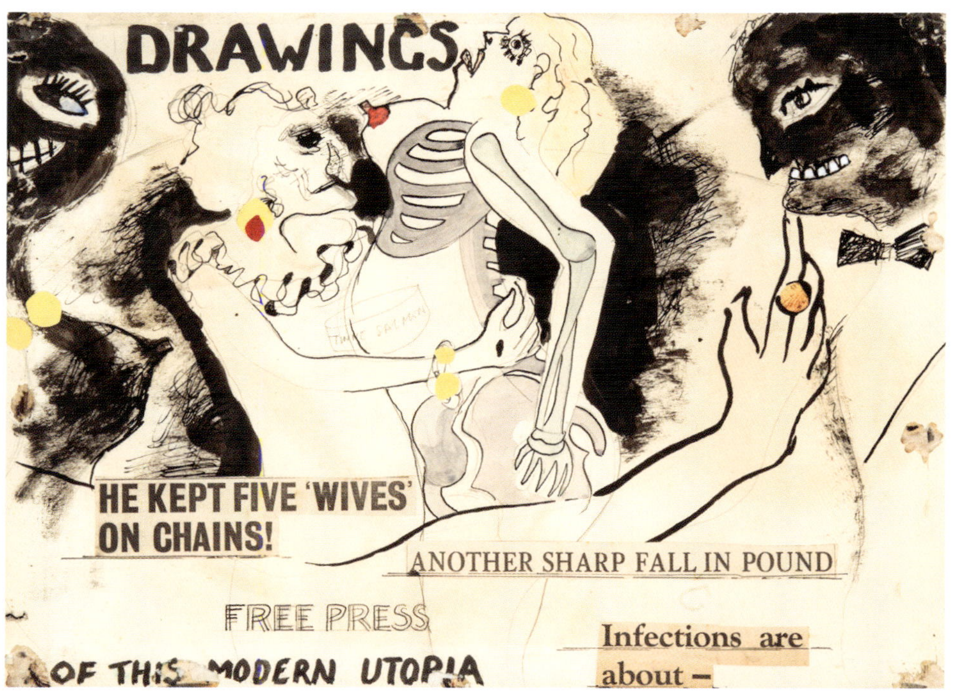

Free Press – Infections Are About from
The Book of the Dead, a 'Comédie humaine'
1939—44, pen and ink, watercolour, gouache
and collage on paper, 38 x 56 cm
private collection

the outbreak of war). Heartfield's 1930s photomontage work lampooned the rise of fascism, the machinery of war and vacuous consumer culture, often using absurdist tropes stemming from the Dada art movement, which itself had emerged in reaction to the horrors of the First World War.

One work in *The Book of the Dead* depicts the gruesome embrace of a cadaverous-seeming couple in what seems to be the death throes of an orgasm [above]. Here, some hand-written text by the artist — stating 'FREE PRESS OF THIS MODERN UTOPIA' — is ironically juxtaposed with collaged headlines: the sensationalist 'HE KEPT FIVE "WIVES" ON CHAINS!';

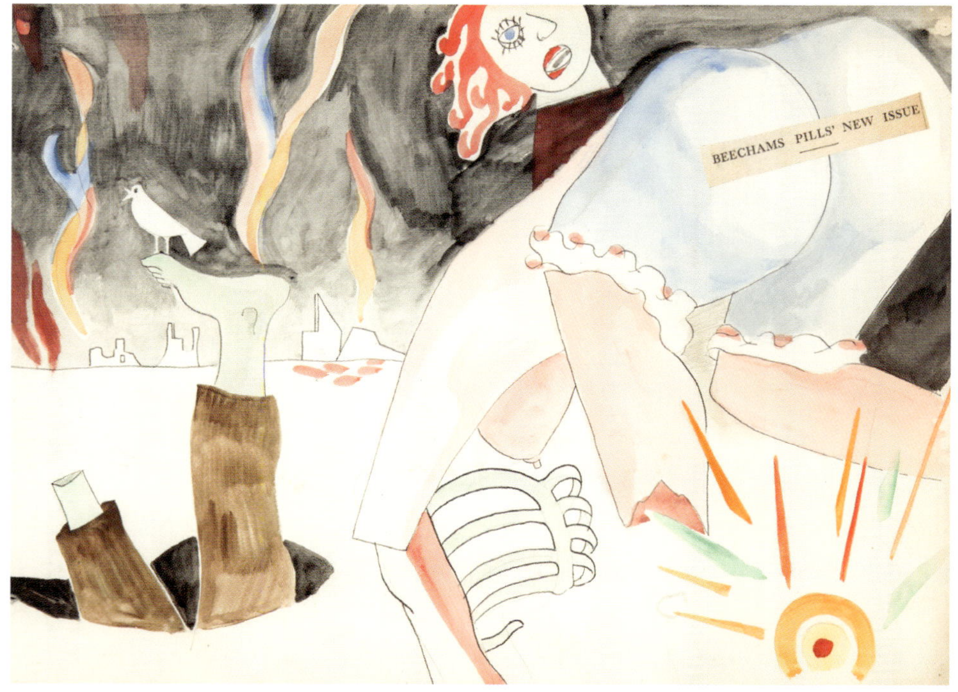

Beecham Pills' New Issue from
The Book of the Dead, a 'Comédie humaine'
1939—44, pen and ink, watercolour, gouache
and collage on paper, 38 x 56 cm
private collection

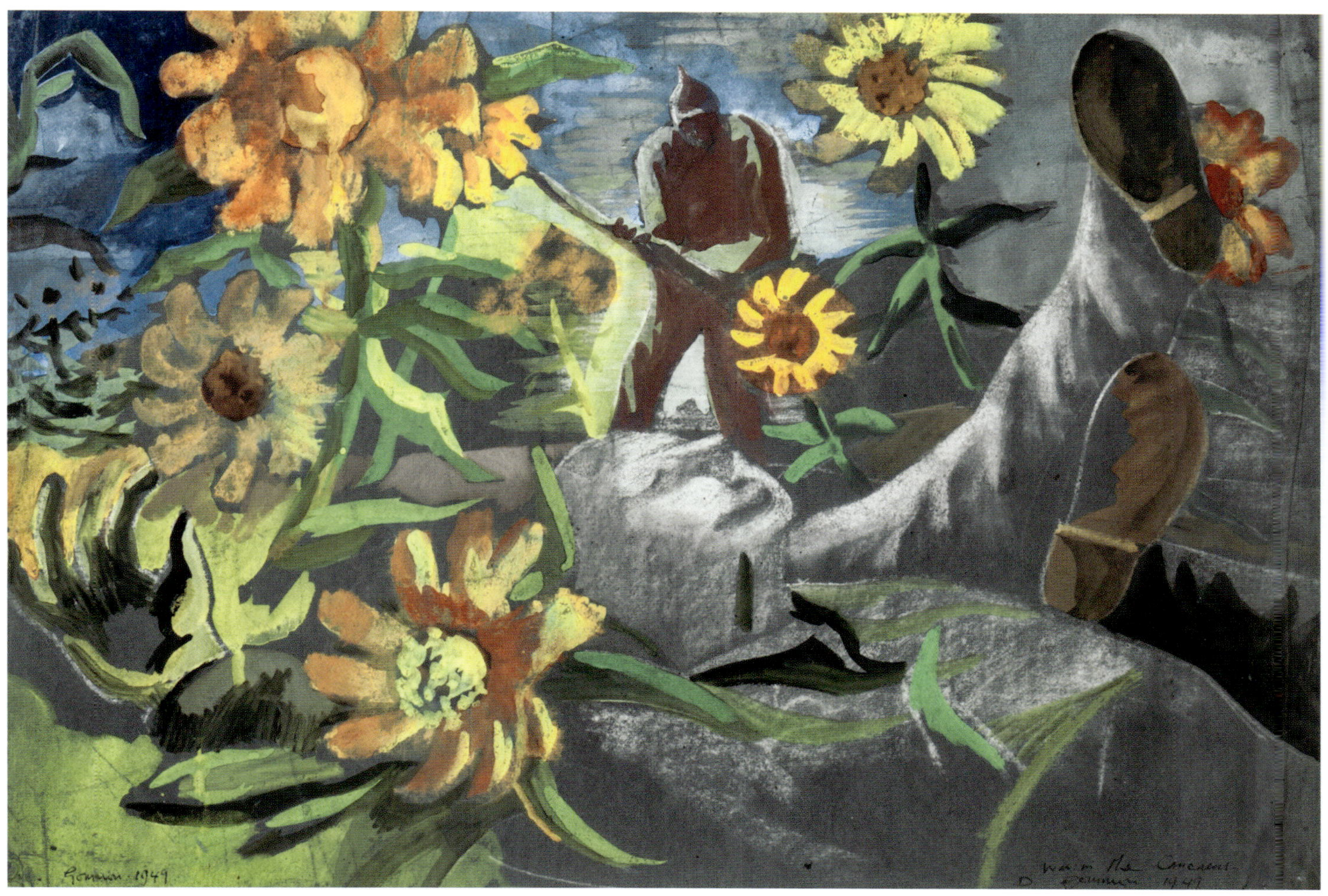

War in the Caucasus / 1949, gouache on paper, 51 x 74 cm / private collection

'ANOTHER SHARP FALL IN THE POUND'; and the matter-of-fact yet sinister-sounding statement: 'Infections are about'.

On another page [left], the printed line 'BEECHAMS PILLS' NEW ISSUE' is facetiously pasted over the bloomer-covered buttocks of a woman in the process of being literally blown to pieces by a descending bomb; the insertion of that ad line here (promising a medicinal quick fix) is bitterly ironical. By the dazed look on her face the victim appears still alive — as simultaneously her severed legs are seen to plunge into a pothole, and one breast signals down towards her horribly sundered ribcage. One foot has gone, and on the other foot — protruding towards the burning city on the horizon — perches what is apparently a cooing dove (iconic symbol of peace): a bizarrely surreal image with a Dadaist edge to it.

Gommon's 1949 painting *War in the Caucasus* [above] reflects on the horrors of the Second World War. The contrast here between the anaemic greyish tones of a male corpse on the ground, and around him gorgeous palpitating sunflowers, is truly disturbing. In the background is the gloomy, foul figure of their murderer, a soldier seen wielding a bayonet.

Kate Currie says this is a picture 'of dead soldiers lying among sunflowers which was caused by my father reading a report of bodies lying around the

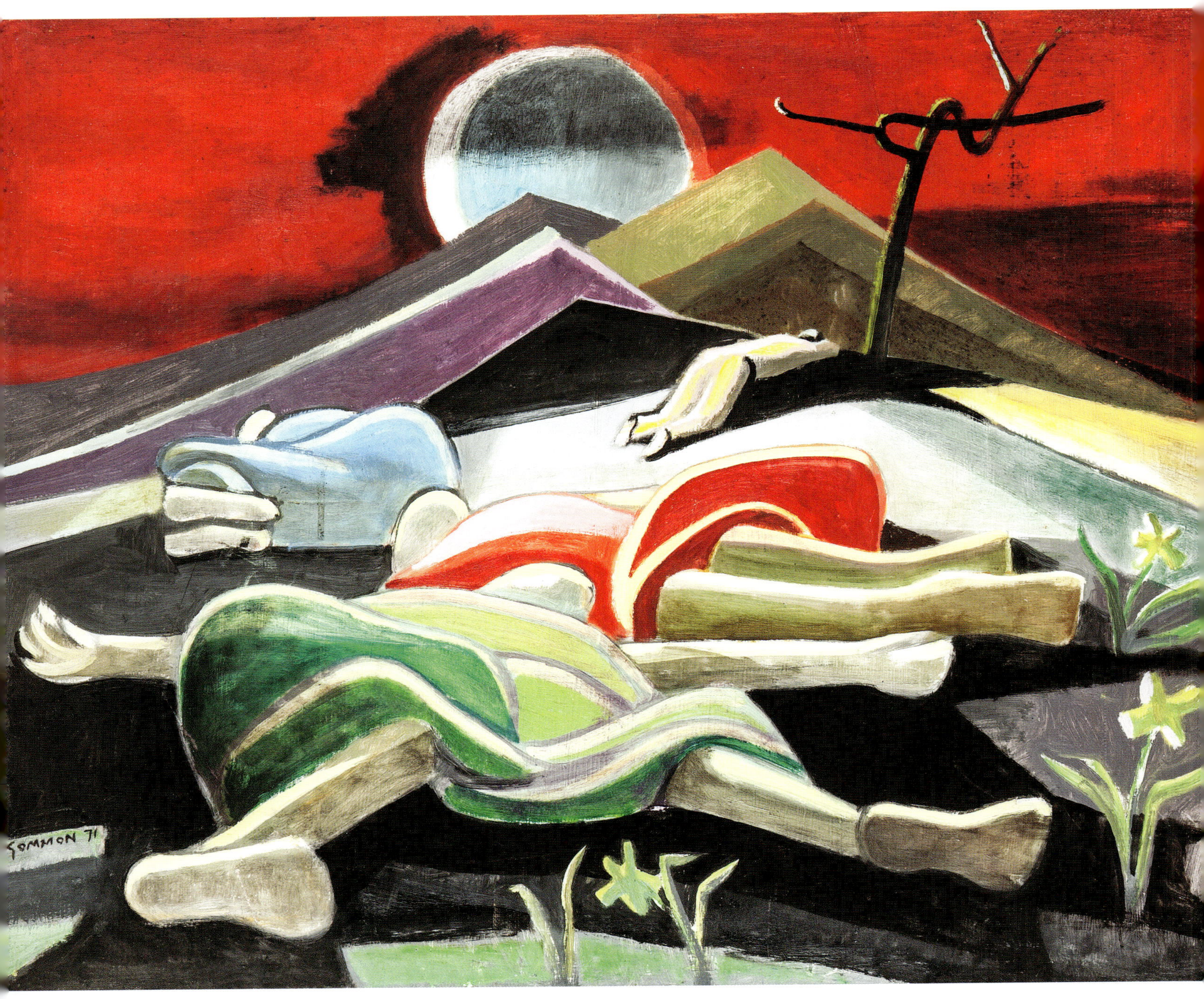

Agony in the Garden / 1971, oil on board, 76 x 101 cm / private collection

city of Stalingrad with sunflowers growing over and around them'. In the Battle of Stalingrad (17 July 1942 to 2 February 1943) German and Soviet armies fought to gain control of the city; by the time the Germans surrendered it is estimated over a million civilians and soldiers had been killed in an unprecedentedly large-scale military bloodbath.

The mystical symbol of the sunflower resonated deeply with Gommon, with its echoes of William Blake's poem beginning:

> Ah! Sun-flower! weary of time
> Who Countest the steps of the Sun,
> Seeking after that sweet golden clime
> Where the traveller's journey is done[3]

It parallels too Van Gogh's own portrayals, which (as the latter wrote in 1890) were 'almost a cry of anguish although in the rustic sunflower they may symbolise gratitude'.[4]

This 1949 painting, evoking what the poet Wilfred Owen called 'the pity of war',[5] finds certain echoes in a 1971 painting, *Agony in the Garden* [facing page]. The latter depicts four sleeping disciples of Jesus lying on the ground at Gethsemane, in what appears to be an angularised hellscape overlooked by a twisting bare tree (its spiky, minatory form in various ways a portent of the Crucifixion) under an ominously reddened sky (like a Francis Bacon backdrop) with a huge sullen, pallid blue moon.

The figure of Jesus does not appear in this picture. In the New Testament Gospel of Matthew, it is related that Jesus, whose 'heart [was] was ready to break with grief',[6] had addressed the recumbent men: 'Still sleeping? Still taking your rest? The hour has come! The Son of Man is betrayed to sinful men. Up, let us go forward; the traitor is upon us.'[7] In Gommon's painting, three lustrous daffodils are seen to be dancing plaintively on the edges of this grisly, at times heart-wrenching. tableau.

3. William Blake, 'Ah! Sun-flower', *William Blake* (Penguin Books, Harmondsworth, Middlesex 1976), p.51.
4. Quoted from a letter from Vincent Van Gogh to his sister Wilhemina J. Van Gogh, dated 'middle of February 1890', *The Complete Letters of Vincent van Gogh*, vol. 3 (Thames & Hudson, London, 1988).
5. Wilfred Owen, phrase quoted in 'Strange Meeting', *The Poems of Wilfred Owen* (London: Chatto and Windus, 1972), p.116.
6. 'The Gospel According to Matthew', *The New English Bible*, 26:38, (Oxford University Press & Cambridge University Press, 1970), p.38.
7. Ibid.

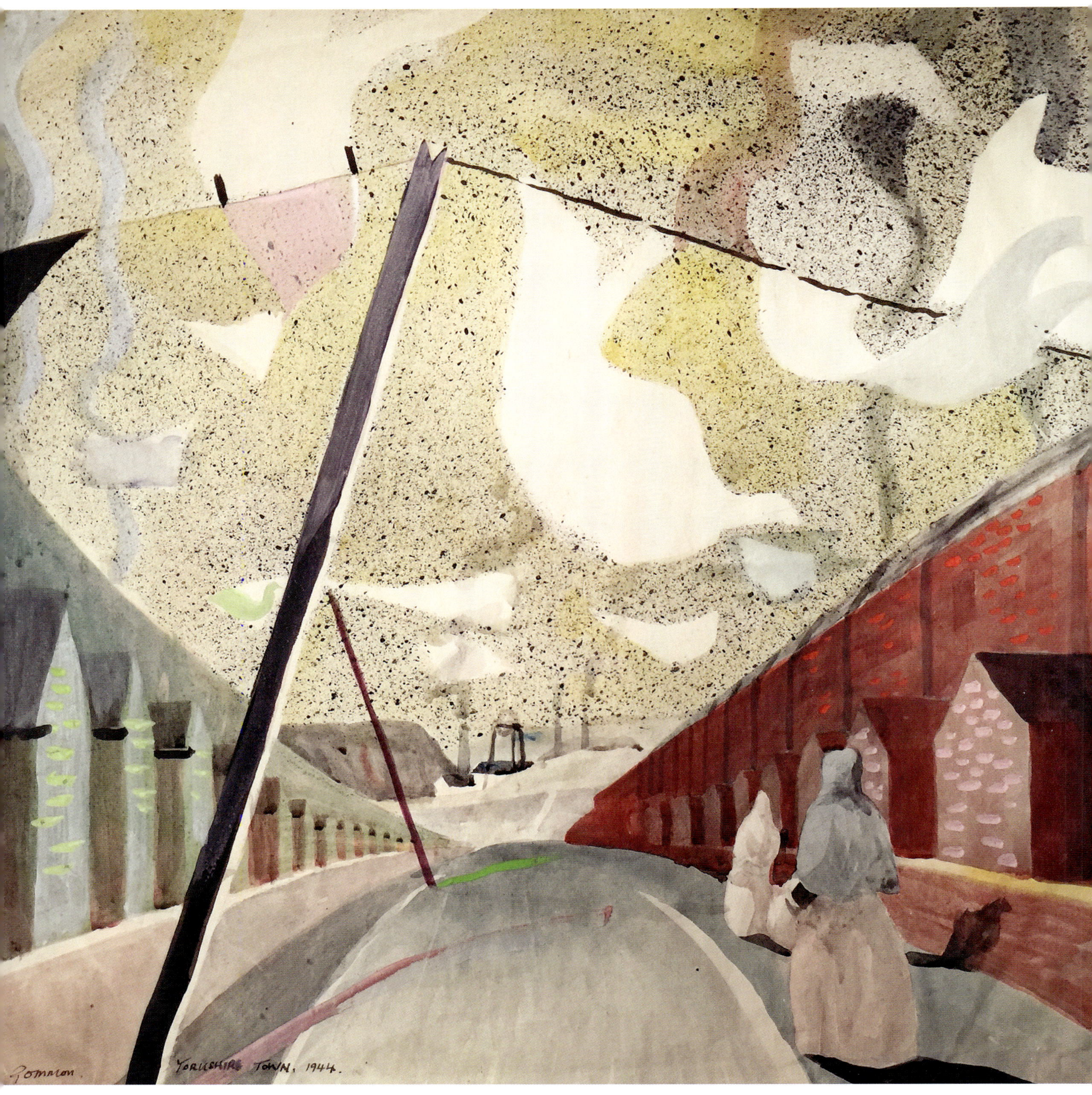

Yorkshire Town / 1944, gouache and airbrush on paper, 55.5 x 62 cm / private collection

Empathetic teacher and portraitist

IT WAS DURING THE SECOND WORLD WAR THAT DAVID MET JEAN Vipond, and they married in 1943. Their initial encounter was auspicious and serendipitous, as Kate Currie has recounted. Employed as a telephone operator in Leeds, Jean tried to put through a call from David in London but this failed. The two then started chatting on the line. He asked, 'What are you reading?' but, unimpressed by her answer, exclaimed, 'God, I'll have to send you something worth reading!' A couple of days later Jean was summoned by her supervisor, querying why a parcel had arrived for her. She opened it to find a copy of Tolstoy's *Anna Karenina* and a note from David. From then on they corresponded regularly.

Jean's mother suggested that David come to stay with them in Leeds. Kate says, 'So my mother waited at Leeds Station — with another friend hiding behind a pillar, who could come to the rescue if need be. Instead of which this handsome man got off the train — and I think that was it, they both fell for one another. A kind of *Brief Encounter* in reverse!'

David recalled, 'The marriage service was sandwiched between an air raid warning and an all-clear. It was one of those very cold and frosty November days' (and he went on then to quote here these lines from 'Little Gidding' [first published separately in 1942], the fourth and final poem of T.S. Eliot's *Four Quartets*)

> When the short day is brightest, with frost and fire,
> The brief sun flames the ice, on pond and ditches ...[1]

Peter Gommon recalls his parents as being 'a very affectionate and loving couple. You'll see that in the many cards and little notes he wrote to her over the years. In their different ways, they both adored each other. His communication was much more gestural; she was much more loquacious.'

Soon after they married, the couple moved to the village of Chiddingstone in Kent, where David got a job teaching in a progressive co-educational school set in a castle 'with views across the North Downs, and an open-air swimming pool. The arts were an important feature ... sometimes we would start the day singing songs by Brahms. I was able to draw and paint again for the first time since 1939.'

Unfortunately, the school could only pay a meagre wage so he applied for and obtained a teaching post as head of the art department at Northampton

1. D. Gommon, from notes ... 1980, p.7. The Eliot quote here is from T.S. Eliot, 'Little Gidding', *Four Quartets* (London: Faber & Faber, 1979), p.41.

Grammar School. 'I went intending to stay a short time, and stayed thirty years. My son was born at the end of my first term there!'[2]

One of the first paintings that Gommon made after consciously resuming the art of picture-making in (probably late) 1944 was a gouache, *Yorkshire Town* [p.60], with its dramatic, quasi-cinematic sweep of perspective. The broad vista opens into an alley of claustrophobic back-to-back houses (with their rows of brick-built outside WCs) in a mining town — on one side coloured a muted cyan, on the other a vivid blood-red. From two washing line-poles — one aslant in the foreground, the other further down the street — billow masses of sheets drying in the wind, their abstract shapes suggestive of shifting clouds, mercurial human presences, even uncanny spectral beings. Two women, mournfully shrouded in shawls, scarves and long heavy dresses, are seen walking towards each other, casting quite sinister black shadows onto the pavement.

The curious conceit here — both literal and metaphysical in nature — is that the sky is darkened with myriads of funereal black specks (pollution emanating from three chimneys glimpsed afar, aside a pithead) — and yet the washing itself remains unsullied and pristine despite the foul atmosphere. Gommon seems subtly to be making an at once social and spiritual commentary on the innately pure and resilient qualities of a working-class mining community, subject to all kinds of hardship and grief, even terrible disasters, and yet seen somehow to be able to rise — quite transcendently — above it all.

Jean and David Gommon moved to Northamptonshire in 1945, and soon were living in Little Billing Rectory, a house with a fine Regency frontage, which they rented. Peter Gommon recalls, 'There was a morning room on the sunny side of the house, and it was his studio for quite a while. And then he was set up in a beautiful Georgian room overlooking the fields. He had a big army leather jerkin, which he wore when it was cold in the studio.'

David later recalled his new teaching job as

> enjoyable, frustrating, exciting and varied, certainly very hard work. I played cricket, acted and sang in many of the school productions — from Gilbert and Sullivan to *West Side Story.* I put on exhibitions of school work, and was an officer in the school army cadet force! But at the same time I was painting, especially during the school holidays, and I started to exhibit again. I also began to renew those friendships from before the War — particularly with Mrs Wertheim.[3]

A 'frustrating' aspect to the job lay in the fact that he was required to attain a particular teaching qualification for which he was examined five times, 'each time passing the written part and failing on painting!', as Ian Mayes has written, in a *Guardian* obituary from 2000. 'It was only resolved when Gommon passed the exam... after the MP for Northampton [Reginald Paget] ... had raised the matter ... in the Commons.'

In the same *Guardian* obituary (11 May 2000) — of the artist Henry Bird (1909—2000), like Mayes and Gommon a Hardingstone resident — Mayes

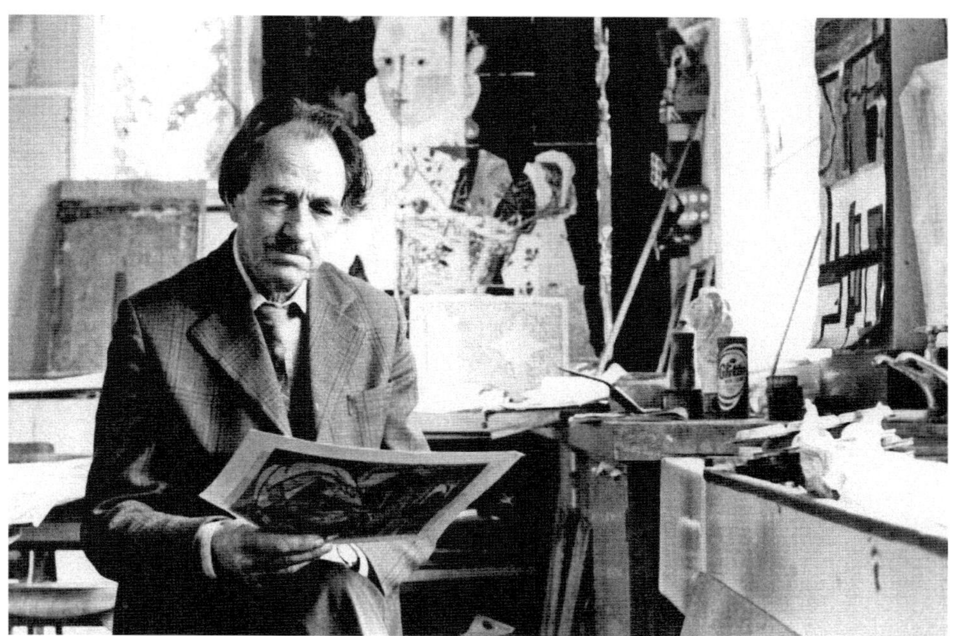

David in the art room at Northampton Grammar School, *c.*1970s

noted that Bird's 'belief in academic skills and qualifications sometimes caused damaging and long-lasting personal conflicts. One of these was with David Gommon, whose appointment as art master at Northampton Grammar School he opposed because Gommon had, to begin with, no conventional qualifications, although he had been rightly praised as a practising artist. Much distress was caused before this was resolved. They lived at opposite ends of the same village and both taught until they reached retirement age, keeping well away from each other.'

The renowned sculptural ceramicist Tony Lattimer, who attended this school from 1956 until 1962, remembers Gommon's inspiring example:

> David's way of teaching had a gentle subtle reality. He was not overtly demonstrative but worked by trailing ideas and suggestions across one's often determined unconscious. I remember examples of artists' work placed by him in the corridor … Matisse's goldfish, Braque's stylised dove, Cubist works of Picasso; images that sunk in subliminally. And then around the art room reproductions of the early Renaissance masters … Giotto, Martini, Duccio and the Botticelli and Piero della Francesca masterpieces.
>
> … he was often working on a painting of his own … The experience of seeing an adult manipulating paint seriously, but with lightness of touch, connected me to the relationship with creativity that I know forty years later in my own work; as a complex and creative freedom.[4]

Peter Howard, who studied at the school from *c.*1957 to 1964 (and who went on to collect David's paintings — as well as being introduced by Gommon to Lucy Wertheim), recalls the art room,

which was remotely housed in a wing on the first floor, at the end of a corridor. Entering it, with its tall ceiling and large windows, seemed like leaving the old world and entering a new one. It was full of light, and

2. D. Gommon, from notes … 1980, p.7.
3. Ibid.
4. Tony Lattimer, quoted from an unpublished short memoir, recalling David Gommon's influence on his own development as an artist, August 2013.

although untidy seemed a calm place to be. Powder paints, mixed in old egg cartons, seemed to be the main medium in use; I suppose they would be called gouache now. It was David's domain, and seemed a world away from the rest of the school.

With his moustache and bent back, David pottered around and seemed rather diffident about 'teaching'. The classes were quite small, as I recall … Sometimes a plate of mackerel or a bowl of oranges or flowers would be waiting for a still life, or someone would be asked to pose, sitting down. When preparing for A level we were often left to our own devices, and David would wander round looking over our shoulders. The most thrilling moment was when — very rarely — he asked for my brush, and making just a couple of careful strokes on the picture hinted at a clarity that I never imagined it could have.

Visiting Jasmine Cottage was a great privilege, and I realise now that its impact, though less, was comparable to visiting Kettle's Yard later on. The approach was across the lawn of a small garden, then under a low canopy. David's pictures were everywhere and he had painted inscriptions over the fireplaces, one of which I later realised was from Sir Thomas Browne. The ceilings were low, the spaces small and dominated by large chimneys which created mysterious alcoves, and all was white. One wall was covered in books of the sort I knew I should have read, and hadn't. Tea would be offered by Jean.[5]

Peter Gommon recalls,

A boundless energy he unleashed on this job, and then he was also starting to paint again. He obviously had a renewal of energy, a rebirth after all the disillusion and horror of war.

I remember going to London on a steam train with my father when I was less than ten, to visit Lucy Wertheim in her flat. She was a rather imposing woman, obviously presenting as an Edwardian-type character in her dark clothes and in her gestures. She was a very welcoming and pleasant person. I distinctly recall that we all looked at Alfred Wallis pictures.

There is a gouache by David of a skull and bones, which strikes me as a kind of *memento mori*. It is dated 1954. I recently came across the burial certificates for my paternal grandparents — they died in 1954 within a couple of months of each other. I recall no conversation with him at the time about my grandma and granddad — but this painting emerged; it seems he just painted it as his way of dealing with it all.

Kate Currie relates that her father was especially friendly with three or four teachers at Northampton Grammar School who were teaching languages — Jewish refugees from Nazi Germany. She says he generally 'found them much more interesting, more flamboyant, with a much more outward-looking view of life — following their difficult experiences in Germany' than their often more insular English colleagues. 'He enjoyed discussing continental affairs and philosophy with them.'

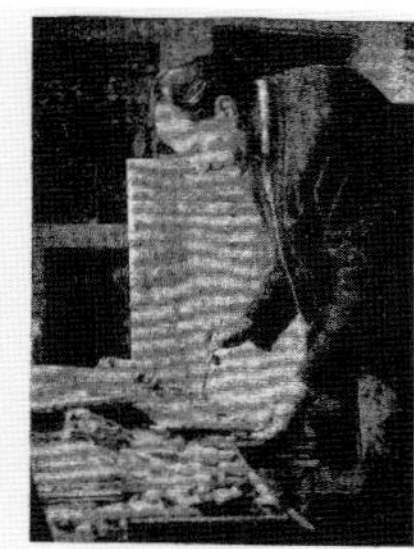

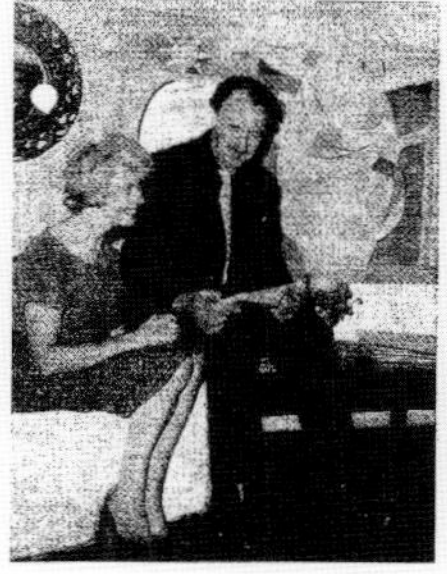

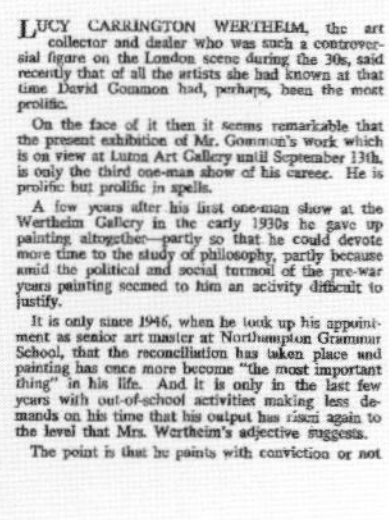

Review of David Gommon's third solo exhibition at Luton Art Gallery; Ian Mayes, *Northampton Independent*, September 1964

In the early 1950s Gommon resumed exhibiting his paintings. However, it was not until 1959 that he succeeded in having his second one-man show — at Northampton Museum and Art Gallery (though there was a display of his work in a Committee Room at the House of Commons in 1952). His third solo show was at Luton Art Gallery in 1964. He had further solo shows at the same Northampton civic venue in 1965 and 1977; at Gainsborough's House, Sudbury, Suffolk in 1965; at St Catherine's College, Oxford in 1975; and at Derby City Art Gallery in 1979. He also exhibited in some mixed exhibitions, notably in 1954 in 'Modern English Paintings from the Wertheim Collection'; and at the Herbert Art Gallery, Coventry, along with his ex-pupil and friend Jonathan Adams in 1963 — a show opened by Lucy Wertheim.

It was at some point in or shortly after 1946 that Gommon befriended the Welsh-born painter and Modernist poet David Jones (1895—1974), and would visit him

> in his one room at Harrow on the Hill in a small private hotel — which had a small table, two chairs and a bed. Books and pictures were everywhere; the bed was covered with books and drawings and so was the floor. The Great War, where he was a private in the infantry, haunted and stayed with him for the rest of his life [this was the subject of his epic Modernist poem In *Parenthesis*, published in 1937]. What a gentle soul David was![6]

A 1965 interview with Jones, talking to his old friend Saunders Lewis (the Welsh writer and politician) for the BBC television series *Writers' World*, is a compelling evocation of Jones as a humane, humorous, acutely thoughtful man in his studio living room at Harrow on the Hill. He is filmed surrounded by masses of books as well as his own propped-up drawings, brushes, paint pots and objects such as 'an old Roman coin or a bit of a Welsh something else'. Jones says that with this daily 'physical contactual thing … [which is] becoming so difficult [to preserve in our modern civilisation] …', he manages to keep alive a primordial connection 'with the whole world of sacraments and signs', which he explains is the foundation of his art.[7]

A 'solitary perfectionist' (writer and poet Kathleen Raine's apt term for him),[8] Jones was a kindred spirit to Gommon. The latter admired his older friend's respect for a quite Blakean marriage of words and image in art, the depth of his questing interior life and his numinous, often beautifully intricate, watercolour portraits and depictions of animal, landscape, religious and legendary subjects.

It was through Jim Ede that David Jones first encountered Helen Sutherland (1881—1965), a wealthy, pioneer collector of avant-garde art from the mid-1920s onwards — including works by Mondrian, Naum Gabo, Brâncuşi, Ben and Winifred Nicholson and Barbara Hepworth as well as pictures by Alfred Wallis — and also (from 1935 onwards) a keen supporter of the gifted, 'unprofessional', so-called Pitmen Painters of the north-eastern Ashington Group. Sutherland went on to become a discerning patron of Jones's art as well as a sympathetic and nurturing friend. Kathleen Raine's description of Sutherland's 'great, yet most personal collection' (including 'above all those superb David Joneses'), 'the finest works of contemporary artists' set (from

5. Peter Howard, quoted from 'David Gommon, Some Recollections', an unpublished reminiscence, June 2020.
6. David Gommon, from notes … 1980, p.8.
7. David Jones, interviewed by Saunders Lewis for the BBC magazine series *Writers' World*, 1965; interview produced by Melvyn Bragg, directed by Tristram Powell, www.youtube.com/watch?v=psQkOT7eNwE.
8. Kathleen Raine, *David Jones: Solitary Perfectionist* (Ipswich: Golgonooza Press, 1974).

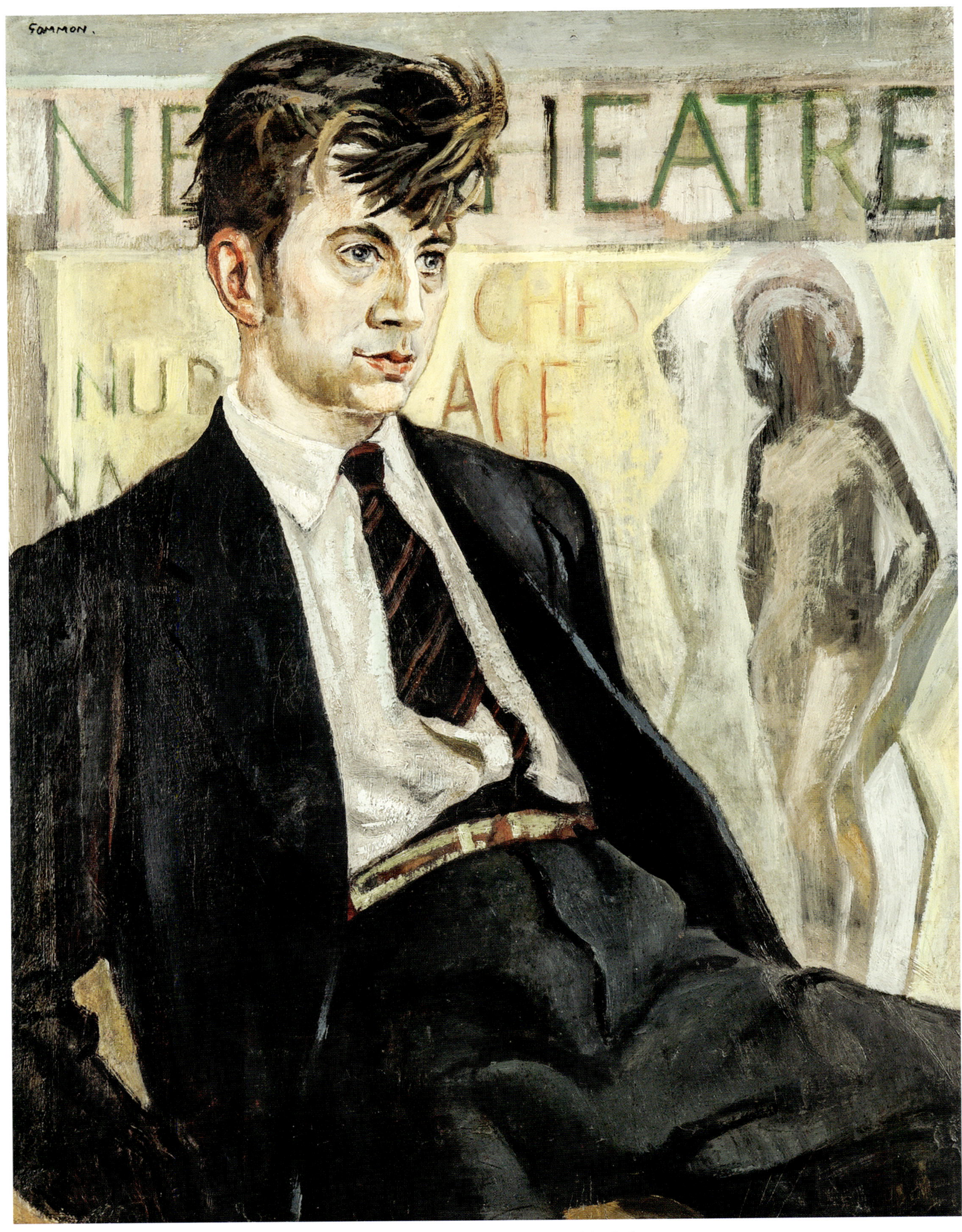

Portrait of Ray Gosling / 1963, oil on canvas, 76 x 61 cm / Northampton Museums and Art Gallery

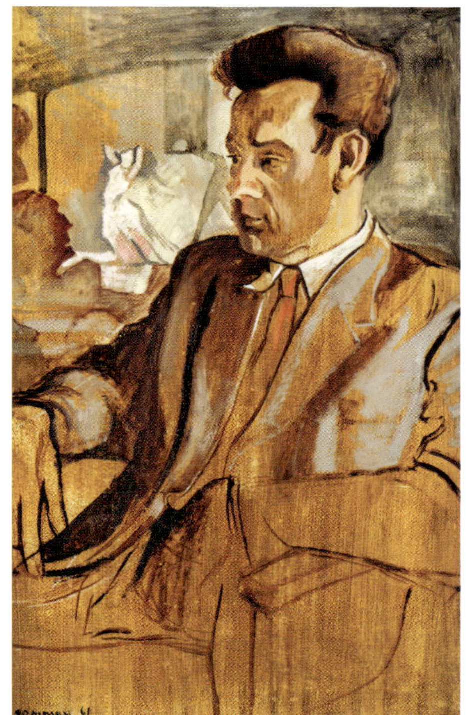

Portrait of Jon Adams
1961, oil on board, 92 x 62 cm
Northampton Museums and Art Gallery

1939) on 'the immaculate white walls'[9] of her extended old farmhouse in Cumbria, has echoes of contemporaneous 'adventures in art' undertaken by both Ede and Wertheim.

Gommon's 1930s art commonly displayed a fusion of landscape and the human element. He once said, 'Landscape has always been the kind of subject matter which I have enjoyed most — and also portrait painting — but never with any sort of great continuity; but I keep on coming back to painting portraits because they are always such challenging things.'[10] During the 1950s he continued to make fine pictures portraying people set within and against the landscape, but increasingly after that — though not invariably — there is a separation between landscape and portrait elements in his work.

In 1961 Gommon made a portrait of a former pupil of his, Jon Adams (1931—2005) [left], who had been at the school at the time David joined the staff. Adams, who showed gifts as an actor, cartoonist and painter early on, became a longstanding friend. Peter Gommon recalls the two of them listening with pleasure to LPs of weirdly raucous *musique concrète* (fashionable in the 1950s), compositions using recorded sounds as raw material. Adams trained as an artist at Northampton Art College and Chelsea School of Art and became known for his surrealist collages and witty cartoons. As an actor, under the name Jonathan Adams, he was renowned for roles in both the London theatre production (1973) and the film version (1975) of *The Rocky Horror Show*.

Gommon acknowledges here Adams's theatrical background — literally so as he is shown seated with his back to the proscenium arch of a stage where an actress performs with brio. His suit, tie, complexion and full head of hair are evoked in a range of rich sepia tones. Adams's character here is one of bedrock resoluteness yet his mien seems morosely introspective.

Gommon's *Portrait of Ray Gosling* (1963) [facing page], who was a pupil at Northampton Grammar School in the 1950s, shows the then 24-year-old seated in relaxed slouching posture, dressed in a black suit and dark tie, with a tousled, Teddy Boy quiff, a quizzically alert expression on a rather strained-looking face. The previous year Gosling had written an autobiographical account, *Sum Total*, in which he stated, 'See the Strand [cigarette] Ad: lonely young man, trilby, raincoat, in the middle of the night, any street, any city — that's me ... One of the rootless, self-made refugees ...'[11]

In 1963 Gosling (1939—2013) had just started to make a name for himself as a wry, poetic TV and radio documentary chronicler of apparently humdrum scenes from British life. As Ian Mayes noted in his *Guardian* obituary (20 November 2013), 'He wanted a classless society in which people looked outward towards each other, not upward or downward. He cared intensely about people, and about his writing. He put the two things together in a way that is still quite rare.'

The backdrop to this portrait is partly obscured by signage announcing the 'NEW THEATRE' — alongside a faintly displayed slim, naked, androgynous-looking young figure. Gommon does convey a sense here of Gosling as

9. Kathleen Raine, *The Land Unknown* (London: Hamish Hamilton, 1975), p.135.
10. 'An Interview with David Gommon, the Painter from Northamptonshire ...', p.40.
11. Ray Gosling, *Sum Total* (Hebden Bridge: Pomona Books, 2004), p.4.

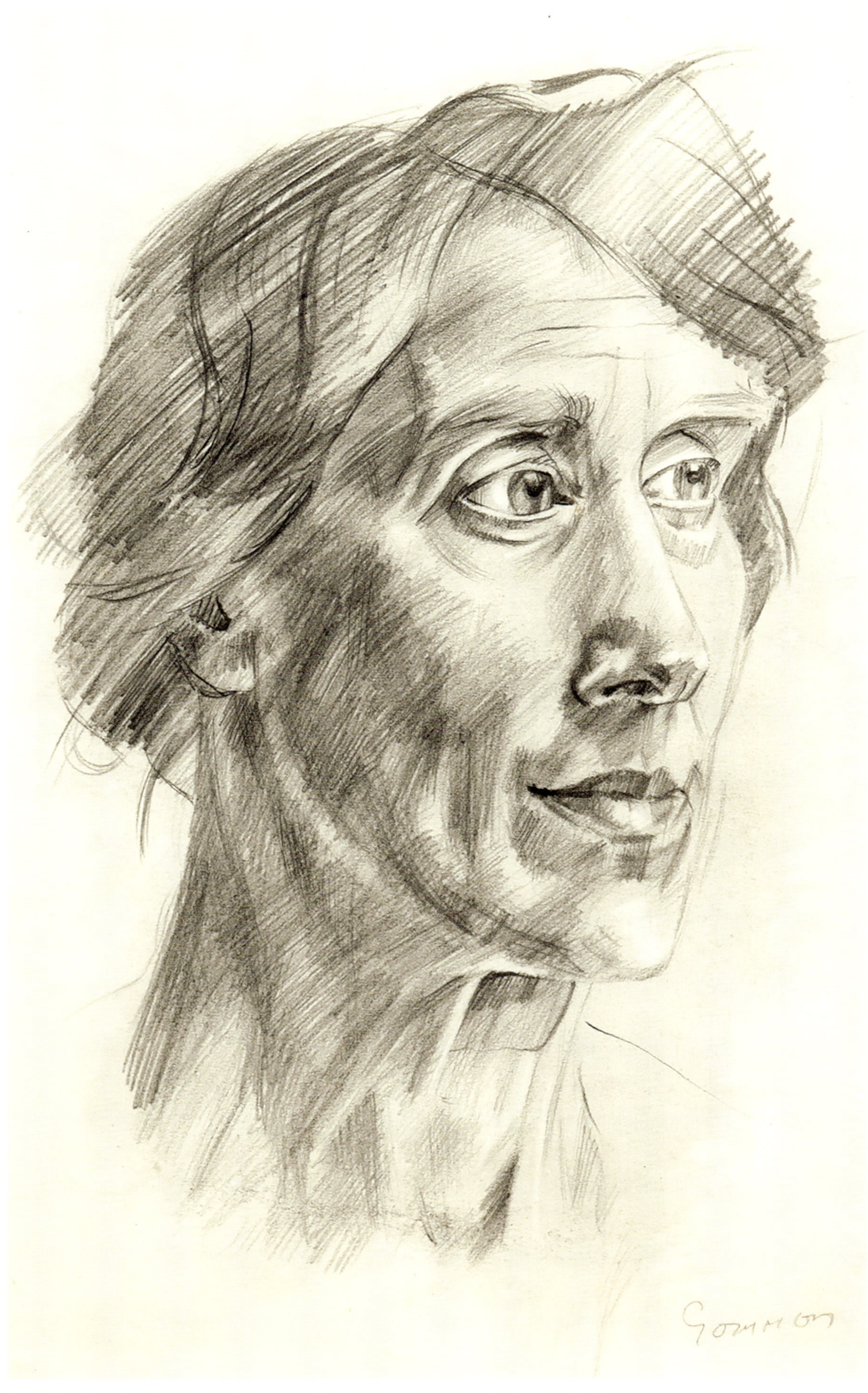

Portrait of Jemima Gommon / 1941, pencil on paper, 40 x 30 cm / private collection

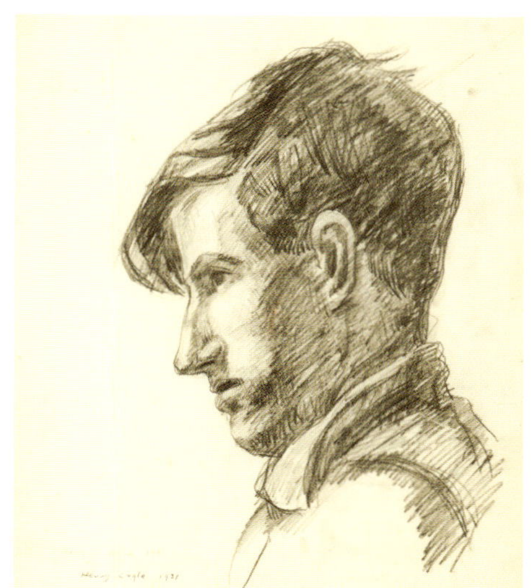

Portrait of David Gommon
[possibly a self-portrait with help from
Henry Cogle]
1931, pencil on paper, 42 x 36.5 cm
private collection

'an intelligent and fiercely positive anarchist' (as he was later called), which revealed itself in his documentaries and his role as a pioneering gay rights activist.

Many of Gommon's portrait drawings and paintings show how nourished he was by keen observational and life-drawing skills he had attained at art school — and by studying Old Master portraits. Henry Cogle (1875—1957), Head of Battersea Polytechnic — and himself a talented artist, fairly open to modern art trends — was his art teacher at that college. A 1931 portrait drawing of Gommon in semi-profile [left] is a skilful study of a thoughtful and determined-looking young man; it seems likely that this is a self-portrait made with help from Cogle (whose name is signed, or at least written, on the drawing).

In the same year Gommon made a pen-and-ink drawing, *Boy*, of a late-adolescent young man — maybe a self-portrait — whose upper body is summoned up with a chic facility of line and graceful simplicity; a sensuous accent is added here by the reddening of the lips. At about the same time he was making touching, piercingly observed pencil drawings of the head of his paternal grandmother asleep. Gommon's 1941 pencil portrait of his mother, Jemima [facing page], rigorously and tenderly scrutinises each and every aspect of her face, hair and neck, the lines and crevices of late-middle age, conjuring up the radiance of her features and character and what is clearly a wise, empathetic gaze.

Gommon's 1934 ink-and-wash *Self-Portrait* [unillustrated] depicts a poised, earnest-looking, dark-tousle-haired young man casually dressed in luminous, open-necked white shirt and sweater — with a pipe held firmly between his lips. The subtle variations of black and greyish tones are adroitly arranged.

A *c*.1953 *Self-Portrait* [below] shows the artist attired in brown jacket, white shirt and matching tie. The strained expression on his sombre visage has something of the emotionally pent-up, even neurasthenic, quality seen in some of Edvard Munch's self-portraits. The backdrop here is Gommon's own gauzy version of Pieter Bruegel the Elder's *c*.1562 painting *The Triumph of Death*; he has retained some of the grim, fantastic details of the original sea-and-landscape, including a skeleton on horseback, figures ringing a bell signifying the death knell of the world, a sketchy figure hanging on a gallows by the seashore and people being dragged to their deaths in a pond and on the ground. Interestingly, what may be a Horse of the Apocalypse in the left foreground here appears as a paltry nag, a mere shadow presence — a far cry from the full-bodied splendour of Gommon's earlier equine renditions.

It seems that in this intense self-portrait he was finding a way of coming to terms with experiences of London in the Blitz (as well as with his painful understanding of the brutal effects of the wider war). Kate Currie recalls her father once telling her that he

had come back from fire-watching to the alarming sight of his parents sitting under the kitchen table after a bombing raid. He said he'd cycled

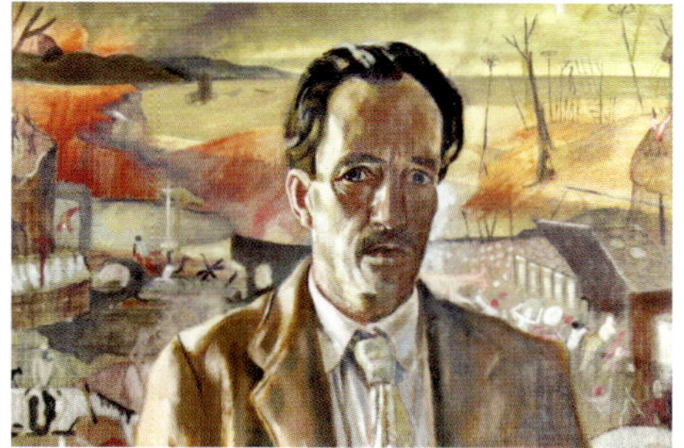

Self-Portrait
c.1953, oil on board, dimensions unknown
private collection

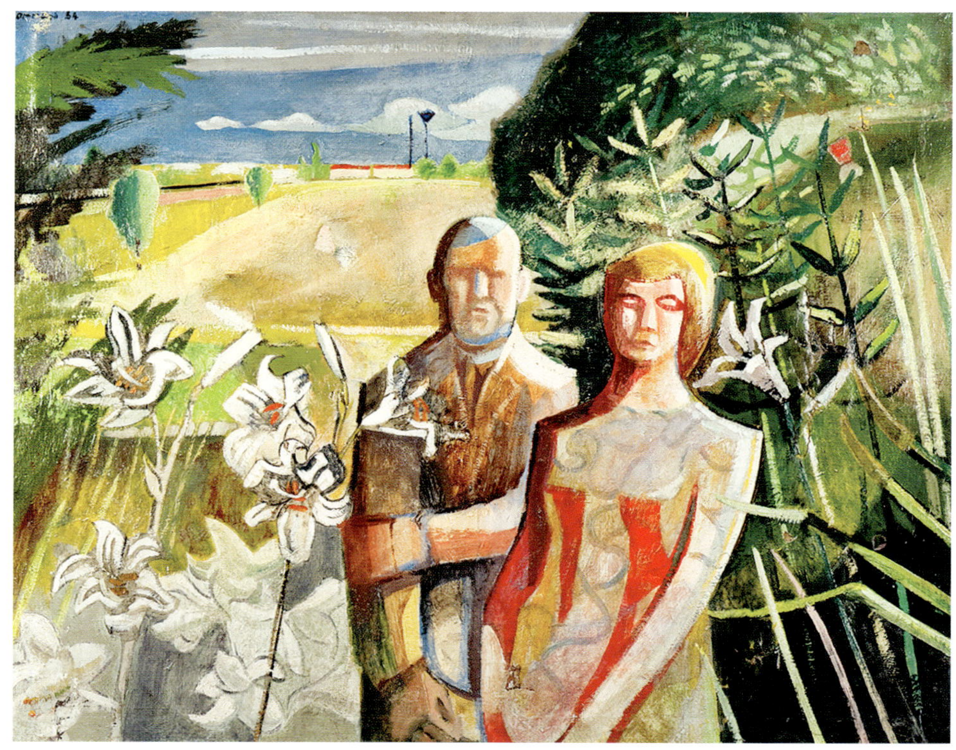

The Walled Garden, Little Billing
1954, oil on canvas, 75 x 96 cm
private collection

past Chelsea Old Church when it had been bombed, seeing bodies lying
in the streets, and how ineffectual you felt because you had a hosepipe
with a trickle coming out of it with all these fires burning around you.
My mother said for years after the War he used to go pale grey when
an aeroplane went over — but the Blitz was generally something he
didn't want to talk about.

Peter Gommon says that the Old Rectory, Little Billing — where the family
lived in the years just after the war — 'was a lovely house, then surrounded
by countryside. Its surroundings have since been altered out of all recognition by the Expressway and Northampton's new town housing.' The
large private walled garden here helped afford David the kind of poetic
and imaginative sanctuary he surely desperately needed at this time.

The 1954 painting *The Walled Garden, Little Billing* [above] shows how, after
the dark, disorientating war years, David was rediscovering a kind of pre-
lapsarian innocence by realigning human subjects with the natural world. The
curiously sculpted-looking forms of a young man and woman are portrayed
here as pensive presences — eyes withdrawn in brown study — amid elegant
white lilies and lush vegetation. The fecund landscape appears intimately
entwined with seeming romantic and sexual bonds between the couple.

In *Lilacs and New Moon* [facing page] a young labouring man, probably
a farm worker, in dungarees, an open-necked top and a russet cloth cap
— a figure again with eyes obscured — is seen loafing against a stretch of
blackened wall illumined in part a vibrant yellow-gold. Moonlight picks out
a profusion of conical-shaped lilac blossoms to the right, which seem somehow to be inclining urgently towards the subject; these could be seen as
aromatic emblems of a young man's yearning.

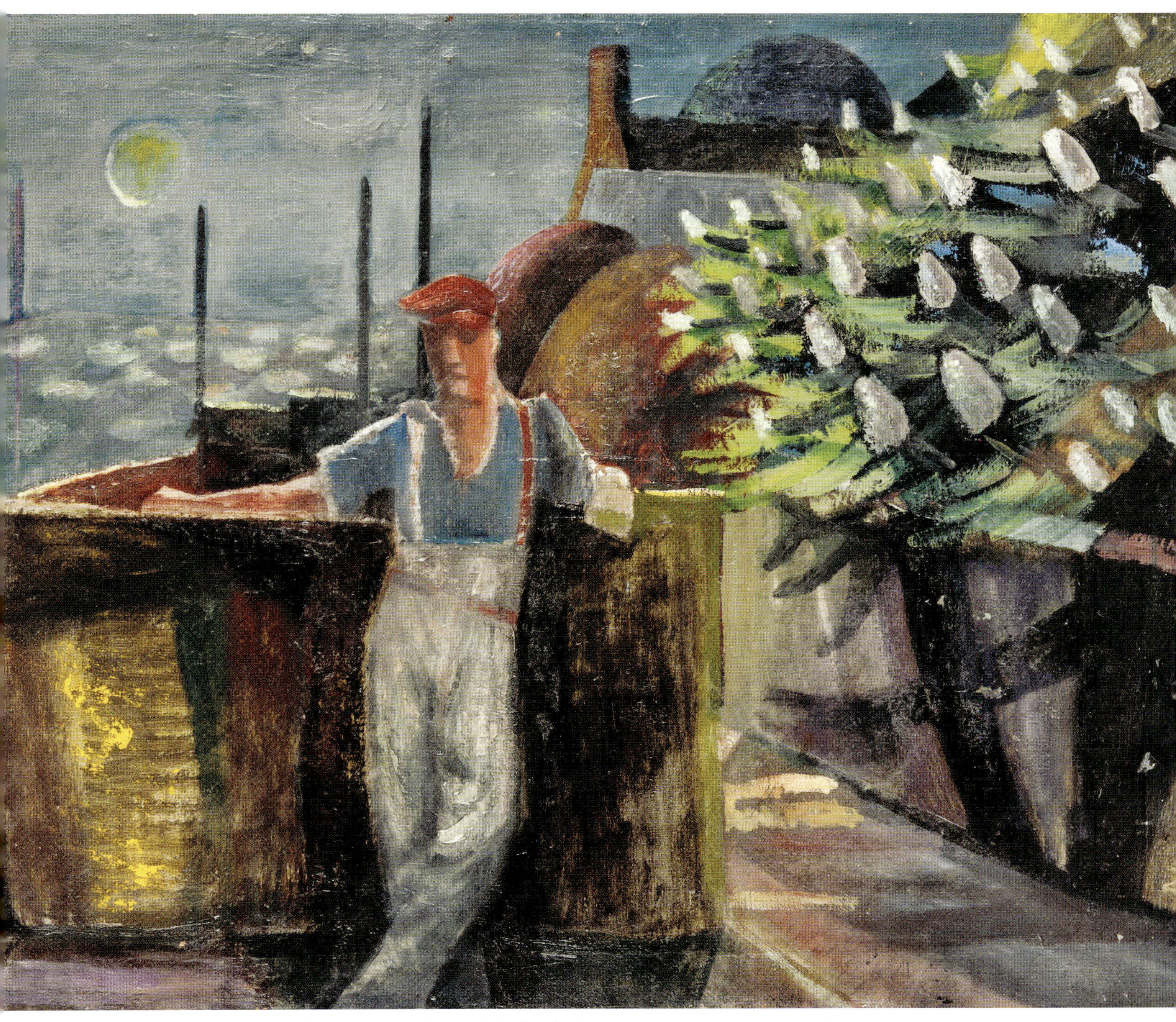

Lilacs and New Moon / 1957, oil on canvas, 47 x 65 cm / private collection

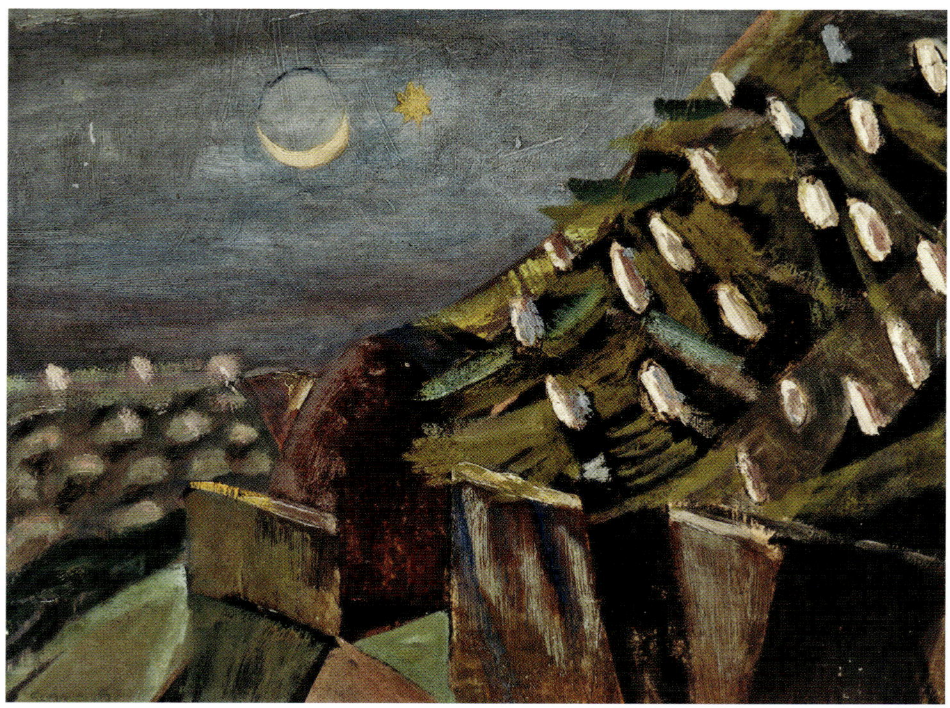

There is an affinity here with pictures by British artists of the period, such as Keith Vaughan (1912—1977) and John Craxton (1922—2009), both of whose many sultry young male subjects also often have something of the poetic lustre of a shepherd under a full or crescent moon in a Samuel Palmer painting. In troubled times the visionary examples of Palmer and William Blake gave Gommon and such fellow artists succour and solace.

The brooding romantic quietude of Gommon's 1950s pictures of figures in the landscape contrasts in spirit with some of his dramatically wrought, erotically charged 1930s paintings, such as the ecstatic watercolour and

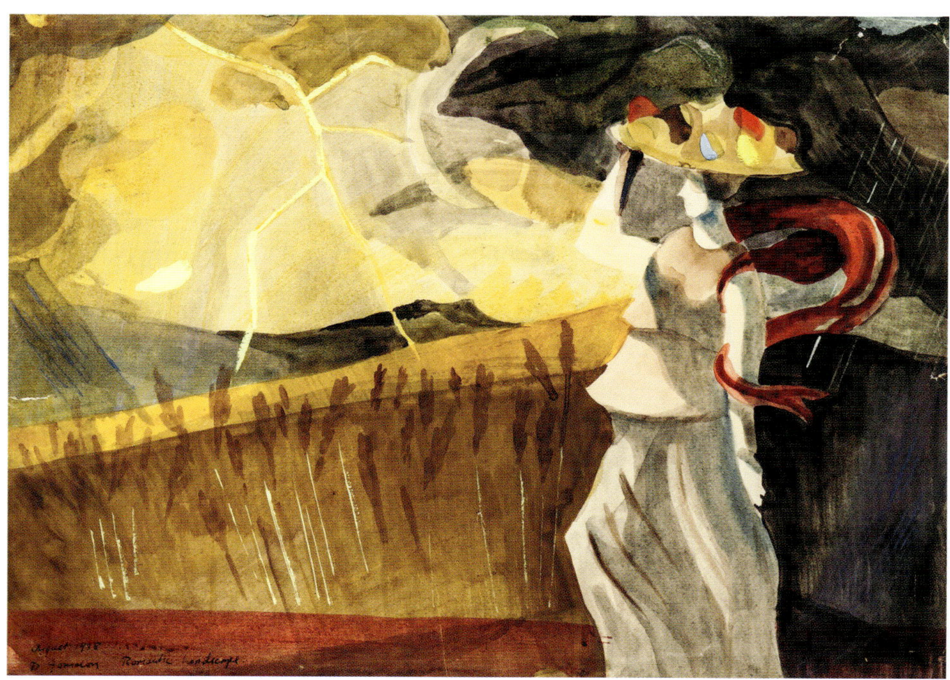

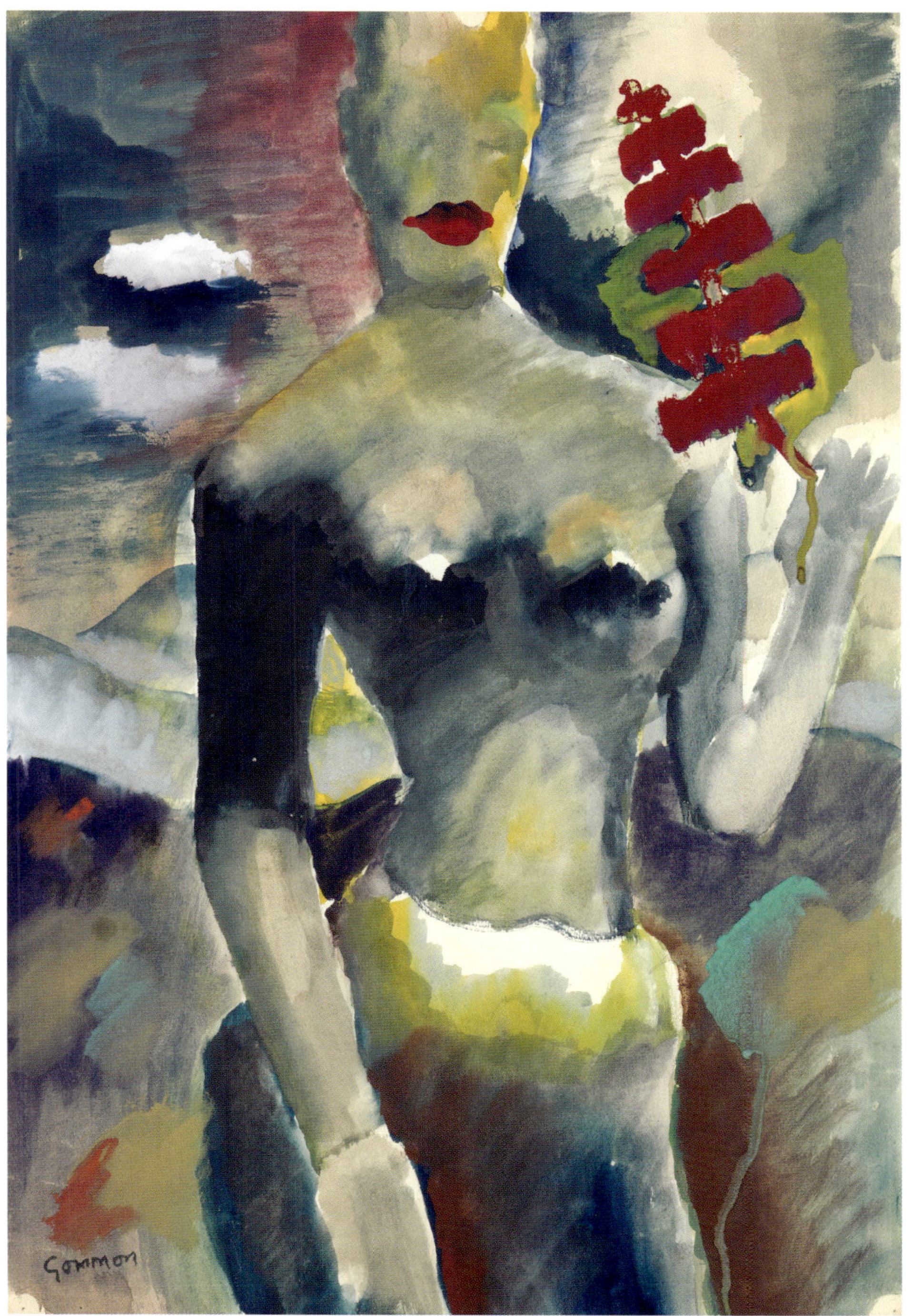

Untitled
(Tess Holding a Geometrised Flower)
*c.*1931—9, watercolour and gouache on paper,
56 x 38.5 cm
Wertheim Estate

gouache — *Tess* (1934) [p. 34]— depicting Thomas Hardy's Tess as a tall,
half-naked young woman leaning onto a noble, in part pale azure horse
(the slight figure of a male onlooker in the distance). Tess is a recurrent
figure in these earlier paintings (often seen holding aloft a single, curiously
geometricised flower) [eg. above], as an archetype of the beautiful, rural girl
contending with elemental natural forces [eg. facing page] as well as with
harsh social mores and stigma.

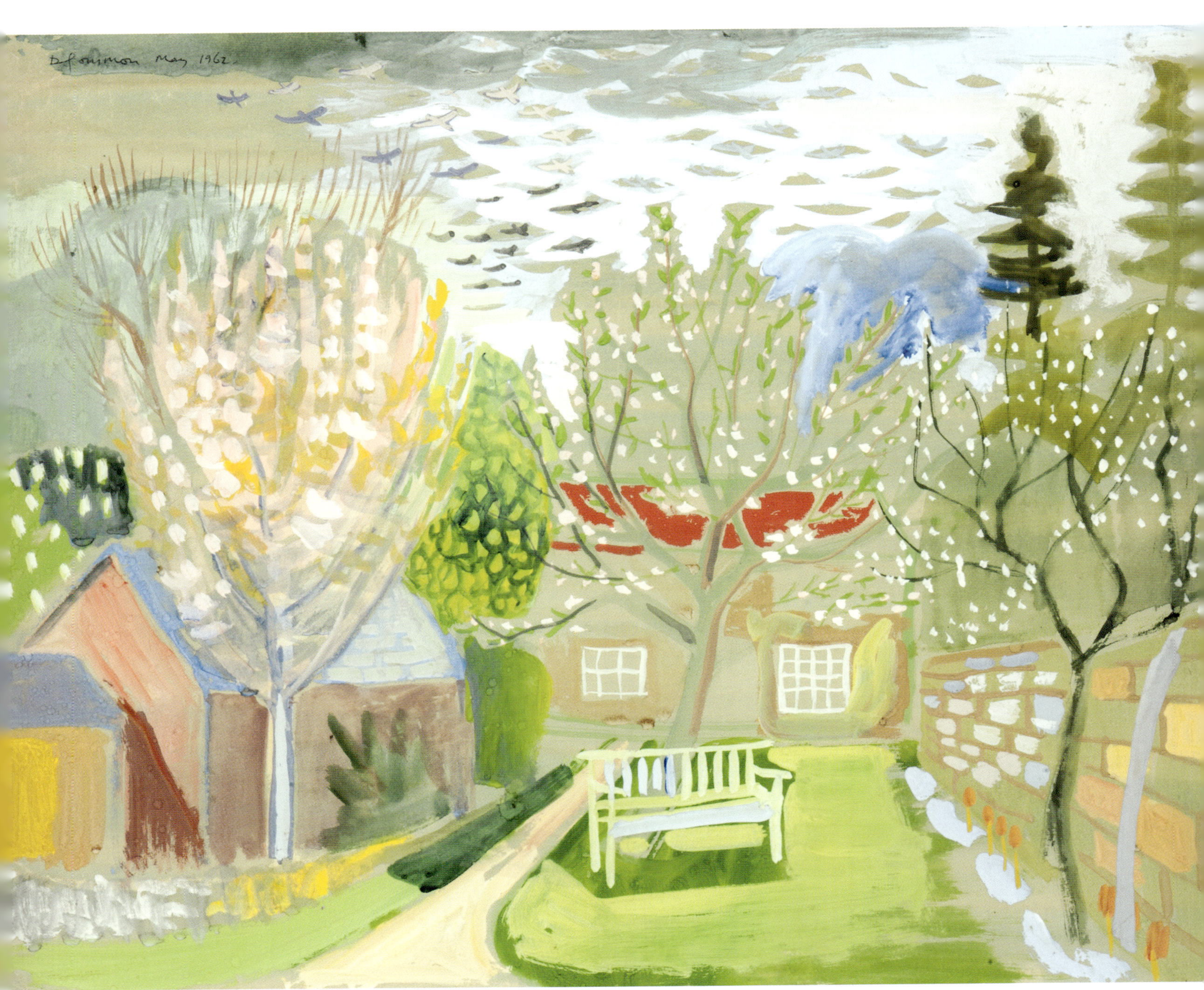

Cottage Garden (The Garden Seat) / 1962, gouache on paper, 55.5 x 76 cm / private collection

The garden that Gommon loved

IN 1958 PETER GOMMON BECAME A PUPIL AT NORTHAMPTON GRAMMAR School at the age of 12, and he thinks it was around this time that the family moved from Little Billing to Hardingstone (about six miles away), a village to the south of Northampton (it is now a suburb of the town). Jean's parents had already moved to the village from Manchester and suggested that David and his family move to the house next door, as the current tenants were leaving. So the Gommons then moved to Jasmine Cottage, the middle property of three largely eighteenth-century, stone-walled cottages in Coldstream Lane, a quiet backwater. It had three storeys with three bedrooms; on the ground floor there was a small kitchen, plus a dining room and a sitting room which had great inglenook fireplaces with hefty beams running over them, above which David had written texts in bold script (see overleaf). These included Sir Thomas Browne's line, 'Life is a pure flame, and we live by an invisible Sun within us' (from *Hydriotaphia, Urne Burial*, 1658).[1]

Peter recalls, 'When you opened the door at Jasmine Cottage there were cut-out images he had made of his heroes on the wall — the poets T.S. Eliot and W.B. Yeats were there, and [the French-Algerian Existentialist or Absurdist writer] Albert Camus — along with the Death Mask of William Blake.' On one wall David had also made his own transfer of mystical words from the fifteenth-century writer and anchorite, Julian of Norwich, in this slightly abbreviated form: 'All shall be well, and all manner of thing shall be well.' Peter says that his parents were 'very fond of her, and attached to her writing. This particular phrase came across like a mantra to them; at the time she wasn't so well known ... they admired her as a wonderful spirit, who — living in tough times — in "a little thing, the quantity of a hazel nut, lying in the palm of my hand" saw the extent of God's entire benign creation, filled with love'.

A bedroom upstairs in the cottage was used as Gommon's studio, one wall covered in shelves displaying hundreds of books of German, French and English literature and philosophy (Peter describes him in this respect as 'Pan-European') and innumerable artbooks. He often worked on works of paper at a small table by the window — with a view of the garden.

Peter says that his mother created the garden — which had a lawn with a sinuous line of stepping stones down the middle — all the way to a wooden bench at the end. On either side were densely planted borders with curving edges to the lawn. In spring and summer the borders were scintillatingly colourful, with a wide variety of flowers.

1. Sir Thomas Browne, 'Hydriotaphia. Urne Burial', from Sir Geoffrey Keynes (ed.), *Sir Thomas Browne: Selected Writings* (London: Faber & Faber, 1968), p.153.

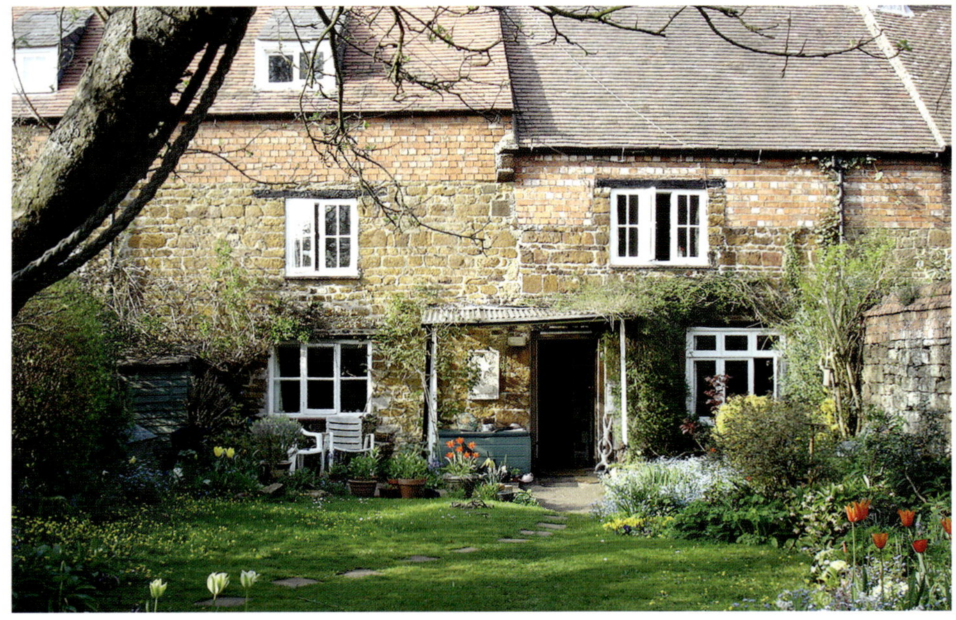

Jasmine Cottage photos, *c.*1984

David in his first floor studio;
the sitting room window

The sitting room

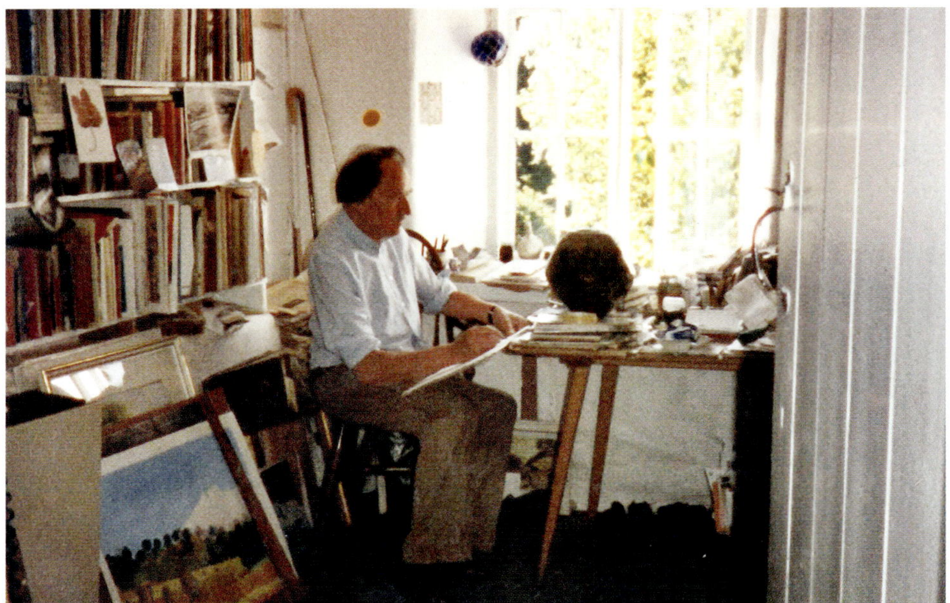

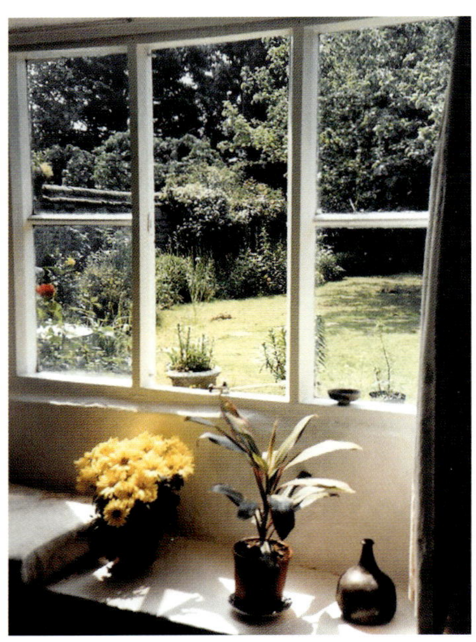

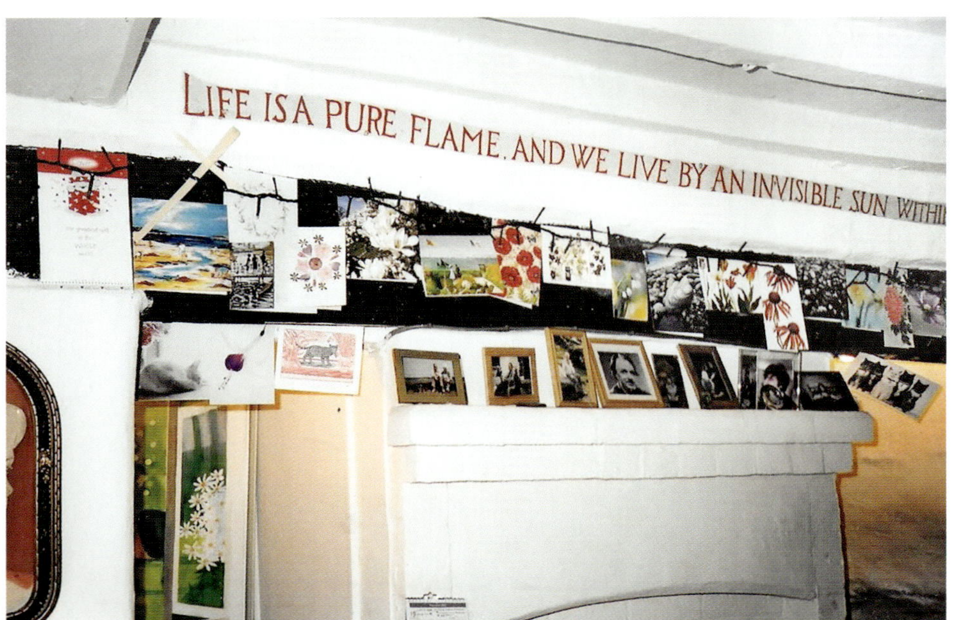

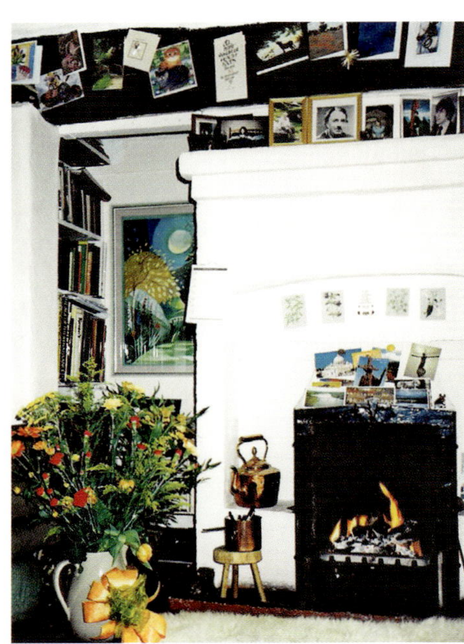

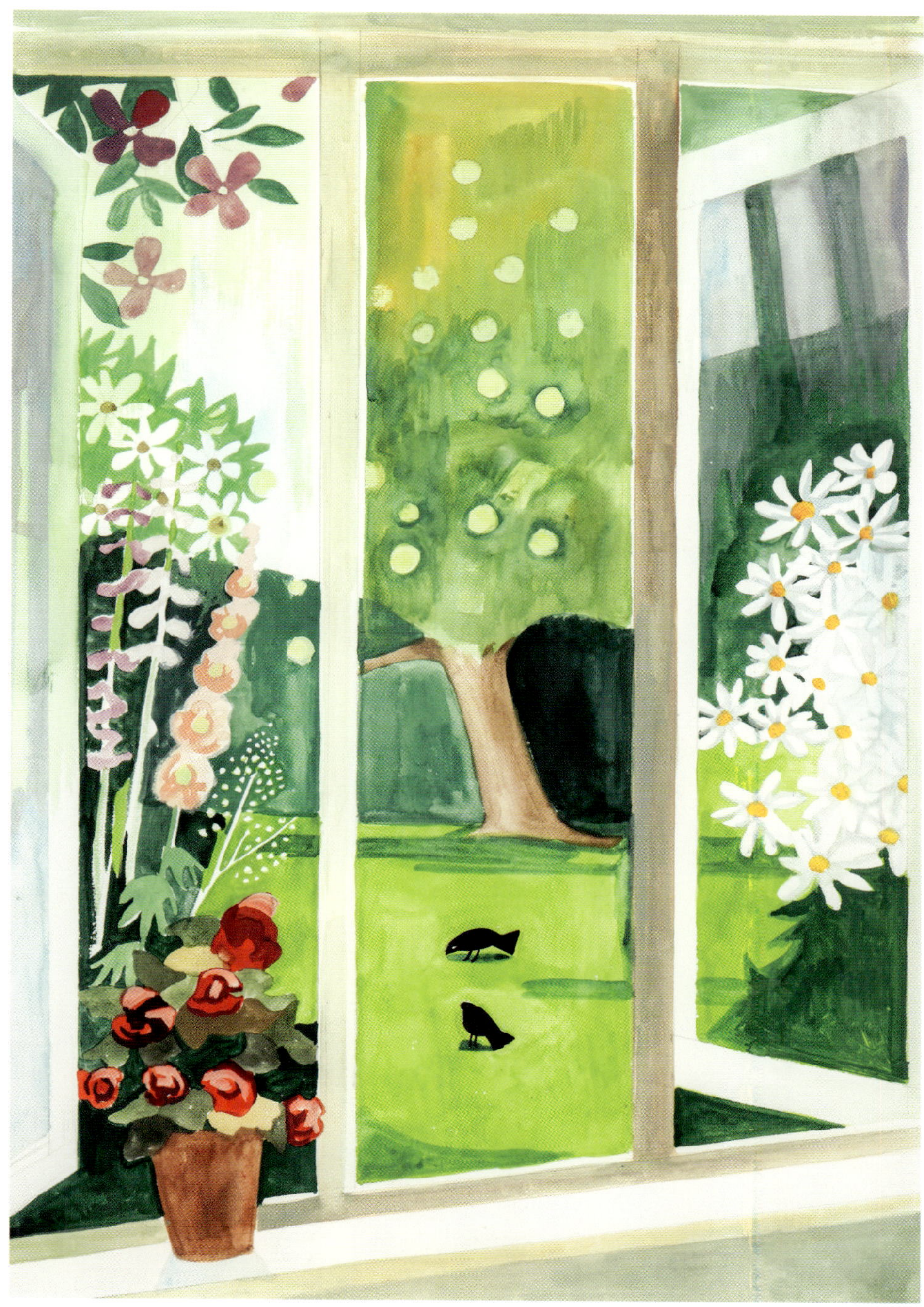

The Garden (with Two Blackbirds)
date unknown, gouache on paper, 73 x 53 cm
private collection

My mother provided the garden that he then loved. She did the gardening, and my father responded to it and painted it. In nearly all the paintings of the garden standing in the centre is the huge Bramley apple tree. My mother used to sit looking out at the garden, where little blackbirds used to nest in the fragrant climbing jasmine under her window — that's why it was called Jasmine Cottage.

This is just the kind of garden that the writer Vita Sackville-West (1892—1962) was referring to in her 1951 book, *In Your Garden*, when she wrote: 'the sort of garden I like best … is a cottage garden of the best sort … packed with flowers at all times of the year … I remember specially a planting of the blue primrose mixed with the blue scilla round the base of a grey stone well-head, a perfectly chosen combination.'[2]

2. Vita Sackville-West, *Observer* article, 12 March 1950, included in Sackville-West, *In Your Garden* (London: Michael Joseph, 1951), pp.46—7.

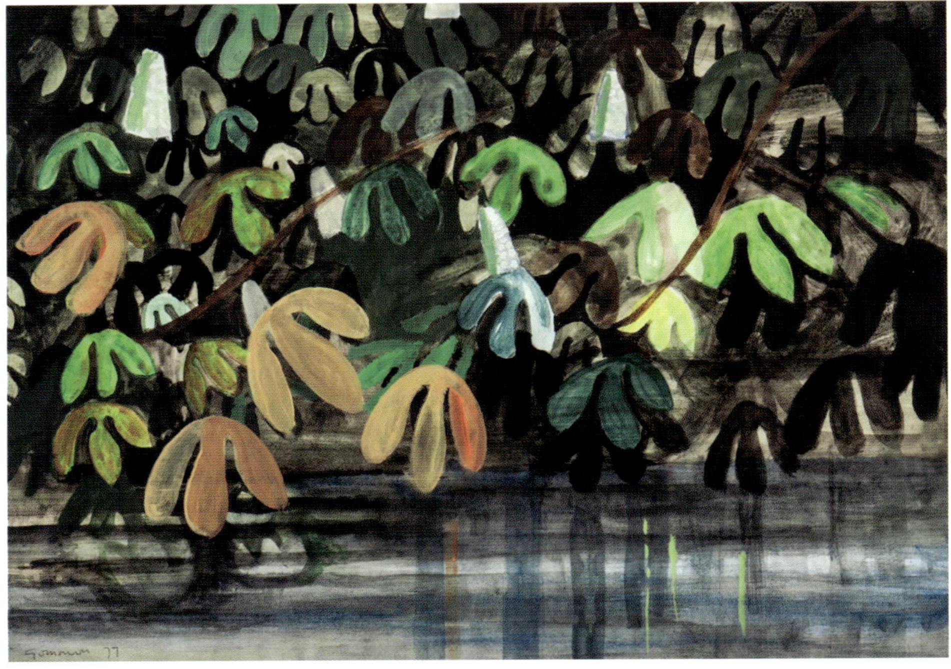

Jasmine Cottage's walled garden quickly became a key subject for Gommon. Also. after he moved to Hardingstone he continued holidaying in, and cycling around, Dorset, and he and Jean sometimes visited Wales; in 1984 he visited Northumberland and the Scottish borders. The landscapes he saw on these trips inspired many paintings. In the summer of 1983 the couple went to the South of France with friends, and he loved seeing places where Cézanne painted.

In December 1979 he visited Australia, commissioned to paint a mural at the Music Centre of Canberra Grammar School. The immense, unspoilt

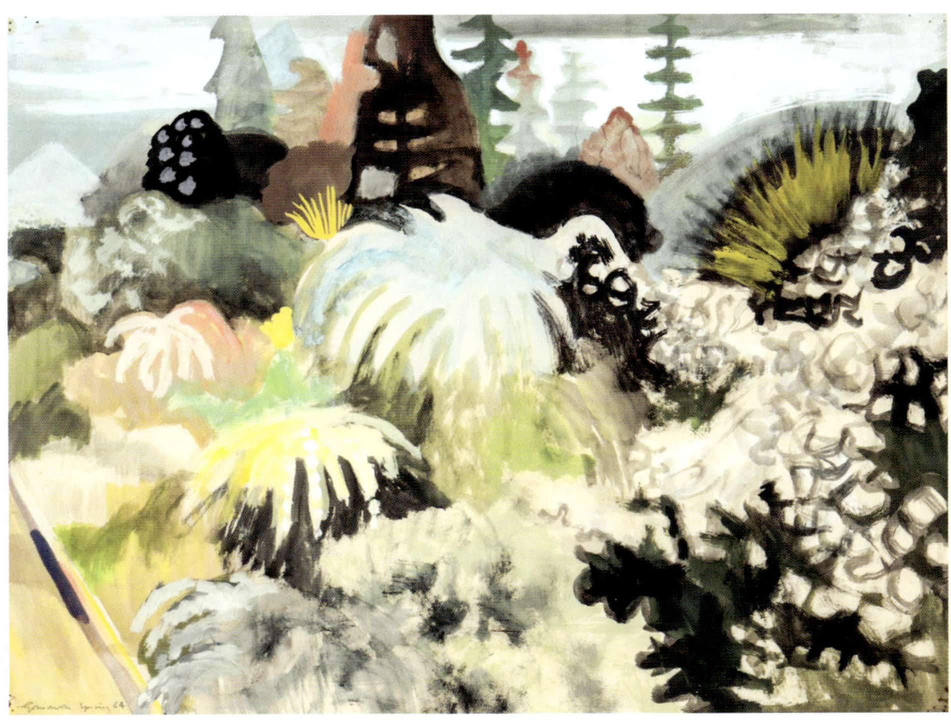

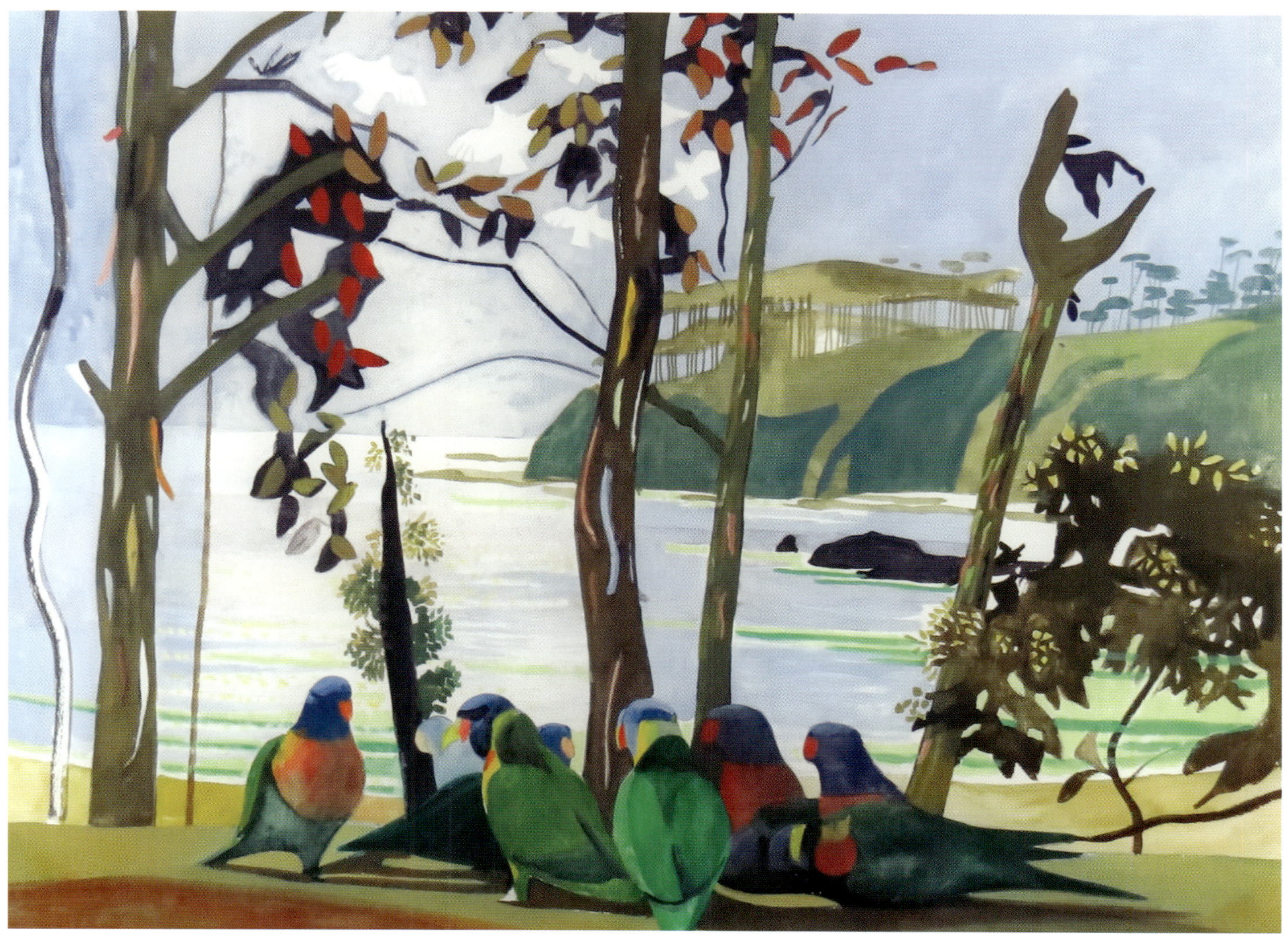

Parakeets / 1980, gouache on paper, dimensions unknown / private collection

landscapes and birdlife he saw in this vast land resulted in paintings with a markedly different tone and a distinctively heightened intensity of light and colour — such as in a 1980 portrayal of a group of subtly vibrant parakeets (above) — the males with scarlet chests, orange throats and bluish-purplish heads, the females with more earthy yellow and green tones — gentle creatures huddling together on a seashore under red-leafed eucalyptus trees.

As a young man Gommon often painted pictures *en plein air*, but in later years he tended to make quick sketches and colour notes outside, subsequently working them up in the studio into complete works of art. Peter Gommon notes that 'he was a very fast draughtsman — as many preparatory draw-ings, gouaches and notations show'. He made numerous quick mono-chrome sketches, sometimes using Biro — often writing individual colour names over particular details as an *aide-mémoire*.

In one A5 sketchbook (p.81) there are some fine rudimentary studies in gouache towards a 1981 series of garden pictures — one of a bare tree and foliage on a moonlit, starry night — which are quite intuitively abstracted. Another sketch here depicts some of nature's forms and colour accents as a riveting assortment of purely abstract shapes and rhythmic dabs.

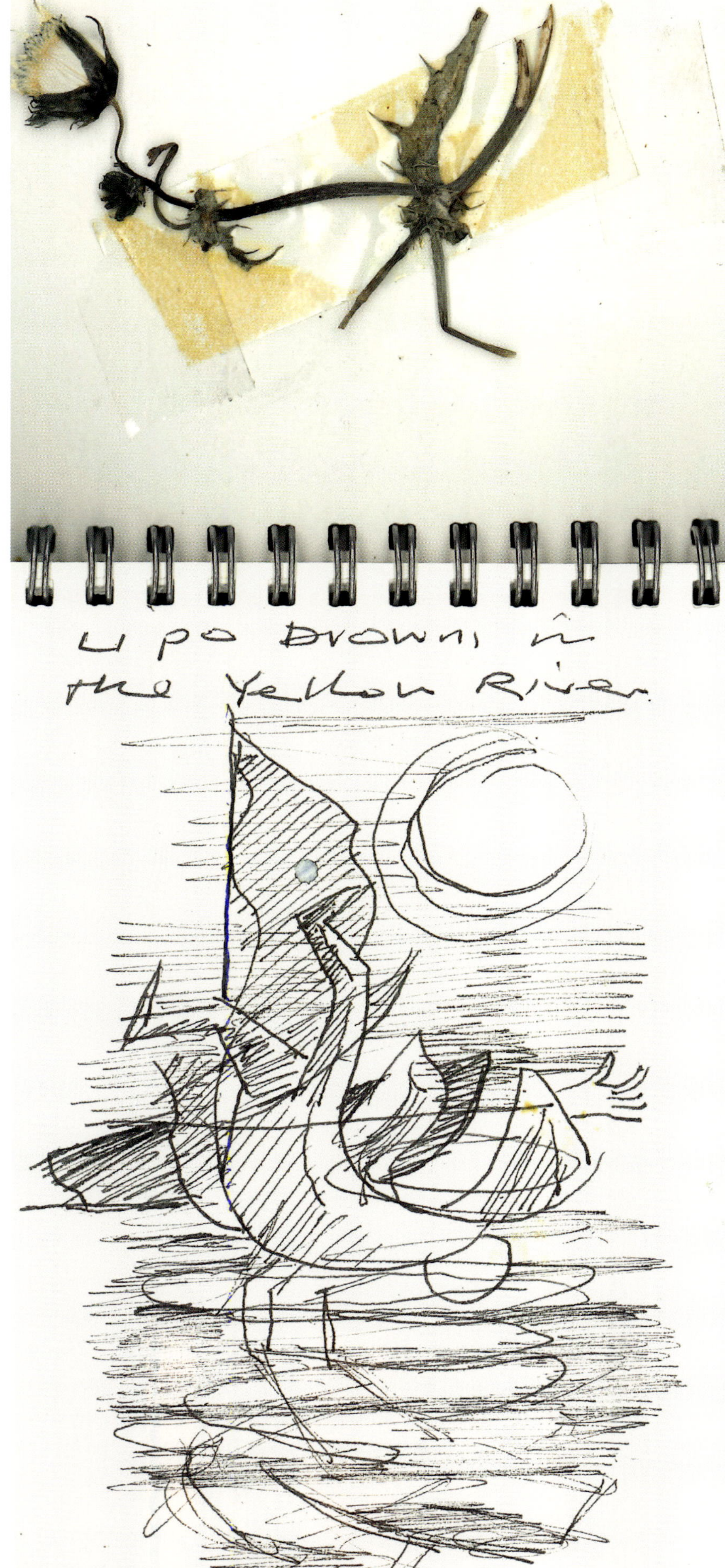

Pages from an A6 sketchbook, 1984;
'Thursday 11th Oct 1984 Flodden Field',
pen and ink and Sellotaped pressed flower on paper;
'Li Po Drowns in the Yellow River', Biro on paper
private collection

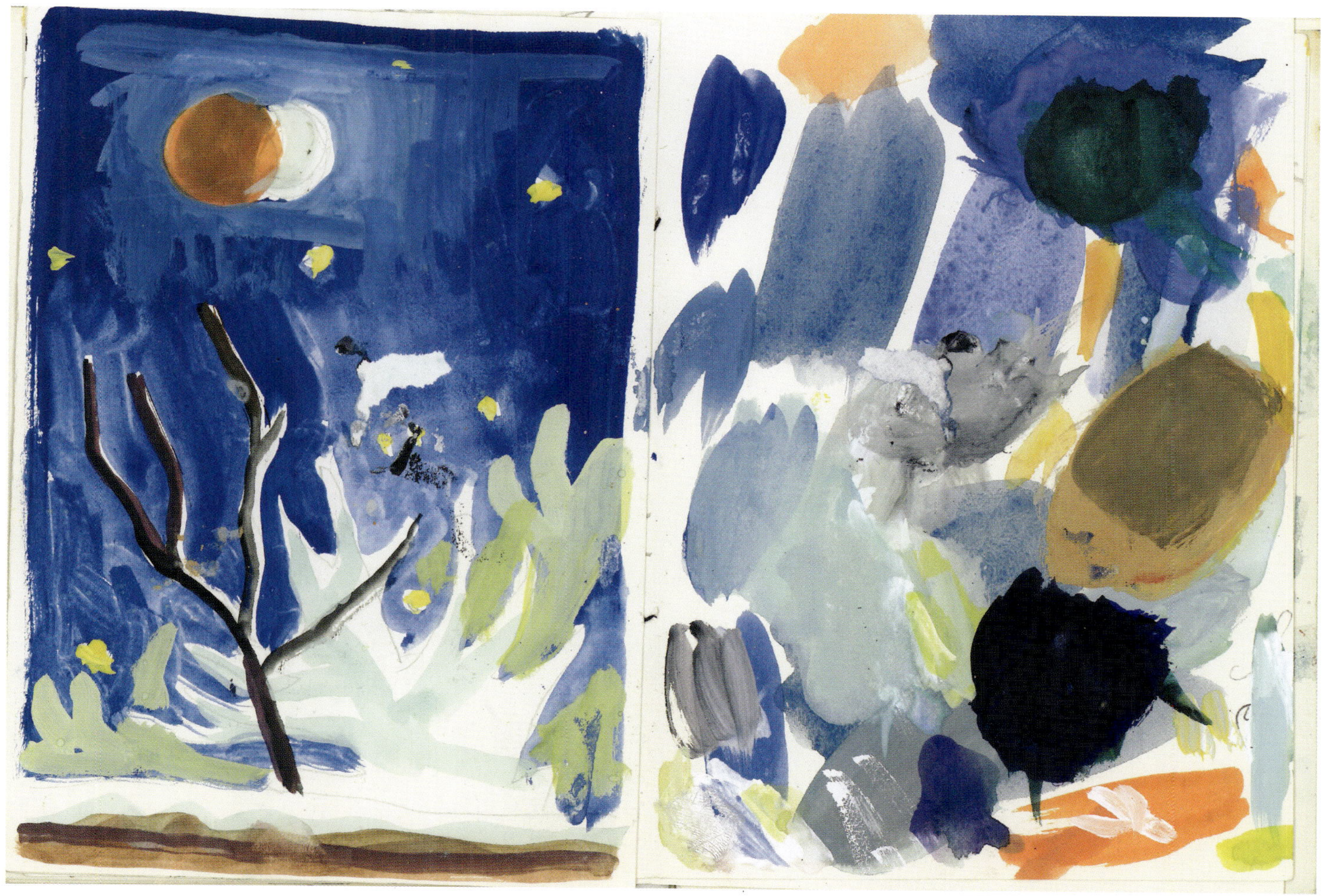

Pages from an A5 sketchbook with studies towards a 1981 series of garden pictures, gouache on paper / private collection

Three years later, in an A6 sketchbook [facing page], Gommon Sellotaped a pressed white-flowered thistle to the page, noting above in black pen, 'Thursday 11th oct [*sic*] 84. Flodden Field'. The thistle is often seen as emblematic of a resilient independent Scotland; he had picked this flower in peaceful green fields which in 1513 had been the boggy, impassable site of the Battle of Flodden Field, in which 10,000 Scottish soldiers, including King James IV of Scotland, were killed whilst fighting the English army. In this simple assemblage are surely echoes too of his own paintings evoking Second World War battlefields — with dead soldiers and civilians depicted with sunflowers growing around them (see p. 57).

On the adjoining page is a sketch in black Biro, inscribed with this title: 'Li Po Drowns in the Yellow River'. Li Po (701—762) was the revered Chinese Tang Dynasty poet; in China he is known as Li Bai. This dramatic scene evokes the dreadful velocity of the poet falling from a sailboat into the river, captured while he is still above the water line with his legs in the air, one hand seen flailing pitiably and his head as vacant and featureless as the moon's vast face looming above — the latter reflected multiple times in the rippling water. A myth had developed later on that Li Po had drowned after falling from his boat one day while drunk (he has been described as a poet 'rapt with wine') and in the process of reaching out to catch a moonbeam or attempting to embrace a lunar reflection in the river.

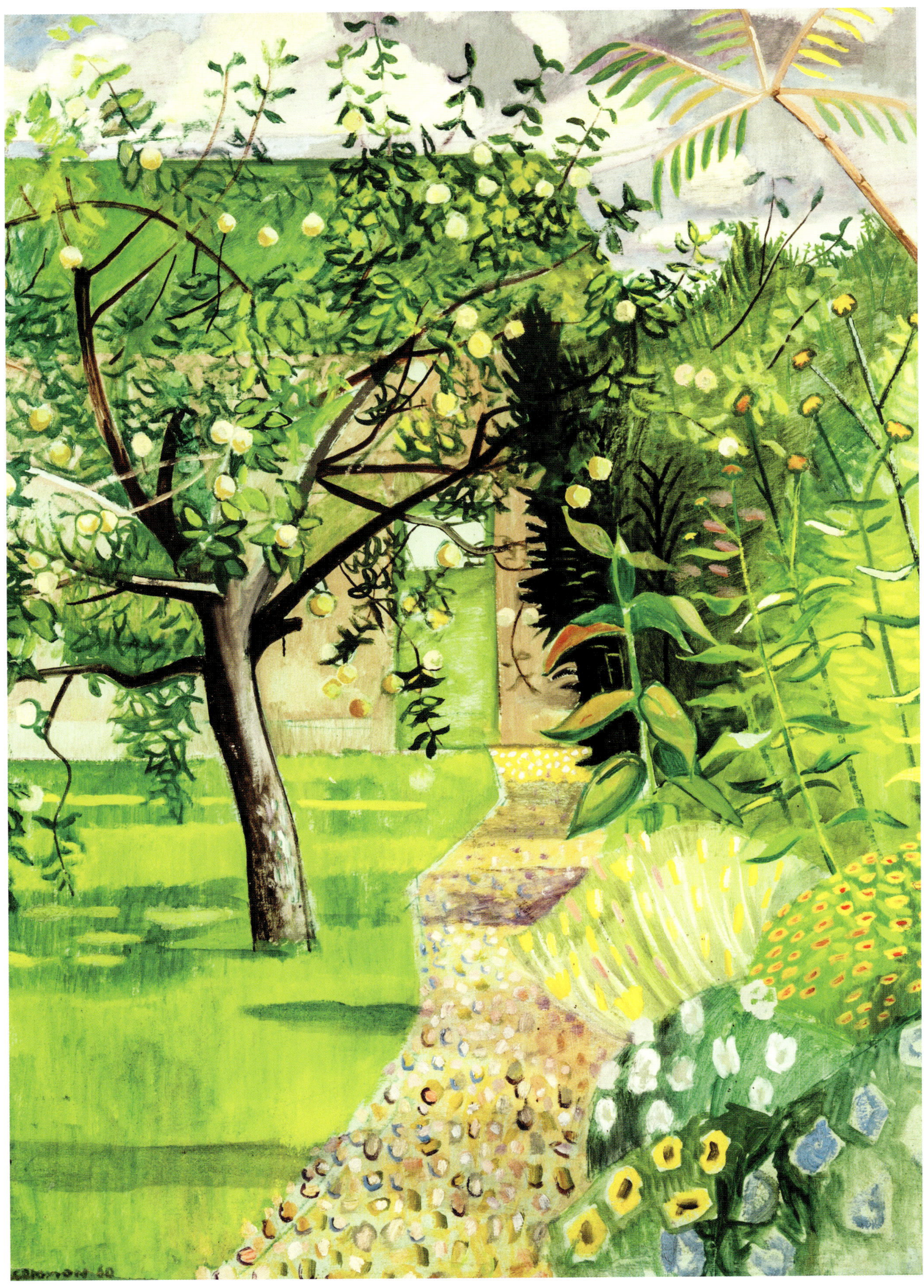

Garden — Apple Tree / 1960, oil on board, 121 x 92 cm / *private collection*

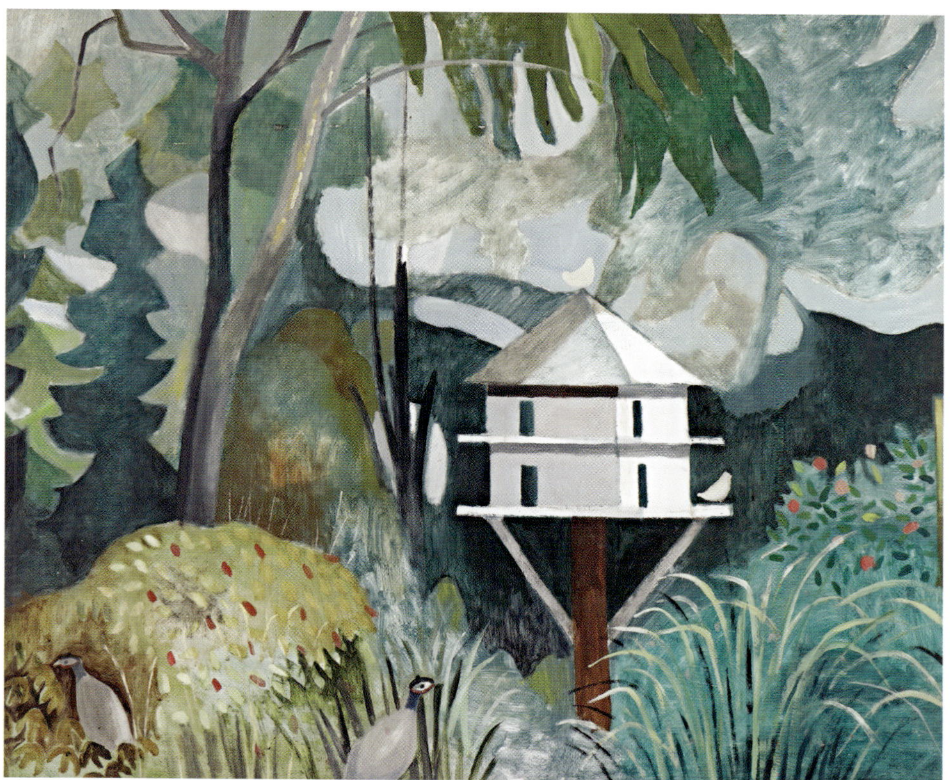

**Scaldwell, Northamptonshire
(Gerald Kendall's Garden)**
1976, oil on board, 122 x 153 cm
private collection

It is likely that Gommon knew Li Po's poems from the critically acclaimed 1915 volume *Cathay*, a collection of classical Chinese poems sensitively interpreted by the poet Ezra Pound. In fact Pound's rather Imagistic rendition of Li Po's hauntingly lovely poem 'Taking Leave of a Friend' could almost be a lyrical evocation of the *inscape* (as well as landscape) of one of Gommon's 1930s gouaches:

> Blue mountains to the north of the walls,
> White river winding about them;
> Here we must make separation
> And go out through a thousand miles of dead grass.
>
> Mind like a floating white cloud,
> Sunset like the parting of old acquaintances
> Who bow over their clasped hands at a distance.
> Our horses neigh to each other
>   as we are departing.[3]

Li Po's poems celebrate the sublime nature of mountains and the inspiring tranquillity of hermitages away from the stresses of the world. In Gommon's paintings, the symbolism of the paradisical garden as a place of meditative retreat and focus is a recurrent theme, one which has deep roots both in Islamic, notably Sufi, mysticism — in Persian, the word *pardis* signifies both paradise and an enclosed garden — and in the Judeo-Christian biblical story of the Garden of Eden (*Gan Eden* in Hebrew).

In the 1960 oil painting *Garden — Apple Tree* [facing page], the view to the shed at the bottom of his garden is divided into three main sections,

3. Ezra Pound, his creative rendition of a poem by Li Po (addressed here as Rihaku), 'Taking Leave of a Friend', *Cathay* (London: Elkin Matthews, 1915), pp.28—9.

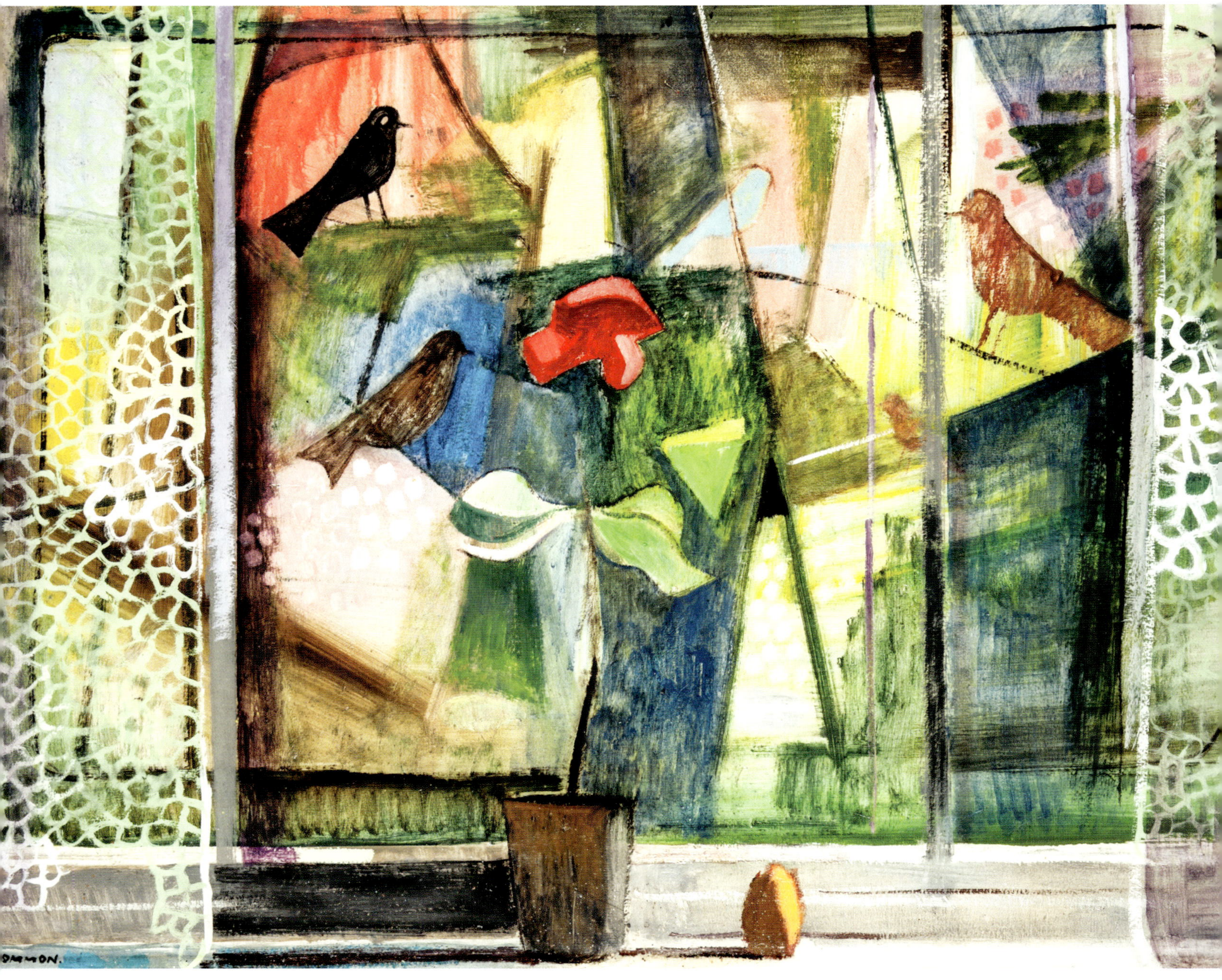

The Red Geranium / 1964, oil on board, 92 x 120 cm / private collection

showing the lawn with its singular apple tree bearing coruscating fruit (echoes here of Samuel Palmer's rhapsodic 1830 painting, *The Magic Apple Tree*), a winding, gravelly pathway and a border with a variety of both tall-stemmed and low-lying plants; the mellifluous stone of the garden shed is seen in the distance. This heightened naturalistic scene gleams with diverse colour accents: those of the apples themselves, different kinds of flowers and multi-hued pebbles or stones on the path. This dictum from a 1753 letter by the writer Horace Walpole is apposite here: 'one's garden ... is to be nothing but riant [cheerful, making one smile], and the gaiety of nature'.[4]

The Red Geranium (1964) [facing page] gives a view of his garden — with four birds observed as imperturbably serene, perching presences — from inside the house. On the windowsill is placed an arrestingly vivid geranium in a simple pot alongside a golden apple. The window, framed on either side with fluttering diaphanous fabric, reveals the theatrical insubstantiality of the garden beyond, rendered in abstracted planes of prismatic colour — in which boldly simplified forms of several birds are seen to perch. The poetic precedent of windowsill still lifes lithely opening up onto the natural world is there in a number of paintings by Christopher Wood and Winifred Nicholson.

In a letter (dated 1 July 1984) to his son Peter, David expressed his pleasure in his garden, its flowers and birds — also making interesting reference to a planned visit to Brighton:

> It's now 7.30 and I am sitting writing this in the evening sun lowering itself down over a [neighbour's] roof; but still quite warm and bright, my gardener [his wife Jean!] is watering her flowers, and the garden is looking very beautiful! I am sitting beside your potentilla [a flowering plant in the rose family] and the Grandpa Dickson rose you gave us is a picture at the moment, insects are buzzing and those birds that just chirp are chirping — sparrows I suppose! I am now going to ring up Mrs Wertheim's daughter to arrange a visit to Brighton [Lucy Wertheim, who herself had spent her later years living in Brighton, had died in 1971 aged 88, and David continued to remain in touch with her family].

In Gommon's post-war art, horses feature hardly at all — and birds have become a prime subject as well as pivotal symbolic focus. Choreographing birds soaring in flight as well as still and peaceful on the ground, his art seems to show the kind of intimate comprehension of this fellow creature as expressed by William Blake:

> How do you know but ev'ry Bird that cuts the airy way,
> Is an immense world of delight, clos'd by your senses five?[5]

Gommon owned several books on medieval European illuminated manuscripts. His own lyrical depictions of songbirds have affinities to avian portrayals in the decorative margins of many such manuscripts — especially in English works from about 1200 to 1400. As creatures formed on the fifth day of Creation in the Book of Genesis, their song is intuited in such works as being imbued with cosmic meaning, resonant with 'the music of the spheres'. In the English *Bird Psalter* (*c.*1280—1300; The Fitzwilliam Museum,

4. *Letters of Horace Walpole, Earl of Orford, to Sir Horace Mann, British Envoy at the Court of Tuscany* (London: Richard Bentley 1833), p.86.
5. William Blake, 'A Memorable Fancy', *William Blake* (Harmondsworth: Penguin Books, 1976), p.96.

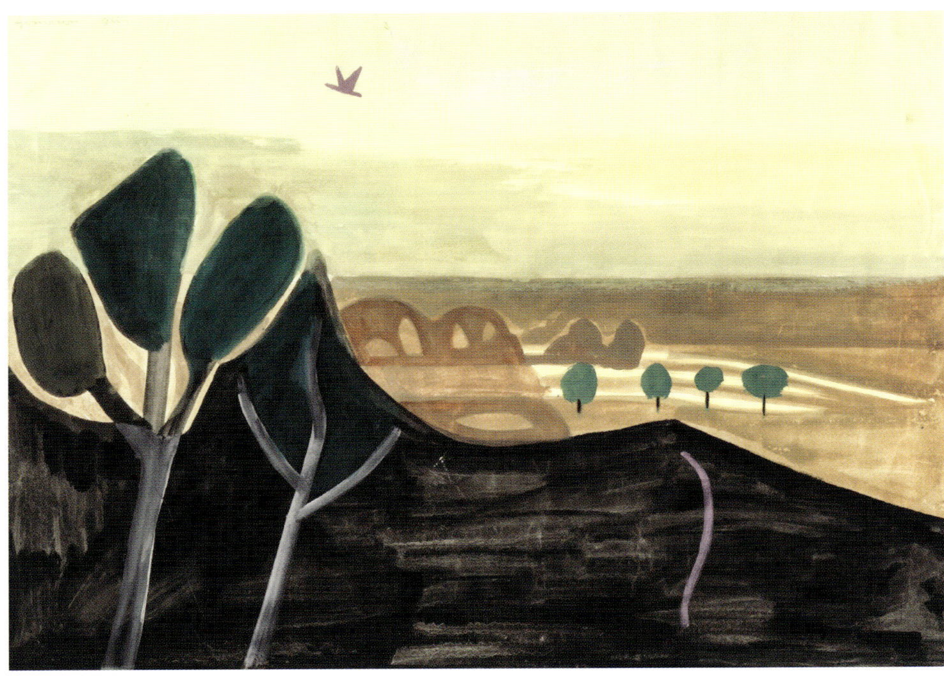

Evening Bird
1966, gouache on paper, 41 x 60 cm
private collection

Cambridge), containing 150 Psalms, about 27 species of birds have been identified; the *vox* of birds was seen as being harmoniously at one with the poet's voice, represented here by an image of King David with his harp.

In 1952 a highly original and observant book, *Birds as Individuals*, appeared, written by a musician and naturalist, Len [Gwendolen] Howard (1894—1973). In her rural Sussex cottage she developed a quick understanding of what soon became 'tame-wild birds'[6] in her area, protecting them from predatory cats and feeling that she had come to appreciate their distinctive characters and what she considered their intelligent minds; she found that her musical training helped her appreciate diverse aspects of birdsong. Many paintings by Gommon express a similar kind of sensibility — at least in their evident appreciation of avian lightness, resilience, quick-wittedness, agility and alacrity of flight, and the variegated beauty of birdsong.

Gommon's 1956 oil painting *Blackbird in Winter* [facing page] shows a full-throated common blackbird (a species of true thrush) perched on the branch of a tree whose form is summoned up in a concatenation of curving, spiky black lines, edged white with snow. The bold, incisive foreground delineation of bird and tree contrasts with the soft-edged delicacy of two distant trees against far fields depicted in a pale palette of light blue, subdued mauve and white. A flock of birds (maybe a murder of crows or a murmuration of starlings) — conjured up by a mass of miniscule black and pale blue specks — is seen flying across part of the sky (glowing an admixed roseate and yellow hue) and the filmy winter sun (with its hazy bluish aureole).

This picture possesses the kind of allusive and graceful mystical quality found in Wallace Stevens's 1954 poem, 'Thirteen Ways of Looking at a Blackbird' — for example in these lines:

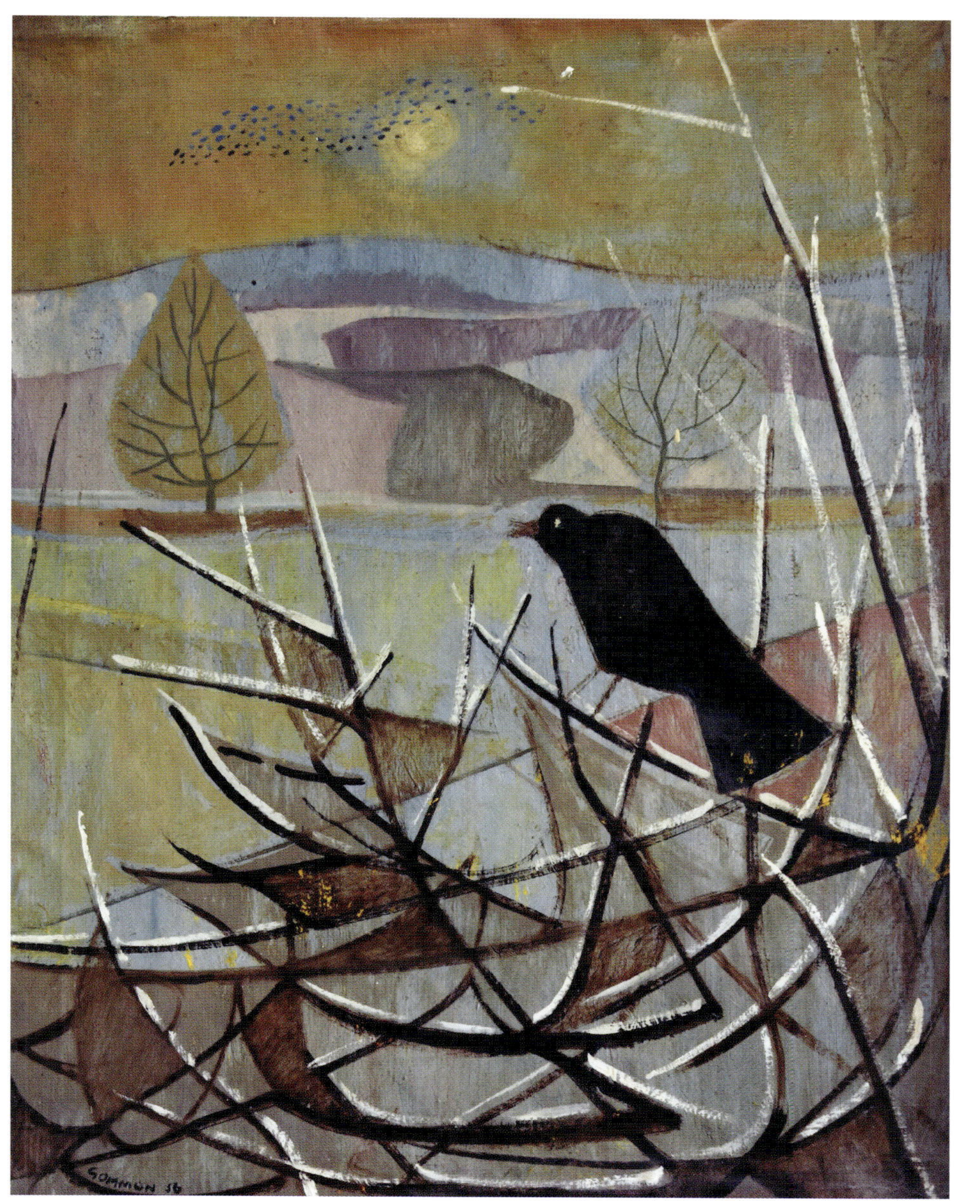

Blackbird in Winter
1956, oil on canvas, 55 x 76 cm
private collection

I know noble accents
And lucid, inescapable rhythms;
But I know, too,
That the blackbird is involved
In what I know.[7]

Gommon also painted a number of pictures conjoining a foreground group of wild irises with a semi-abstract landscape backdrop [eg. p. 89], the latter often containing stylised birds. Over the years, the artist-plantsman Cedric Morris painted irises and other flowers set against landscape too; his flowers are generally more botanically detailed than Gommon's, which nevertheless are also vivid with sensuous exuberance.

In Gommon's *Moonlight and Irises* (1964) [overleaf], three birds, perched on vegetation and branches in the upper air, possess an iconic, archaic simplicity of form. What this particular bird trio actually symbolises is open to question. But the atmosphere here is suggestive of a poignant Symbolist-

6. Len Howard, *Birds as Individuals* (London: Penguin Random House, 2024), p.3.
7. Wallace Stevens, 'Thirteen Ways of Looking at a Blackbird', *Selected Poems: Wallace Stevens* (London: Faber & Faber, 1972), p.45.

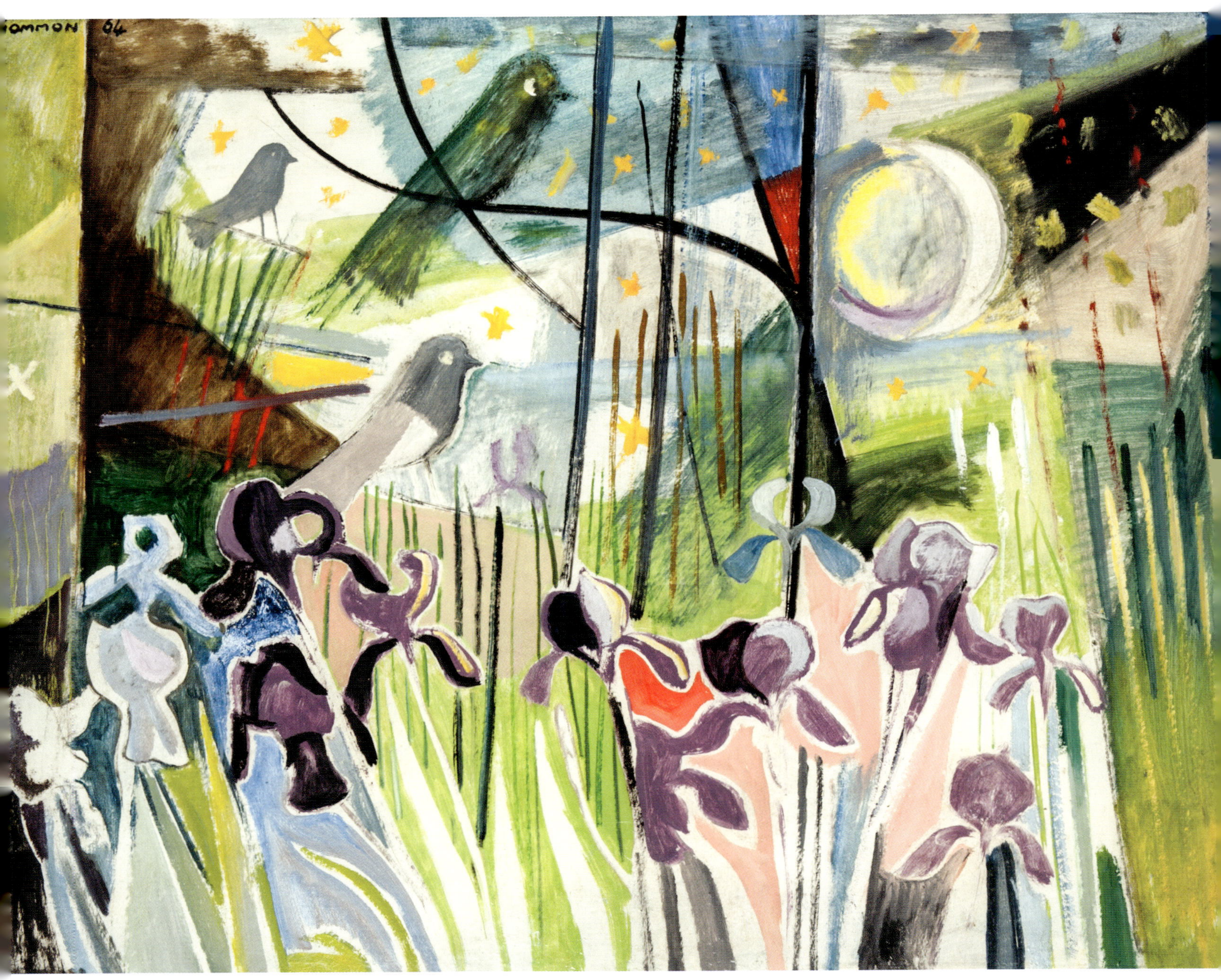

Moonlight and Irises / 1964, oil on board, 92 x 122 cm / private collection

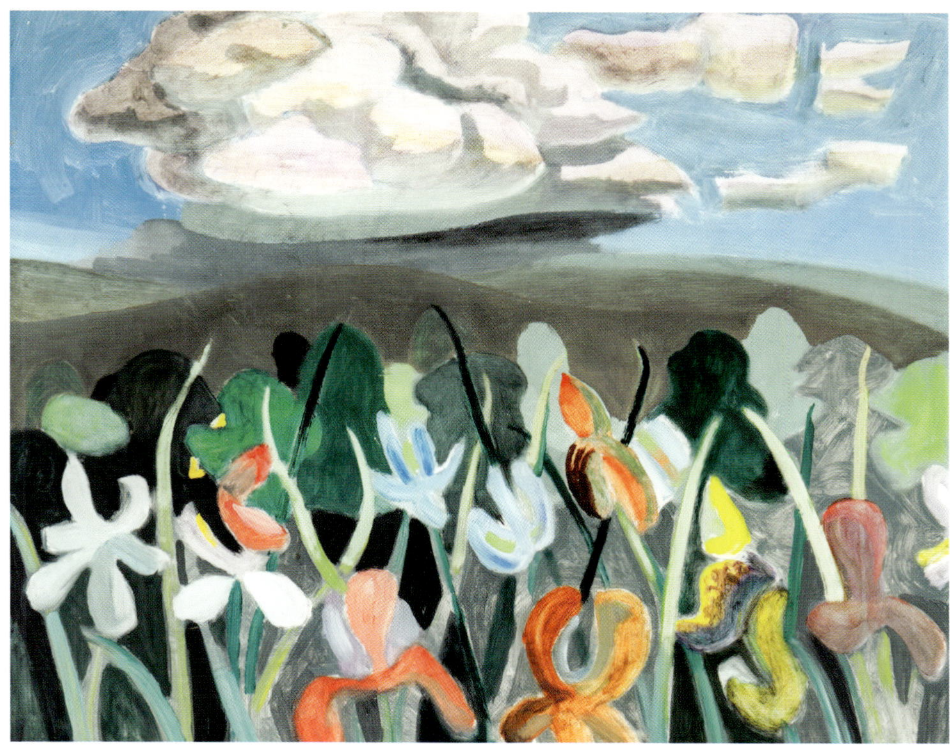

Irises (1)
1976, oil on board, 62 x 77 cm
private collection

like music with an affinity to that of Claude Debussy's 1905 piano piece
'Clair de lune', itself inspired by Paul Verlaine's 1869 poem 'Clair de lune'
('Moonlight') — part of which translates as:

> Your soul is a select landscape
> Where charming masqueraders and bergamaskers go
> Playing the lute and dancing and almost
> Sad beneath their fantastic disguises.
>
> All sing in a minor key
> Of victorious love and the opportune life,
> They do not seem to believe in their happiness
> And their song mingles with the moonlight,
> With the still moonlight, sad and beautiful,
> That sets the birds dreaming in the trees ...[8]

Elements evocative of manifold sounds, sights and even scents which
characterise and pervade gardens all combine in Gommon's pictures to
create a subtle synaesthetic experience for the person contemplating the
work of art. Words by the writer Ronald Blythe (1922—2023) are apposite
here:

> Gardens are for listening as well as looking ... garden noises ... are
> especially and welcomingly intrusive in July, the tell-tale movements
> of unseen creatures, the cry of owls ... and the delicious sound of trees
> caught in the lightest of warm winds ... Birds certainly are the garden's
> main sound-makers ... Like Omar Khayyam, I imagine I hear roses spilling
> on the earth. And if I listen hard I do hear plops which are only a degree
> above silence itself.[9]

8. Paul Verlaine, 'Clair de lune [Moonlight]',
translated by Chris Routledge, 'Featured
Poem', The Reader, 30 March 2009,
www.thereader.org.uk/featured-poem-3.
9. Ronald Blythe, 'The Artist Plantsman',
Going to Meet George [Mackay Brown,
the Orkney poet] *and Other Outings*
(Ebrington, Gloucestershire: Long
Barn Books, 1999), p.11.

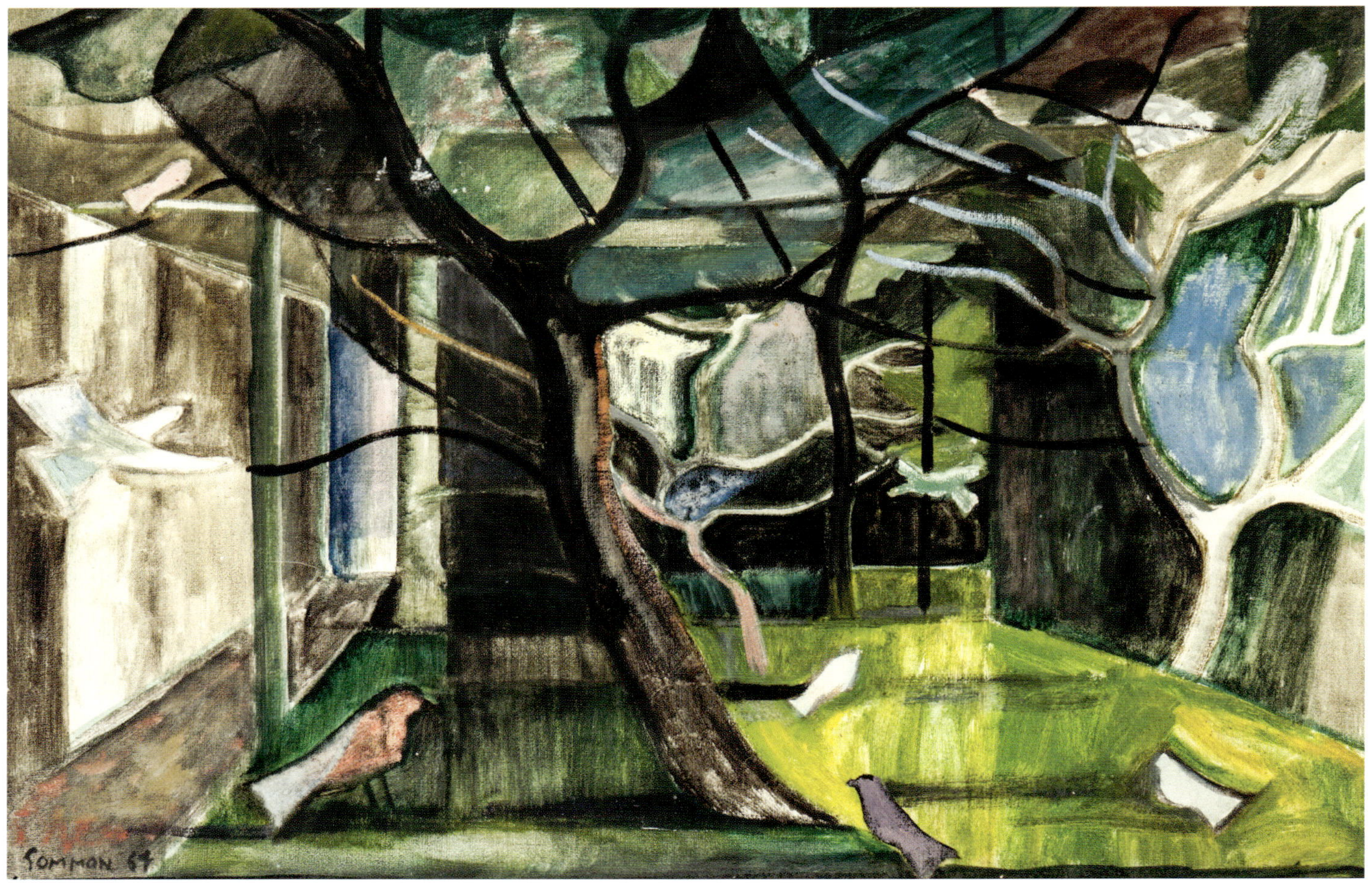

Green Garden / 1964, oil on board, 50 x 75 cm / private collection

In a pair of oil paintings from 1964, *Green Garden* [above] and *Birds in a Green Garden* [facing page], Gommon describes surreally abstracted enclosed spaces based on his own walled garden. The brighter verdancy of the first suggests it is set in spring or summer; the bleak palette of the latter indicates autumn or winter. In each picture, three visible walls take on a surrealistic quality so that some trees appear dynamically flattened onto them rather than standing freely.

The almost monochrome palette of the second picture is complemented by the artist's choice of birds seen flying, hovering, standing and perched in the space: white doves and blackbirds. These are haunting, elaborately stylised, even theatricalised gardens, with only trees and birds, and no shrubs, flowers or plants visible.

Gommon admired T.S. Eliot's poetry enormously, and this passage from Eliot's poem 'Burnt Norton' (one of the *Four Quartets* but first published separately in 1941) — evoking that epiphanic moment when the poet comes across 'a drained pool' in a garden along with an enigmatic, truth-telling bird — would have reverberated with him:

> The surface glittered out of heart of light ...
> Then a cloud passed, and the pool was empty ...
> Go, go, go, said the bird; human kind

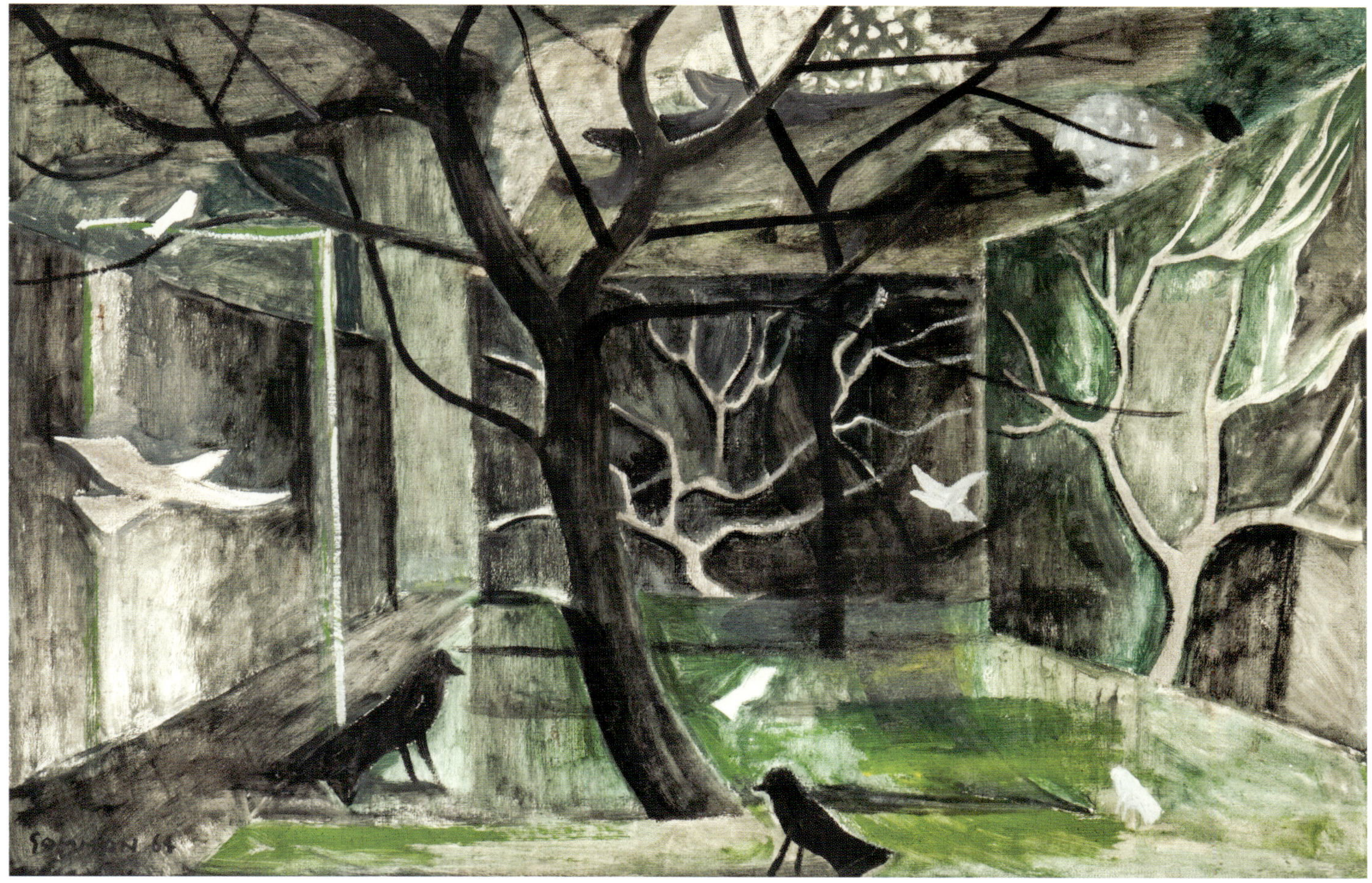

Birds in a Green Garden / 1964, oil on board, 50 x 75 cm / private collection

Cannot bear very much reality.
Time past and time future
What might have been and what has been
Point to one end, which is always present.[10]

In 1985 Gommon made a series of gouaches of his garden — with a pre-ternatural intensity of colour and clarity of form like that seen in Indian and Persian garden miniatures. In *Jasmine Cottage Garden — Magpies* [overleaf] one bird with a greenish sheen stands on the lawn, while a second is seen flying just above the flowerbed — with its brilliant red and yellow tulips as well as slighter, more discreetly coloured flowers. A third magpie is perched on the wall, beyond which we see pink blossom (from a neighbouring garden) set against what at first appears to be a strange backdrop of greenish-black sky (even though it seems to be the height of a fine summer's day); in fact this may simply be an expanse of garden soil, which itself is splattered with tiny blue shapes — abstract inventions perhaps but suggestive of petals or even butterflies.

Gommon's gouache *Jasmine Cottage Garden — Snow* [p.93], shows the uppermost part of a garden wall, topped with snow — with a euphoric-seeming wintry scene beyond, depicting an assortment of trees covered in ice and snow (forms transfigured, it seems, into outlandishly animated sculptural shapes) — set against a night sky with a moon and dazzling stars.

10. T.S. Eliot, 'Burnt Norton', *Four Quartets* (London: Faber & Faber, 1979), p.14.

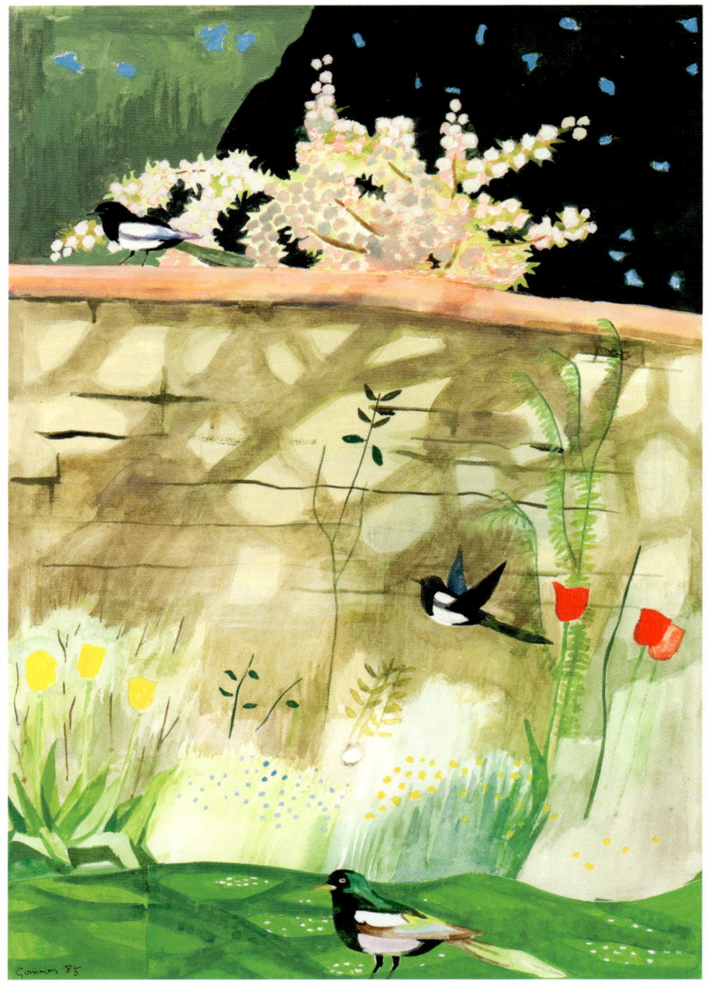

Jasmine Cottage Garden — Magpies
1985, gouache on paper, 76 x 57 cm
private collection

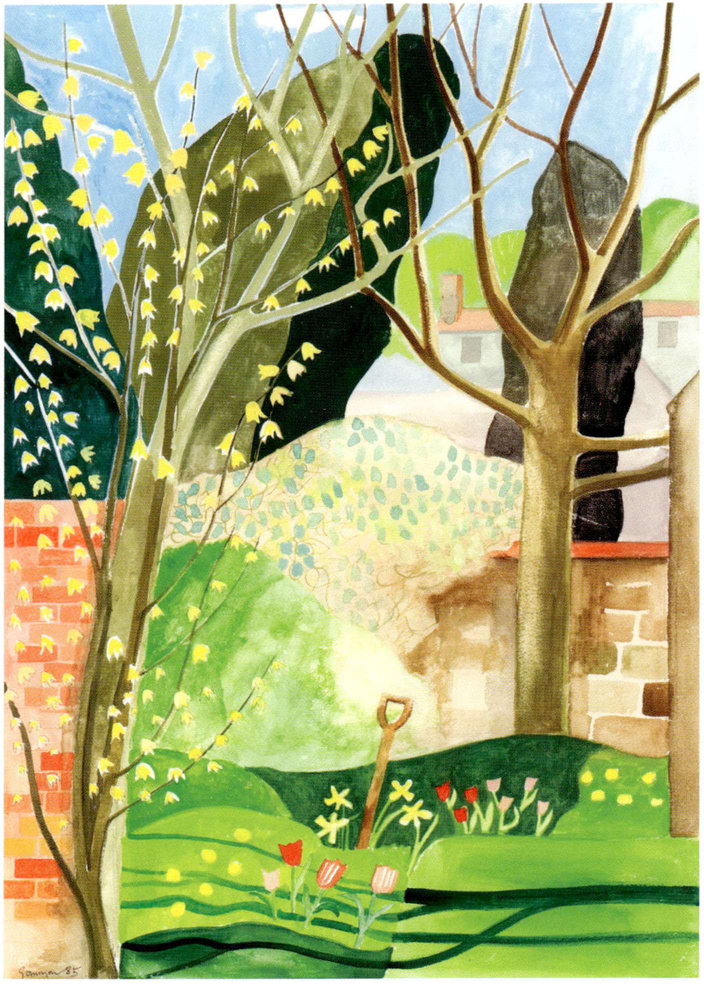

Jasmine Cottage Garden — Spade
1985, gouache on paper, 76 x 57 cm
private collection

This celestial night-time vision appears so resplendent that the viewer may be initially beguiled into believing that it is pictured at the height of a bright winter's day!

John Clare (1793—1864) — the great Romantic poet born in the village of Helpston in Northamptonshire, an impoverished agricultural labourer who achieved fame when his first book of poems was published when he was 27 — evoked this kind of magical locale in his poem 'Snow Storm', describing 'The smallest twig [which] its snowy burthen wears' so that 'the dullest eyes engage / To shape strange things … Domestic spots near home and trod so oft … Trees bushes grass to one wild garb subdued / Are gone and left us in another land.'[11]

Peter Gommon finds

a very strong parallel between Clare's poetry and David's art. Both my parents loved the work of John Clare. His Northamptonshire was quite a bit further east to where we lived. Before the great Enclosure of the people's common land, which he mourned in his poems, the landscape was probably wilder and more open — whereas the bit I grew up in was

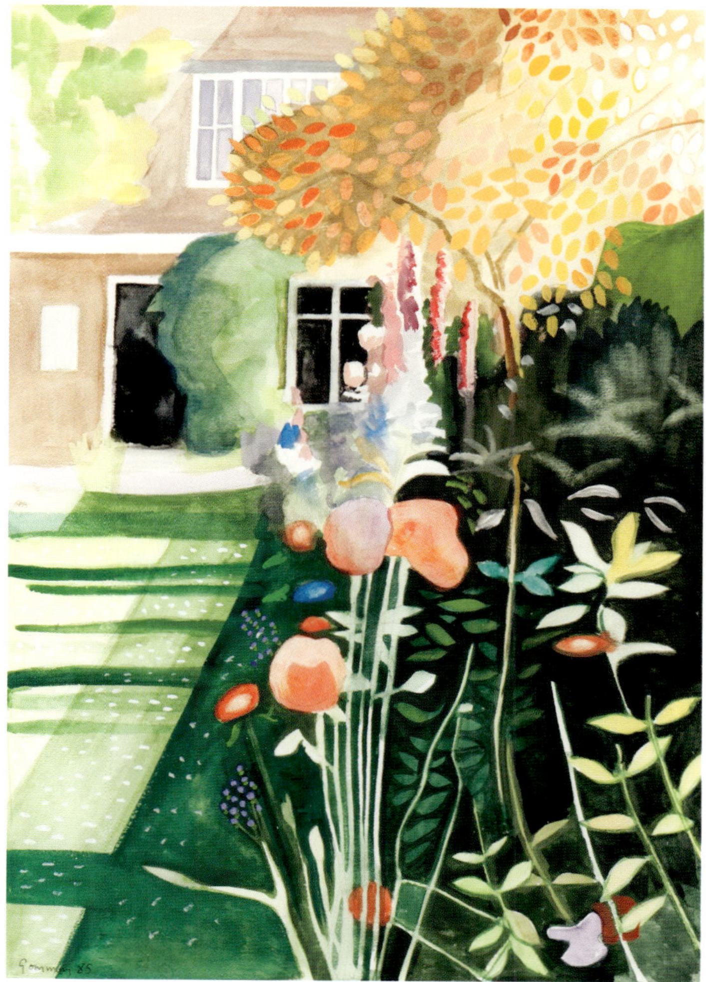

Jasmine Cottage Garden — Afternoon
1985, gouache on paper, 76 x 57 cm
private collection

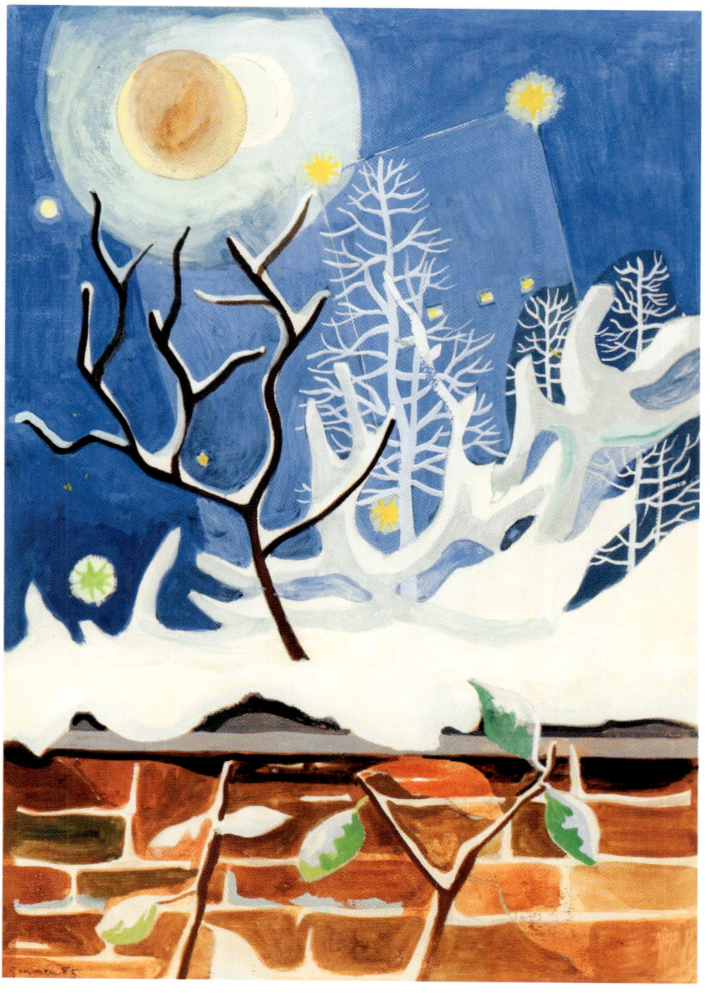

Jasmine Cottage Garden — Snow
1985, gouache on paper, 76 x 57 cm
private collection

lusher and wetter with its water meadows. The Asylum [where Clare was committed in 1841, suffering from fears and delusions, and where he ended his days] was situated next to the Grammar School where my father taught. There was a church in the town where Clare would sit in his later years. You can go to so many of the places locally he would have known.

The environs of Jasmine Cottage were fertile painterly terrain for Gommon. Kate Currie recalls that 'Hardingstone was still a country village when we lived there; there were still men driving cattle to market along the country roads.' In the 1979 painting *Coldstream Lane (with Mrs Ansell's Gate)* [p. 95] the left foreground shows the green gate to his neighbour's house (itself obscured by a polychromatic mass of foliage and flowers), and further to the back is the frontage of his own cottage, with an orange hue — and a light pink roof.

Other pictures explore luminous local wheatfields seen beyond a fence and a kissing gate (a gate that allows pedestrians but not livestock to pass through). In *The Kissing Gate (Cherry Orchard Field)* [overleaf] there is one jarring note in the familiar bucolic scene: a small stretch of barbed wire on

11. John Clare, 'Snow Storm', *John Clare: Major Works* (Oxford University Press, 2008), p. 199.

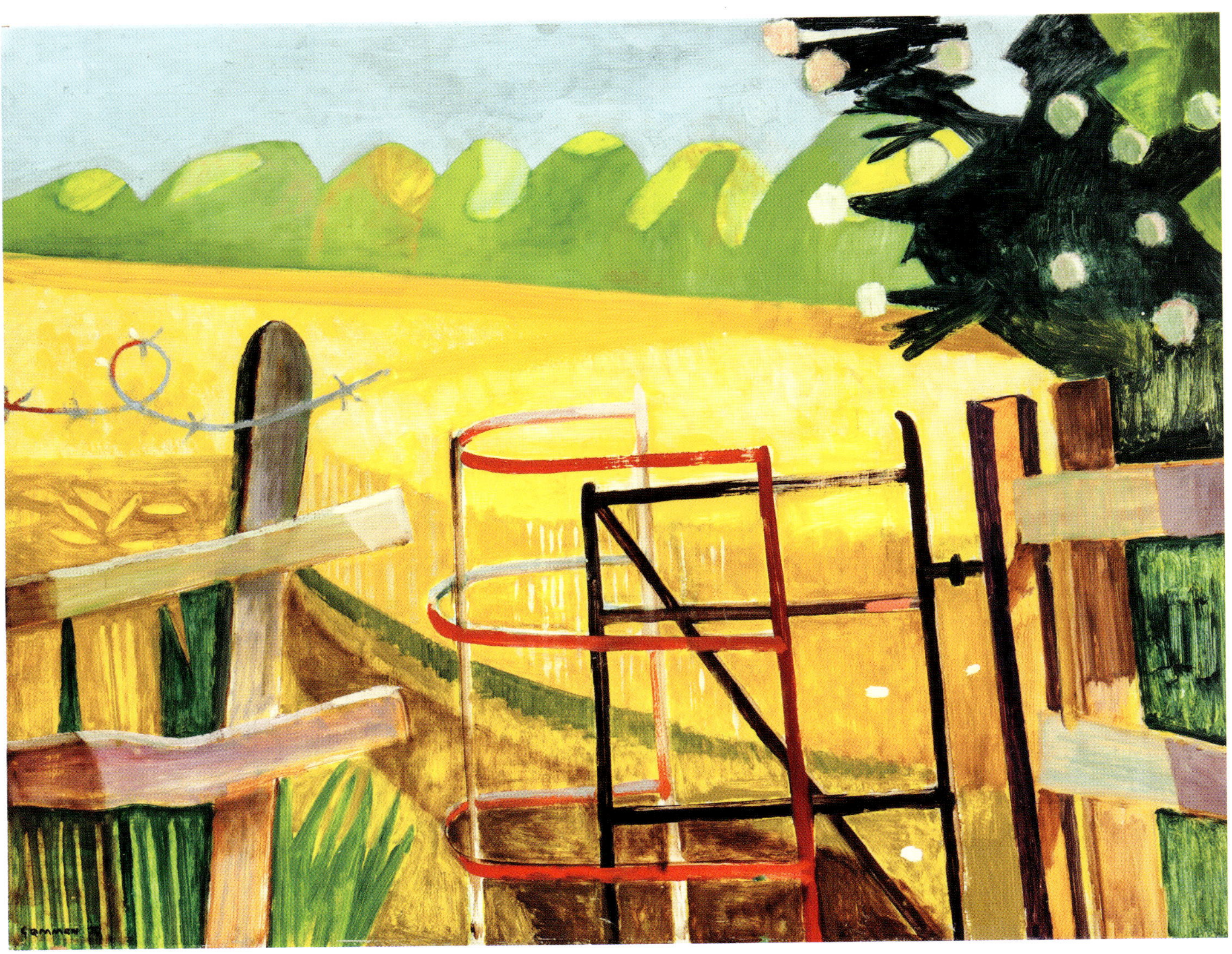

The Kissing Gate (Cherry Orchard Field) / 1970, oil on board, 76 x 101.5 cm / private collection

top of the wooden fence, a minatory accent maybe alluding in part to the historic injustice of the early eighteenth-century Enclosure Act but also to the potential for warring emotions and human conflict even amidst paradisical surroundings.

The 1965 painting *Coldstream Lane, Hardingstone* [facing page] depicts the tree-lined lane where the artist lived. A wide grouping of trees — including a conifer; a compact tree with pink blossom overlooked by a tall, seemingly swivelling, white-blossomed tree; another one skeletal and bare-branched; and a delectable white lilac bush — appears like a disparate crew of eccentric characters, absorbed in animated conversation. Though people are usually absent in his post-war garden and landscape pictures, the arboreal portrayals here often appear effortlessly human in their 'traits' and attributes.

In a 1979 landscape painting, presumably set on a gusty day, the kinetic rhythms of the *Dancing Tree* [overleaf] of the title are conjured up using multi-faceted, twisting planes of variegated greens; the kind of effect realised here is not unlike that of a Futurist portrait of a person dynamically on the move.

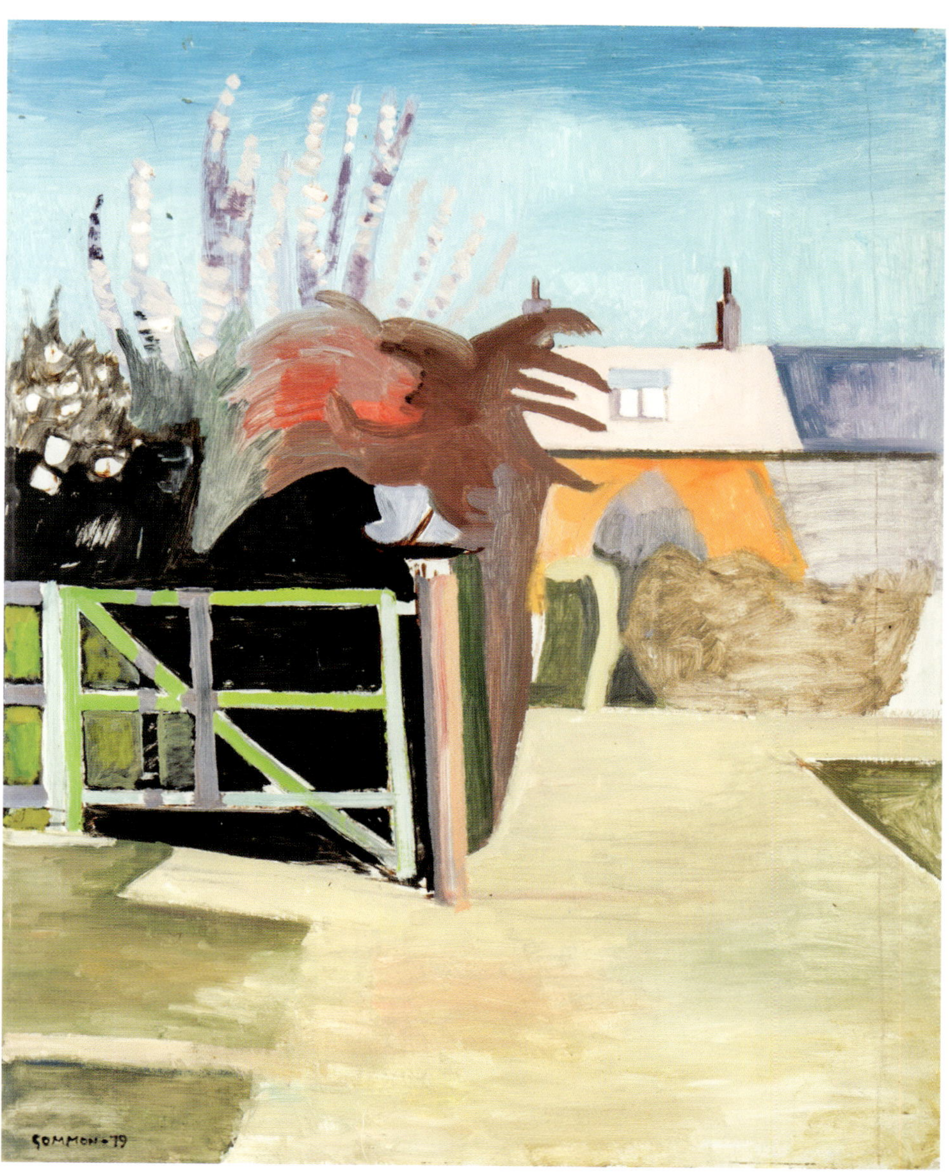

Coldstream Lane (with Mrs Ansell's Gate)
1979, oil on board, 92 x 76 cm
private collection

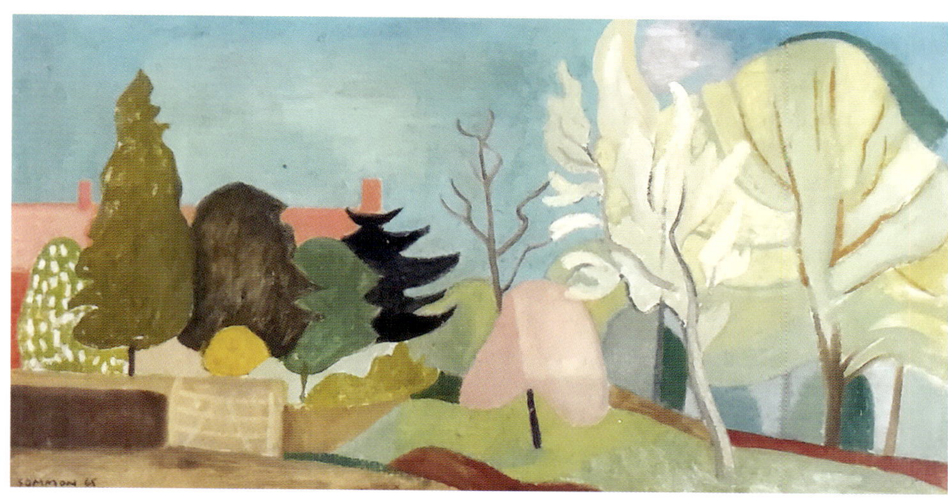

Coldstream Lane, Hardingstone
1965, oil on board, 44 x 87 cm
private collection

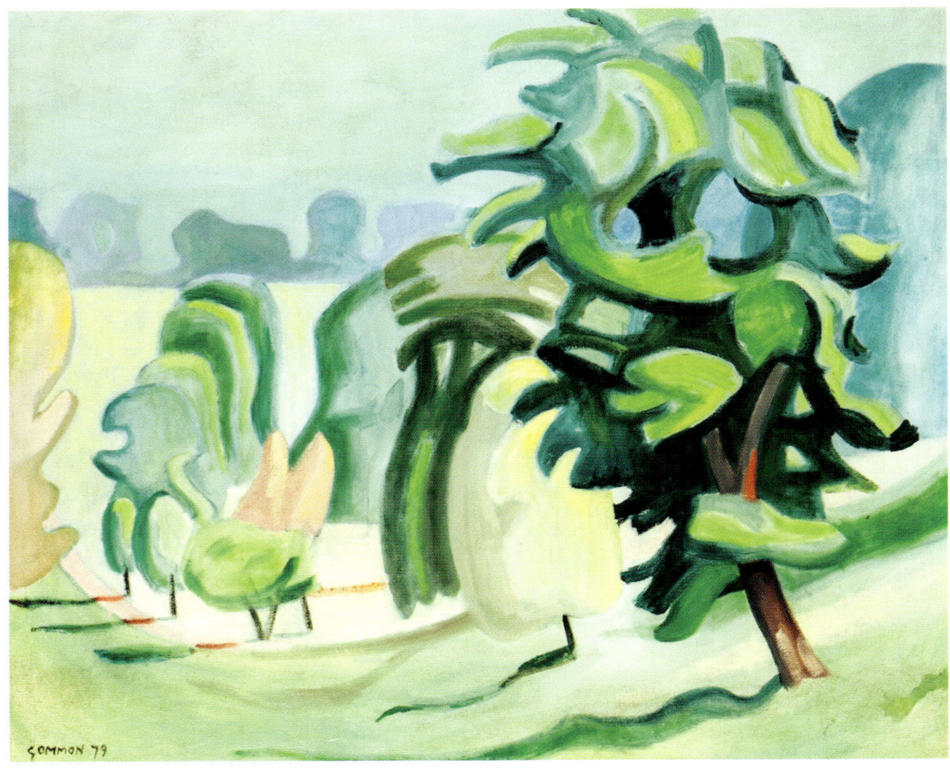

Dancing Tree
1979, oil on canvas, 75.5 × 92 cm
private collection

Gommon enjoyed walking in the nearby Delapre Woods, which are notable for plantings of conifers and oak, beech and sweet chestnut trees. His 1962 gouache, *Autumn Morning (Delapre)* [facing page], is a semi-abstract composition in a palette of mostly yellows, ochres, blacks and browns, summoning up a quite musical maelstrom of whirling, diversely contoured leaves; the Blakean 'Minute Particulars' (from his *Jerusalem*, 1804—1820)[12] of

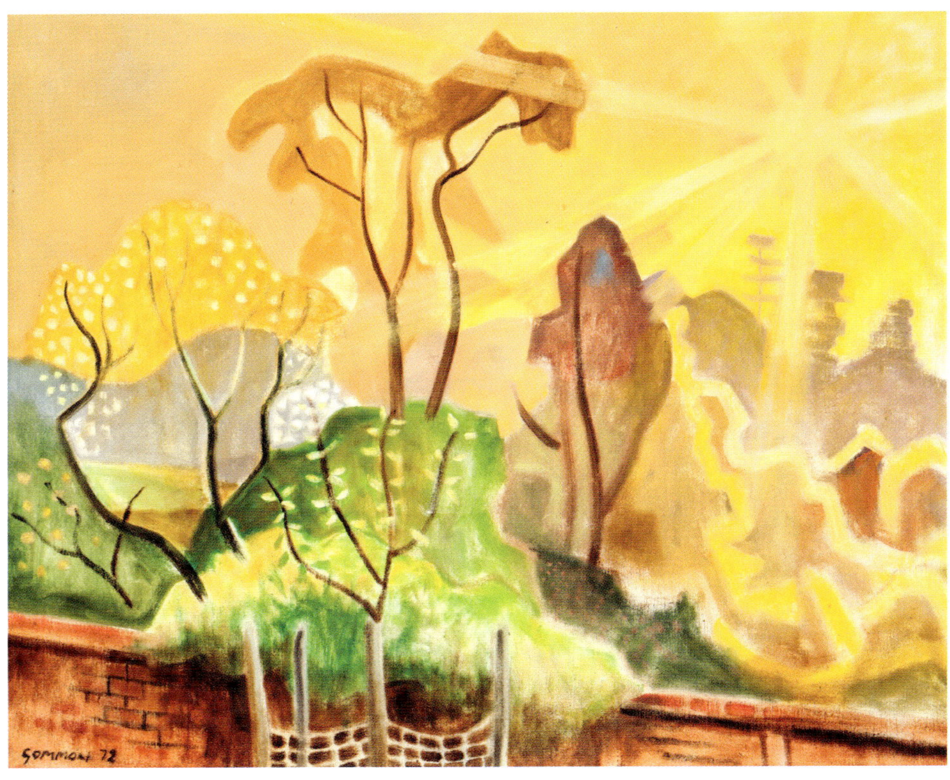

Sunlit Woods (Delapre)
1972, oil on canvas, 76 × 92 cm
private collection

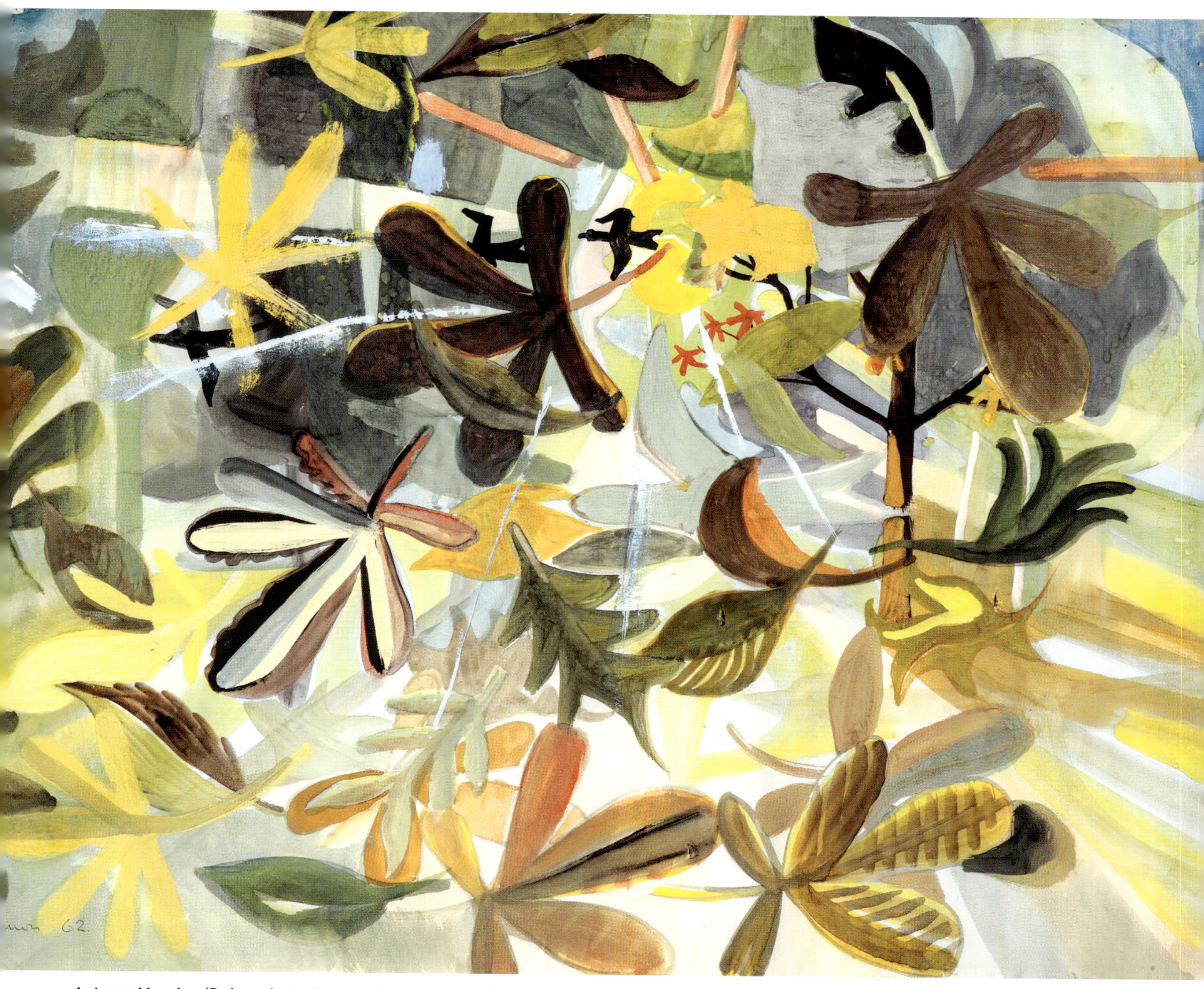

Autumn Morning (Delapre) / 1962, gouache on paper, 56 x 77 cm / private collection

12. William Blake, 'Jerusalem', in David Erdman (ed.), *The Complete Poetry & Prose of William Blake* (Berkeley and Los Angeles: University of California Press, 1984), p.205.

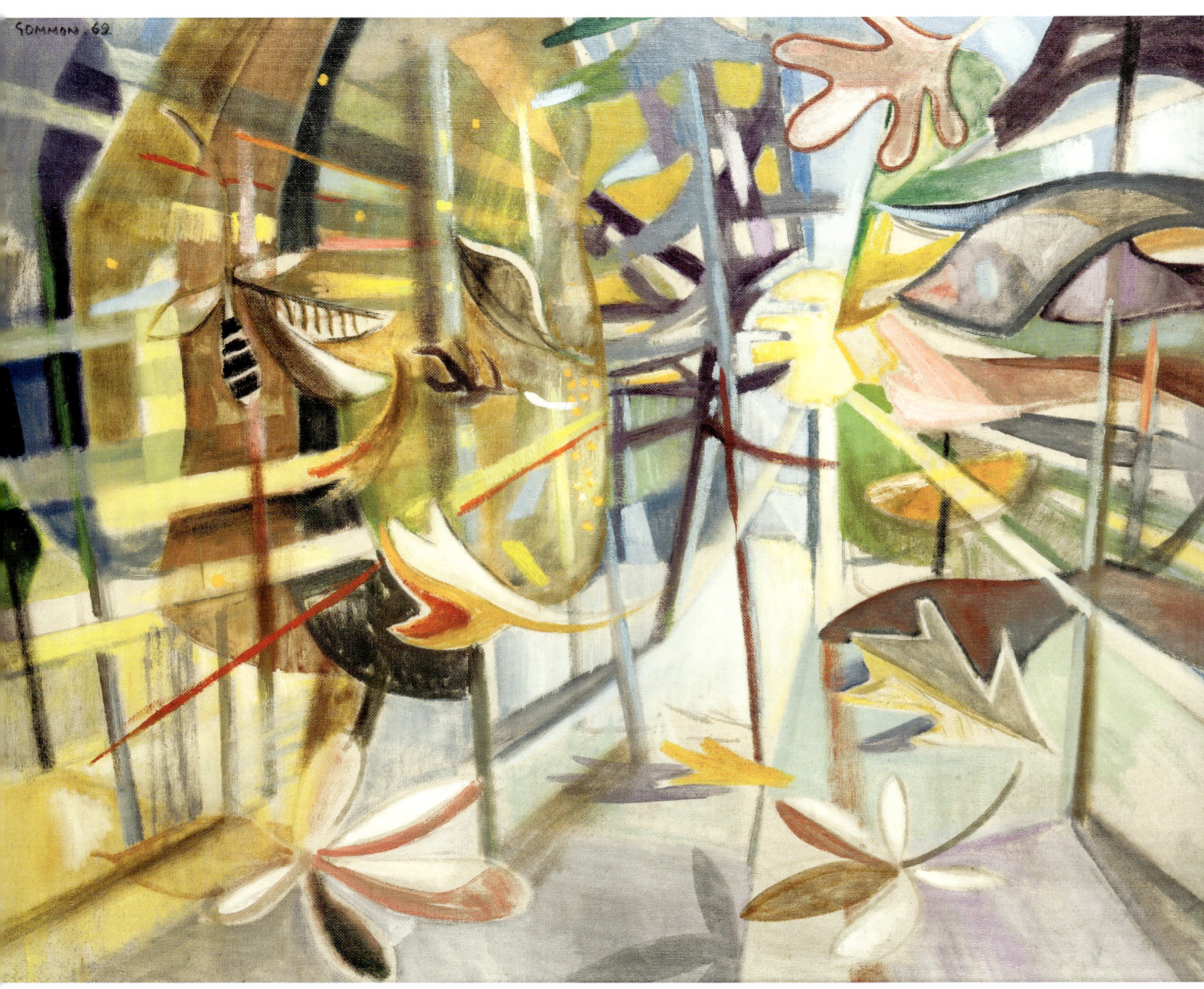

Autumn Morning / 1962, oil on board, 91 x 122 cm / private collection

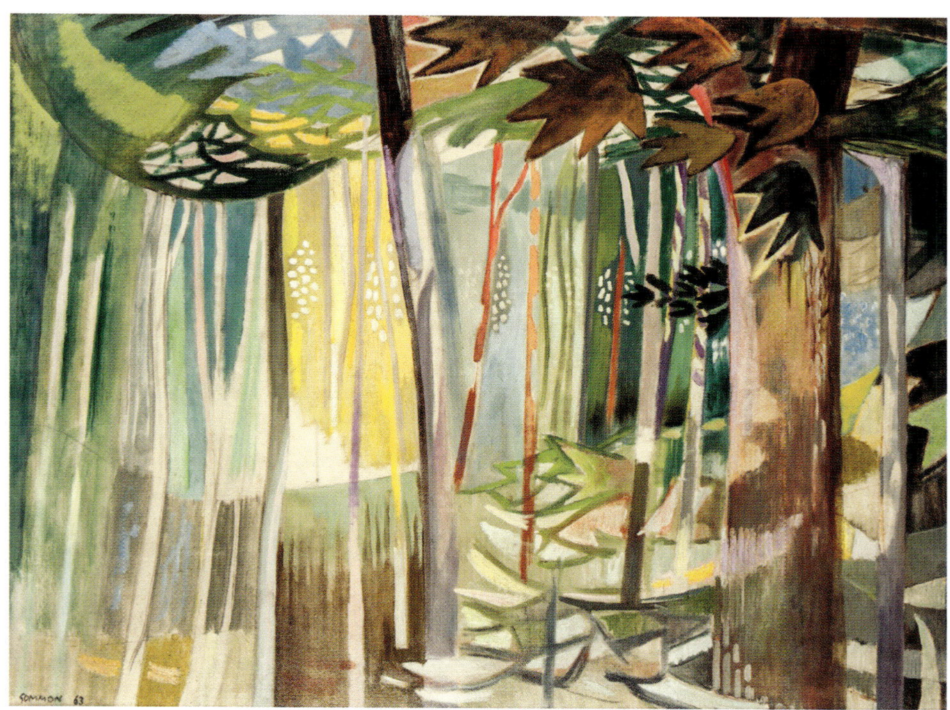

Edge of the Wood
1963, oil on board, 92 x 122 cm
private collection

each leaf are wrought spectacularly large. Just visible in the distance are tiny figures of three black birds flying through wild weather. John Clare's poem 'November' evokes a similar sense of that time 'when the start / Of sudden tempests stirs the forest leaves / Into hoarse fury, till the shower set free'.[13]

In 1970 a plan was created by Northampton Borough Council to redevelop the town's buildings and transport infrastructure. A new motorway was planned, slashing through Delapre Woods and across the valley between Hardingstone and Northampton. A Brutalist carpark was to be built in the middle of town, 'an absolute eyesore', Peter Gommon says. 'My father was apoplectic at all these grandiose proposals, and helped run a concerted local campaign to stop them.' Also (as Ian Mayes noted in a catalogue essay for a 1990s Gommon retrospective at Nottingham's Angel Row Gallery), at this time a new 'golf course disposed of ancient hedgerows; gigantic warehouses smothered green fields'.

David created a booklet with his own text and black-and-white drawings and cartoons, which he called the *Northampton Expansion Manual* ... 'In homage to our town council for building a town fit for [the word 'hero's' [*sic*] crossed out here] offices and car parks to live in'. One succinct drawing [overleaf] depicts a blitzed urban scene in which a rat is seen crawling over rubble, under a distressed sign announcing 'EMPORIUM ARCADE' — a reference to the iconic building in the town's Market Square (built in 1901 with an ornate façade to house over fifty independent shops, offices and stockrooms), demolished in 1972.

With punchy, pungent humour, other pages illustrate what he denotes as 'NORTHAMPTON'S GLORIOUS FUTURE' amid scenes of grieving and fallen citizens, horrendous, polluted traffic jams and claustrophobic clusters of dystopian new housing and office blocks. In one drawing, pointedly headed

13. John Clare, 'November', https://verse.press/poem/november-14877.

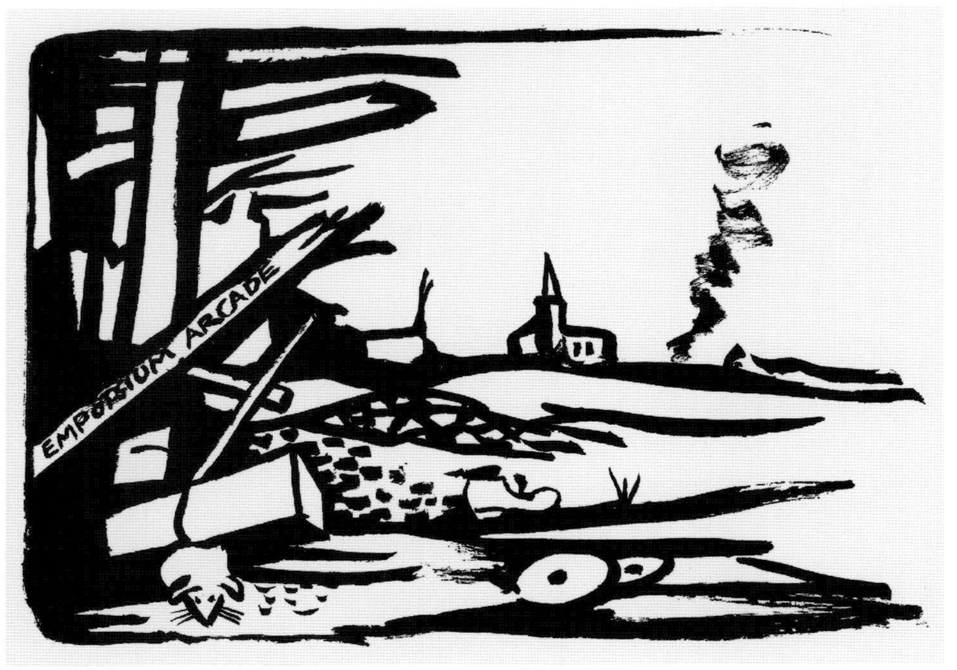

Emporium Arcade
from the **Northampton Expansion Manual**
*c.*1972, brush and pen and ink on paper,
21 x 29,7 cm
private collection

with the admonitory term 'Ssh!' [below], local councillors at a meeting
are depicted. With a tellingly spare use of line and impish irony (which has
a parallel in elegantly quirky, perspicacious drawings and cartoons by the
Jewish Romanian-born American artist Saul Steinberg (1914—1999)), Gommon
shows the councillors as featureless nonentities — seated under a wall of
bombastic official portraits — with, fittingly, a couple of comedic-looking
rats drawn centre-stage.

Peter Gommon recalls how depressing it was for his father after the new
bypass was built. 'Before, you could hear the noise from the road when the
wind was blowing — but with the new and busier Expressway [named the

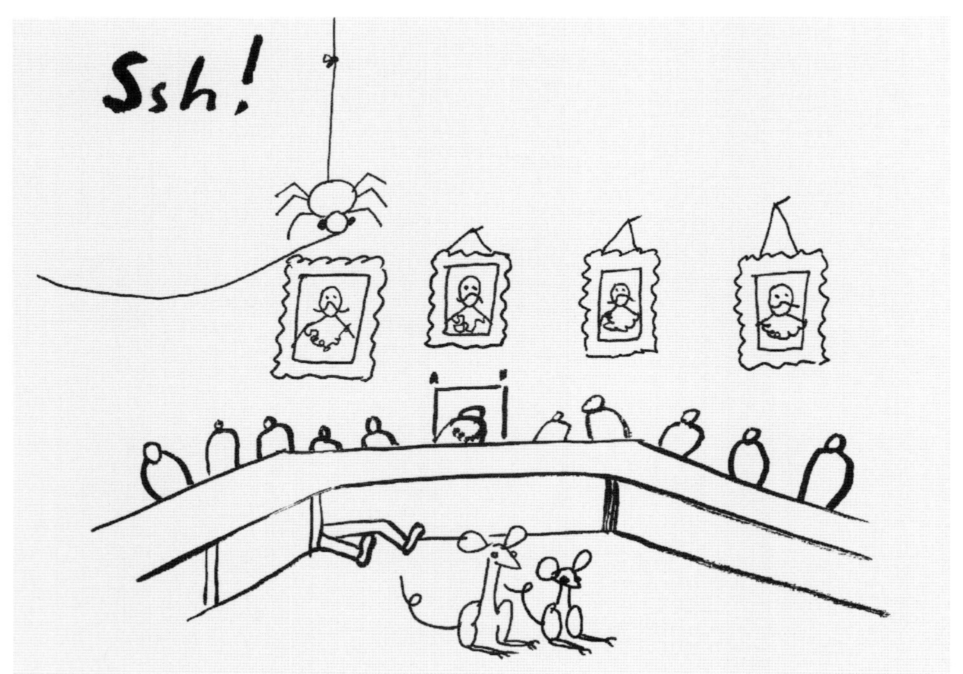

Ssh!
from the **Northampton Expansion Manual**
*c.*1972, brush and pen and ink on paper,
21 x 29,7 cm
private collection

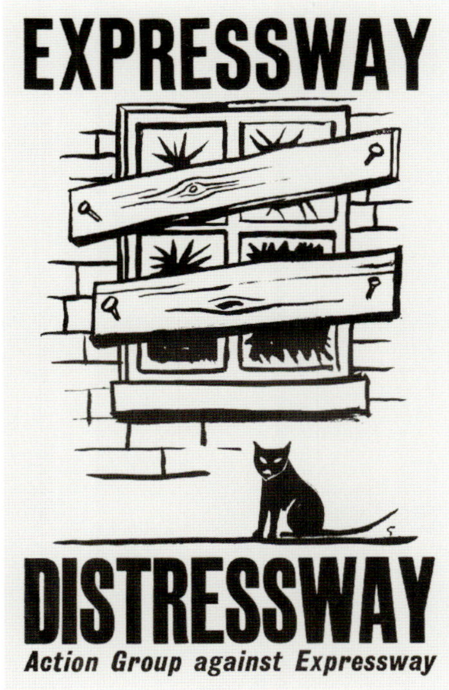

Poster for the campaign against the
Northampton Expressway, *c.*1972, printed
in black-and-white, 55 x 37.5 cm
private collection

14. John Clare, 'Remembrances',
John Clare: Major Works, p.260.

'Distressway' by David, left] you couldn't ever get away from it.' The easy
approach by foot from Hardingstone through Delapre Woods was ruined;
pedestrians now had to navigate a busy roundabout and an underpass.
David was also devastated by the replacement of many fine, historic town
buildings by soulless, grid-like modern architecture. There is a parallel here
with the grief John Clare felt after the Enclosure Act led to commonly held
land passing into private hands, trees being felled, streams diverted, roads
built, and extensive fields parcelled out into rectangles.

Clare lamented:

> Inclosure like a Buonaparte let not a thing remain
> It levelled every bush and tree and levelled every hill
> And hung the moles for traitors — though the brook is running still
> It runs a naked brook, cold and chill.[14]

Gommon produced this booklet at a time when the modern ecological
movement was getting into its stride. His own philosophy was in accord with
that of the German-born British economist and writer E.F. Schumacher, as expressed in his influential 1973 book, *Small Is Beautiful: A Study of Economics
as if People Mattered.* Schumacher argued for small-scale, sustainable economic development and the idea of people working co-operatively with
each other and with Nature.

In Gommon's paintings, Nature itself appears animated and sentient, the
antithesis of the kind of mechanical, inert vision of the natural world which
Schumacher had reacted so vehemently against. In the 1976 picture *Irises (2)*
[below], the glaring sun in an ochreish sky illumines the vivacious display of
wild white, lilac-coloured and yellow irises. On a distant dark green hillock

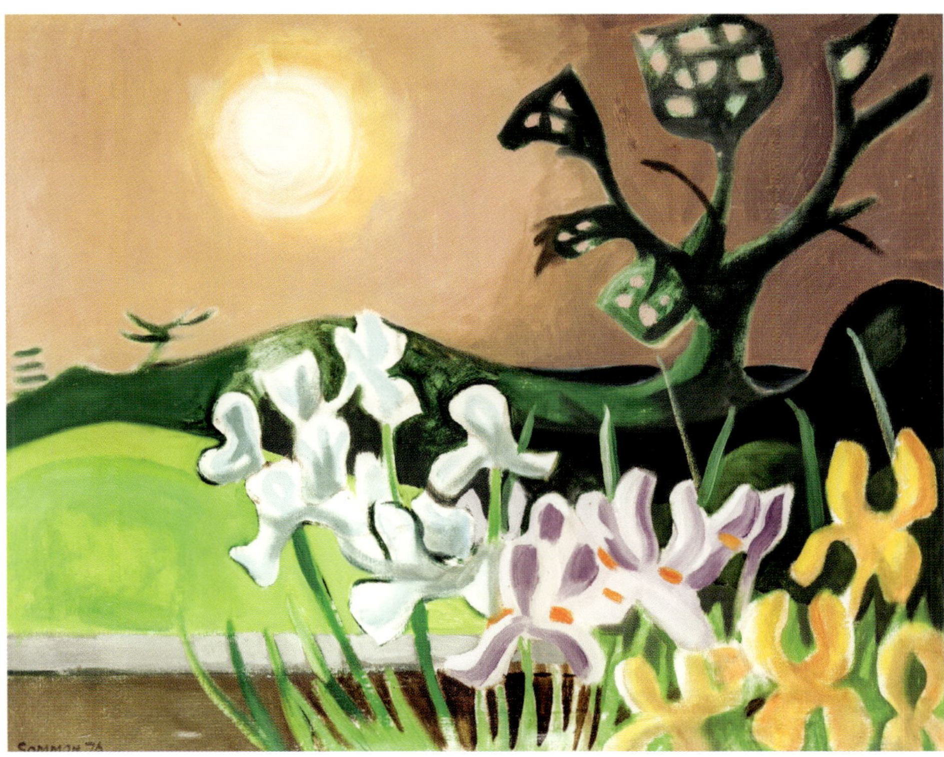

Irises (2)
1976, oil on canvas, 62 x 77 cm
private collection

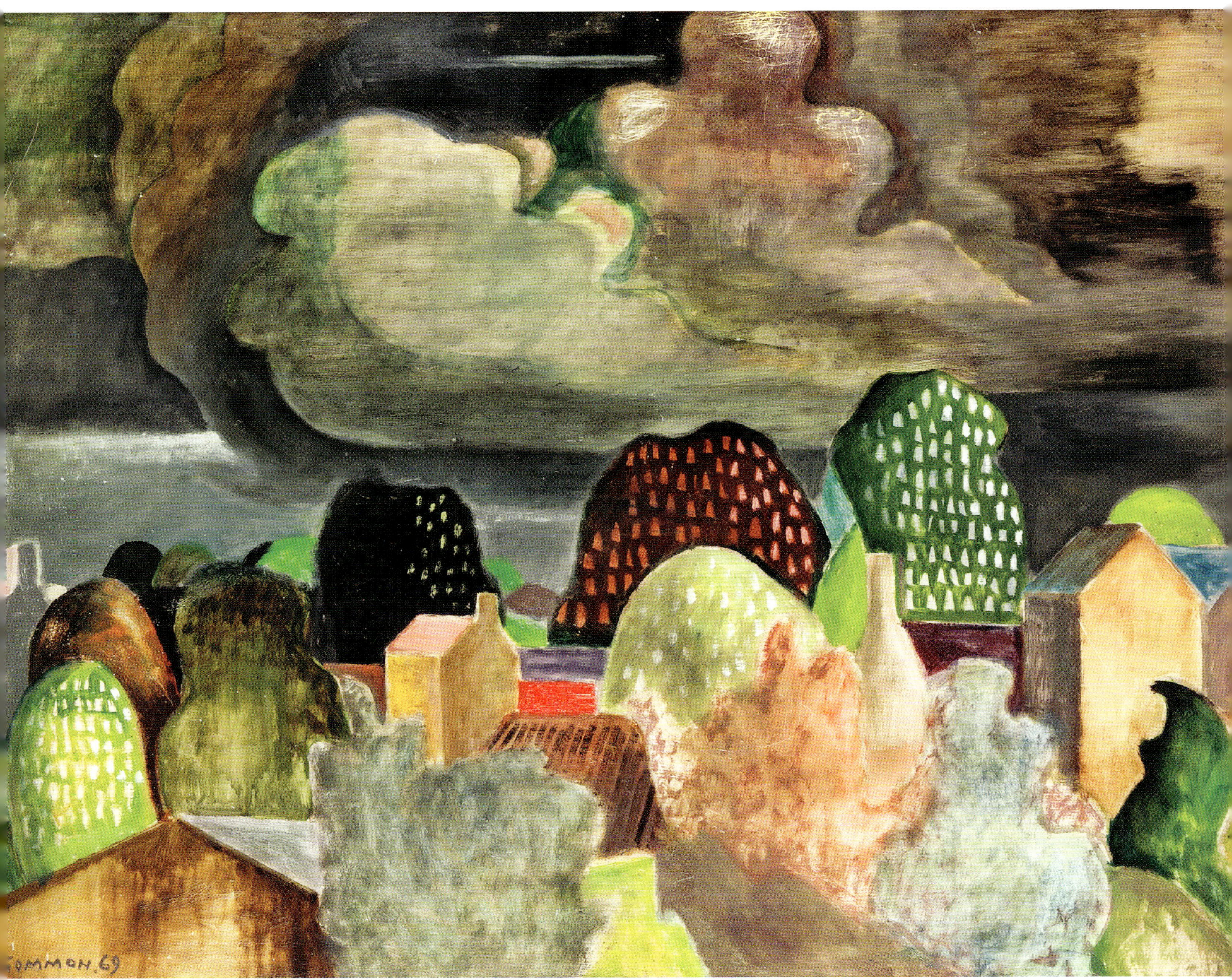

Full Moon / 1969, oil on board, 76 x 101 cm / private collection

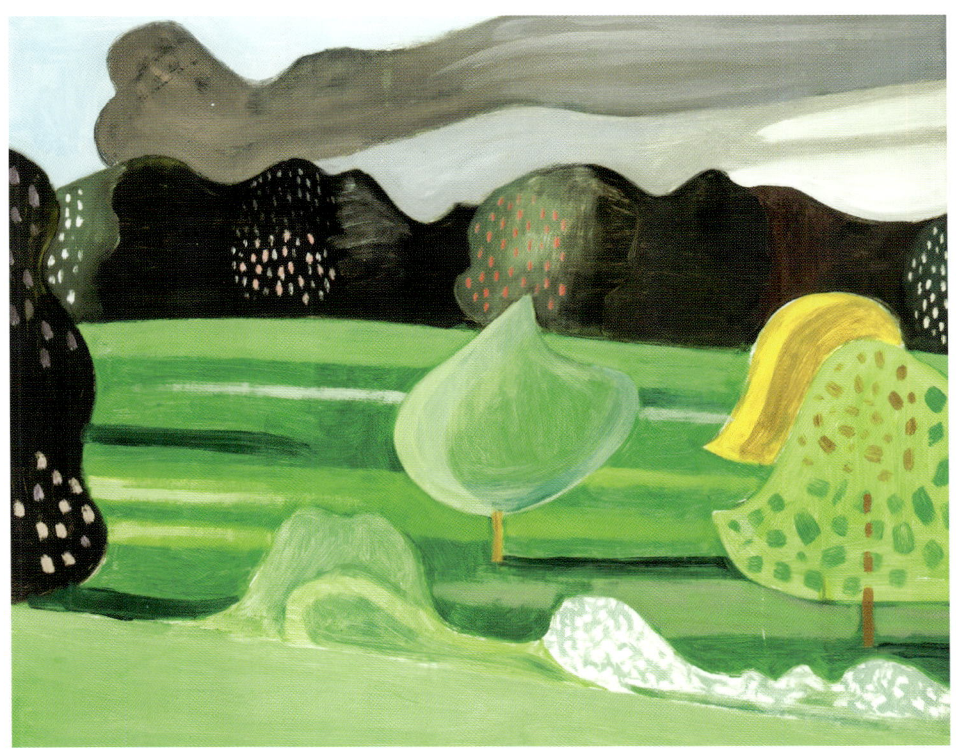

Coming Storm
1976, oil on board, 61 x 77 cm
private collection

looms a massive tree, uncannily resembling a transfigured human character
out of a dark fairy tale; its multiple branches appear like weird gesticulating
limbs and its blossom-laden 'head' seems to cast several bewitching eyes
over the whole scene.

In *Coming Storm* (also 1976) [above], the trimly sculpted, blossoming tree
forms in the landscape are depicted in shades of thrilling contrast — as
either brilliantly lit or in almost unrelieved black — as a vast, elongated
storm cloud is seen to move sinuously across the sky like a phantom.
Painterly specks at one extreme of the cloud conjure up the apparent
aspect of a human face — one with despondent narrowed eyes and the
suggestion of an unsettlingly wraithlike moue.

Gommon's 1969 painting *Full Moon* [facing page] evokes a range of visionary
darks and lights on a tempestuous night. Colours of both blossom trees and
village houses appear almost psychedelic beneath an awe-inspiring cloudscape. The cloud forms themselves seem to resemble ample, curvaceous
female nudes — a type of surreal phenomenon referred to in Shakespeare's
Anthony and Cleopatra:

> Sometime we see a cloud that's dragonish;
> A vapour sometime like a bear or lion,
> A tower'd citadel, a pendent rock …
> … Thou hast seen these signs;
> They are black vesper's pageants.[15]

15. William Shakespeare, 'Anthony
and Cleopatra', *William Shakespeare:
The Complete Works* (London and
Glasgow: Collins, 1968), p.1187.

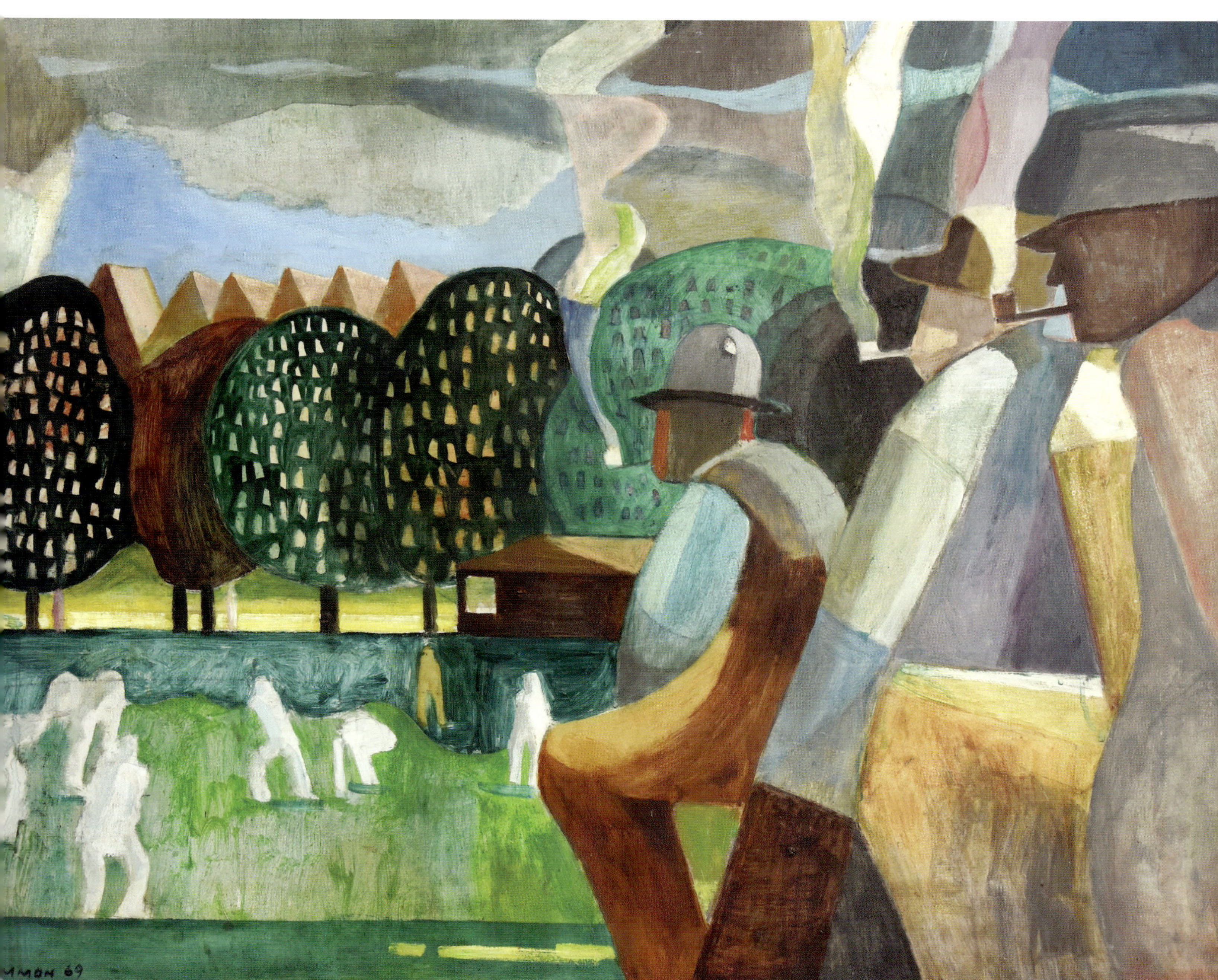

Men Watching Cricket / 1969, oil on board, 75 x 101 cm / private collection

A haunting poignancy
cricketers, naval battles and crucifixions

IN A 1965 INTERVIEW WITH IAN MAYES, GOMMON SAID HE FOUND HIM-self 'haunted by certain subjects … that sometimes live with me for years'. One such subject was the cricket match. 'I was brought up on cricket. As a boy I played on The Oval — at that age it was rather like playing on Mount Olympus.' As Mayes noted, 'Today it is the "ritual dance-like quality of the spectacle" [in Gommon's words] that provides the fascination … It is a sense of "the extraordinary in the ordinary" that Mr. Gommon is trying to convey.' He goes on to quote the artist: '"The struggle begins," he says, "when one tries to find an equivalent in form and colour for this impact of the ordinary. I am all the time striving for greater simplicity and intensity of expression, to create something that has an abundant life of its own."' [1]

A 1930s oil painting on card, *Boys Playing Cricket* [overleaf] (somewhat damaged in both left-hand corners), depicts a match in full flow in front of All Saints Church, Battersea. This richly impastoed work shows the young players fairly luminous in their cricketing whites, with their faces blank; figures bowling, batting, crouching and standing on the grass are delineated with the kind of terse, dynamic and quite sculptural simplification that key London-based linocut artists — such as Cyril Power, Sybil Andrews and Lill Tschudi — made use of to portray sportsmen, athletes and dancers in the early 1930s.

Gommon's 1969 painting *Men Watching Cricket* [facing page] shows a diminu-tive tableau of anonymous cricketers in white (in the left-hand corner) over-looked to the right by a trio of still, faceless, trilby-wearing male villagers (it seems), all massively magnified in close-up. Their attitudes of keen focus are complemented by rippling rhythms of multi-coloured smoke arising from their pipes, which partly merge with, and partly bisect, the cloudscape above.

The 1963 painting *Cricket* [p. 107] shows mature cricketers at play. This time the game is set against the backdrop of an ethereally lit landscape — where faraway assorted trees have the fantastic appearance of a group of absorbed spectators. These featureless sportsmen in their chalky whites, appearing rocklike as much as pliantly human, are in some way reminiscent of the mystery and gravity of Dorset's many ancient standing stones.

In this latter respect, Gommon was surely thinking and feeling along similar lines to the artist Paul Nash (1889—1946) as he expressed himself in his essay 'The Face of Dorset' (commissioned by Jack Beddington) in *Dorset: A Shell Guide* (1935). Here Nash described how he experienced 'an almost unnerving feeling of the latent force of the past' in viewing landscapes at

1. Ian Mayes, 'The Artist-Master Prepares Another One-Man Exhibition', *Northampton Chronicle & Echo*, 1965.

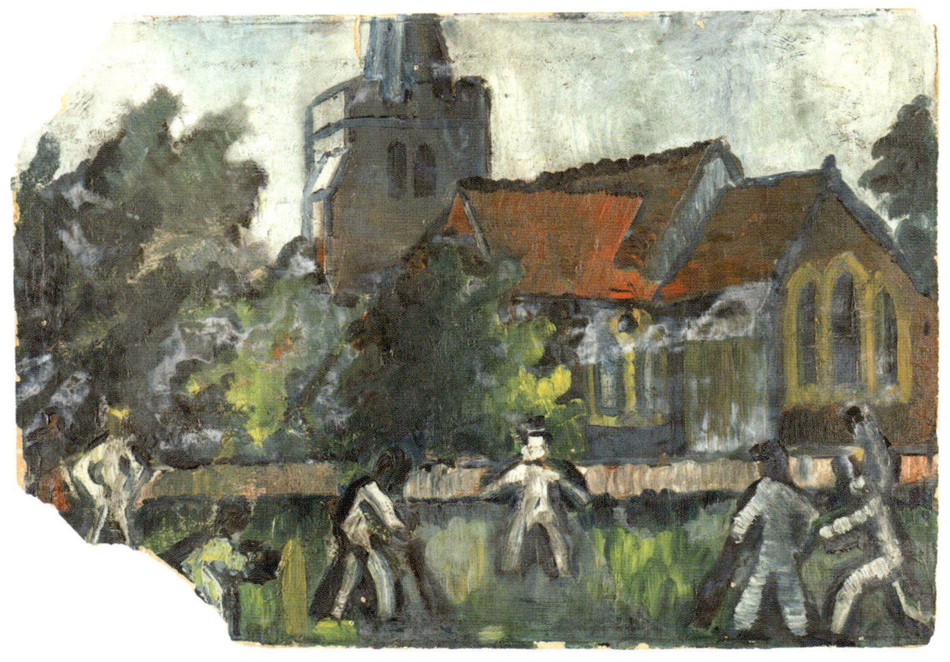

Boys Playing Cricket
1930s, oil on cardboard, 49.5 x 71.1 cm
Auckland Art Gallery Toi o Tāmaki, New Zealand

twilight and in contemplating both prehistoric earthworks and what (in his mission statement for the 1934 avant-garde publication *Unit 1*, edited by Herbert Read) he had called 'rough monoliths'. In the *Guide* Nash wrote, 'I remember nothing so beautifully haunted as the wood in Badbury Rings … Beyond the outer plateau the rings heave up and round in waves 40 feet high. A magic bird in a haunted wood, an ancient cliff washed by a sea changed into earth.'[2]

Gommon's 1967 painting *Dorset Landscape — Badbury Rings* [p.109] is a broad panoramic view of this Iron Age hillfort in chalk grassland (a site abundant in wildlife and flora, with a wood at the top) — all the way to the watery stretch of the Solent and the Isle of Wight beyond. Storm clouds on

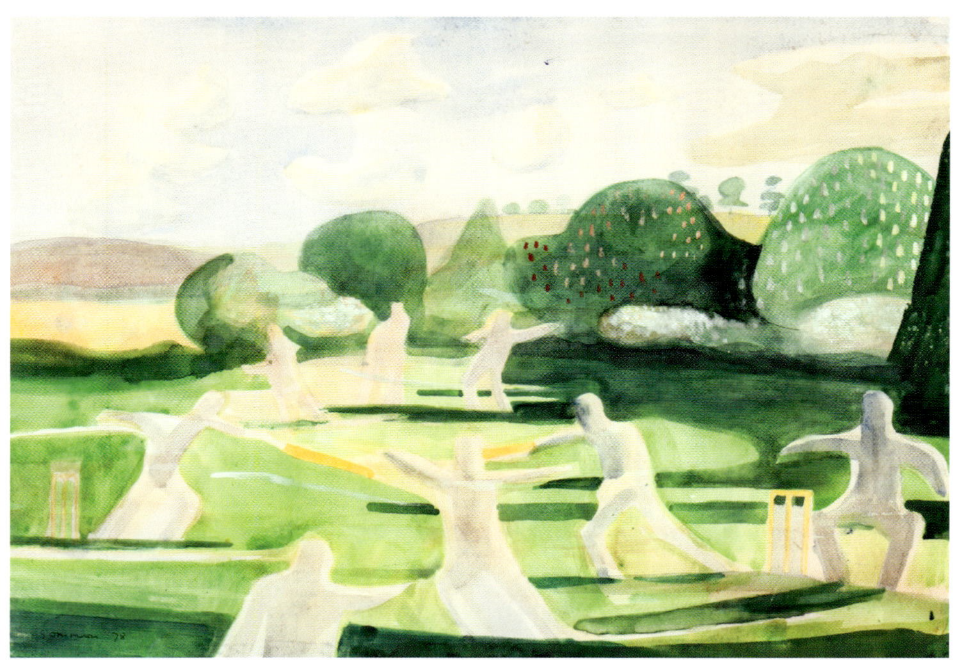

Cricket Match
1978, gouache on paper, 38 x 55 cm
private collection

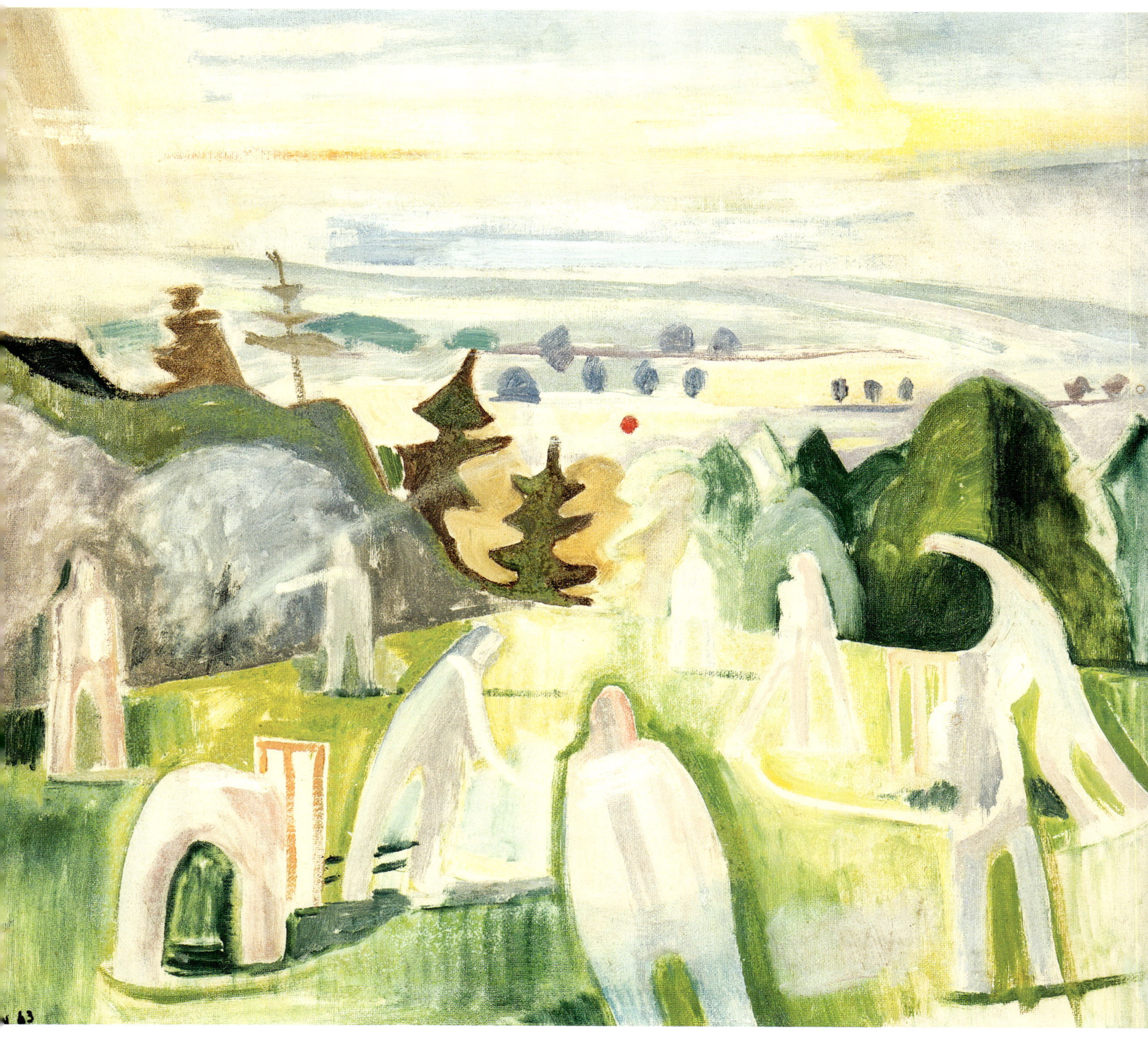

Cricket / 1963, oil on board, 64 x 78.5 cm / private collection

2. Paul Nash, 'The Face of Dorset', in
Michael Pitt-Rivers, *Dorset: A Shell Guide*
(London: Faber & Faber, 1966), pp.10—12.

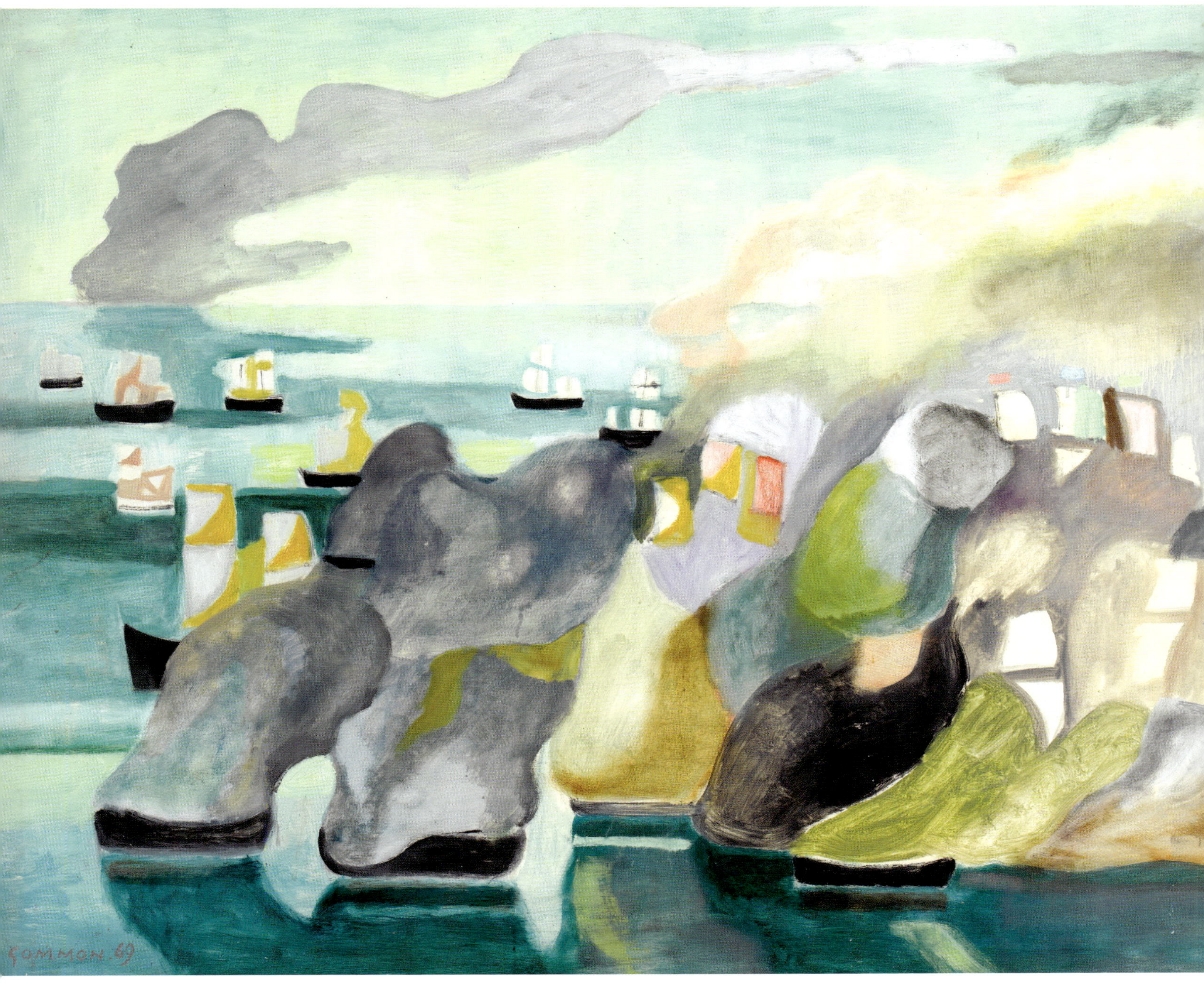

Trafalgar (8): 5.30 pm, End of the Action / 1969, oil on board, 77 x 103 cm / private collection

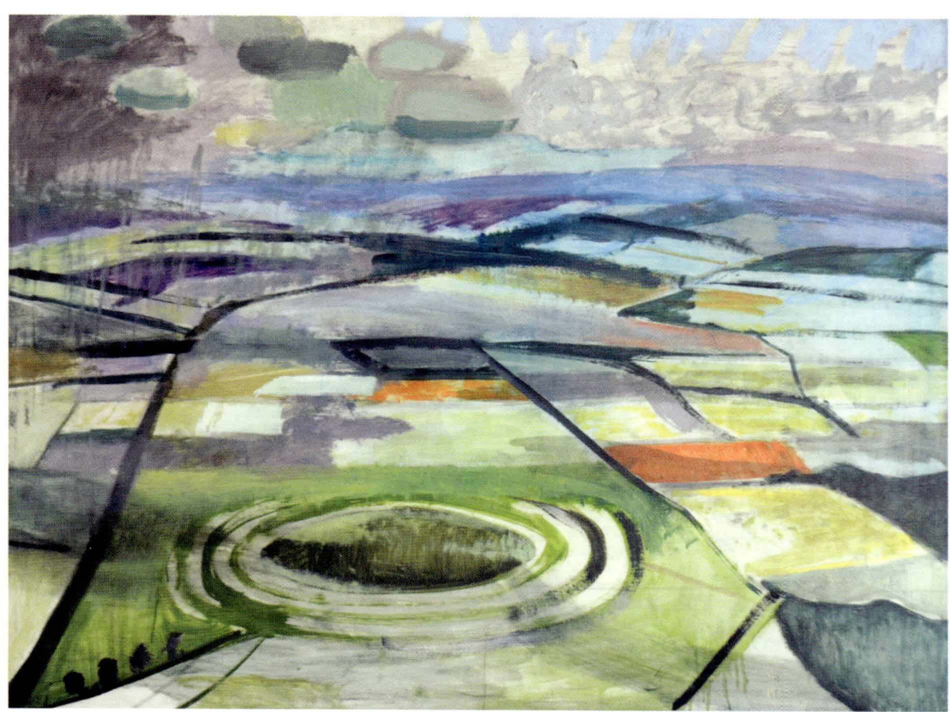

Dorset Landscape — Badbury Rings
1967, oil on board, 92 x 122 cm
private collection

the left-hand side bring rain; the rest of the scene is painted in an attenuated palette with striking accents such as a few orange, pale purple and mauve fields. The three rings of fortifications remind the visitor that this lovely spot had a grim, bloody history right up to the time of the Roman Occupation in 43AD. Yet the picture is pervaded by an expansive sense of peacefulness; this kind of layered ambiguity gives the painting a haunting poignancy.

Gommon's fascination with great historical turning points is evident in a 1969 series of paintings reimagining the narrative of the Battle of Trafalgar on 21 October 1805. He recalled that

> as a boy I had walked the decks of the HMS Victory and I felt I knew people like Collingwood [the Vice-Admiral — Horatio Nelson's Second-in-Command — whose heroic orders succeeded in separating the Spanish and French fleets, helping ensure British victory against all the odds] ... but most of all it was the formal excitement offered by those great ships [that attracted me] ... history offers some marvellous visual subject matter, but I did not want to paint an illustration or a literary anecdote. What fired me was the tragic and heroic quality of the subject and that the subject had become a myth — like Robin Hood.[3]

The series opens with a dramatically filmic overview of the competing fleets lined up in a tranquil turquoise and azure sea. The next few pictures evoke battle episodes in an urgent, yet still cohesive, semi-abstract *mêlée* of curvilinear, biomorphic and explosive shapes — in vibrant, often flaming colours. The eighth and final picture [facing page] is an overview of, in the artist's words, 'the end of the action; the battered British ships lie with their prizes. Nelson is dead.' Huge columns of black and grey smoke are seen to rise from these ravaged hulls, echoed by further plumes on the horizon seeming to metamorphose into one huge, sweeping pacific cloud.

3. David Gommon, quoted from some unpublished notes on his series of Trafalgar paintings, 1969.

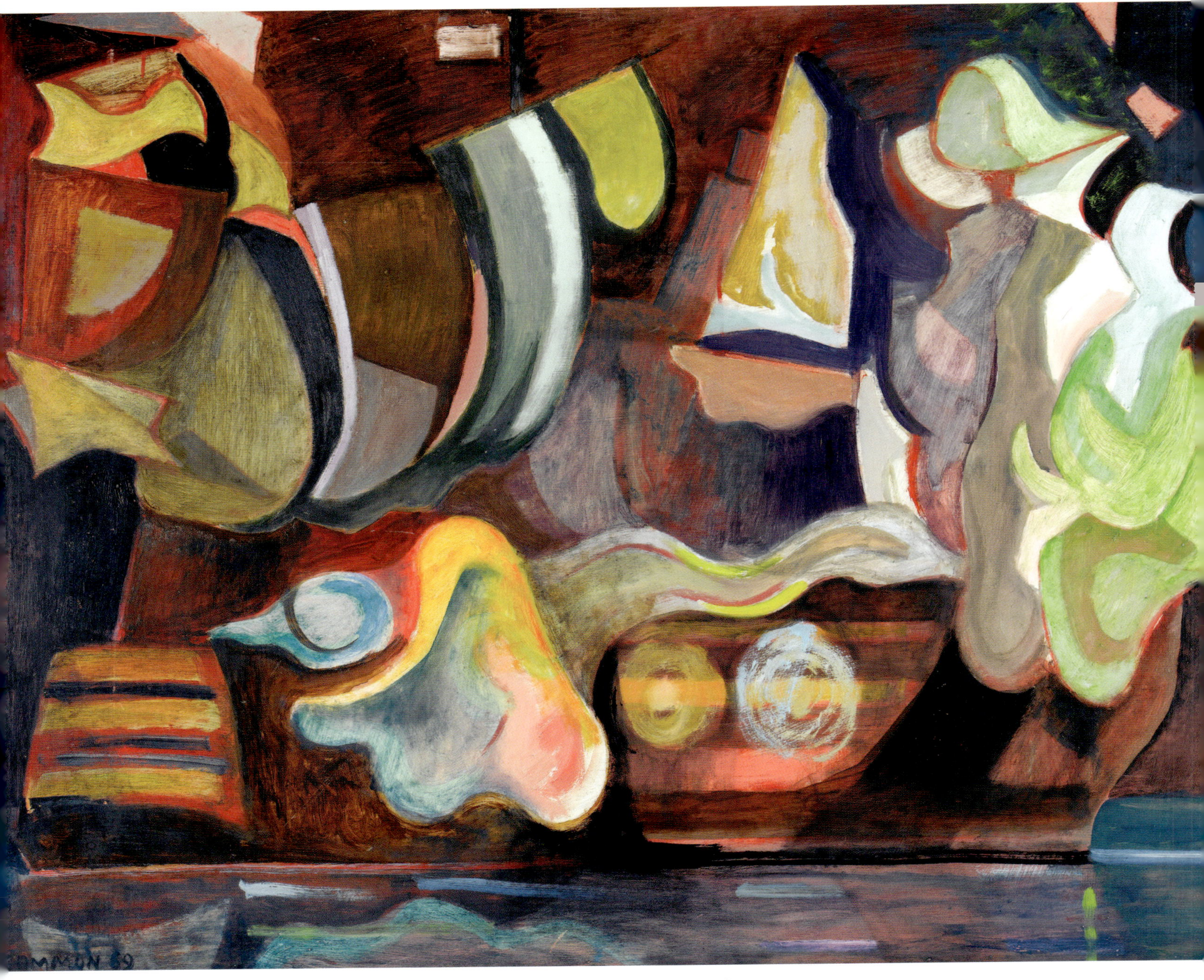

Trafalgar (6): Victory and Bucentaure / 1969, oil on board, 77 x 103 cm / private collection

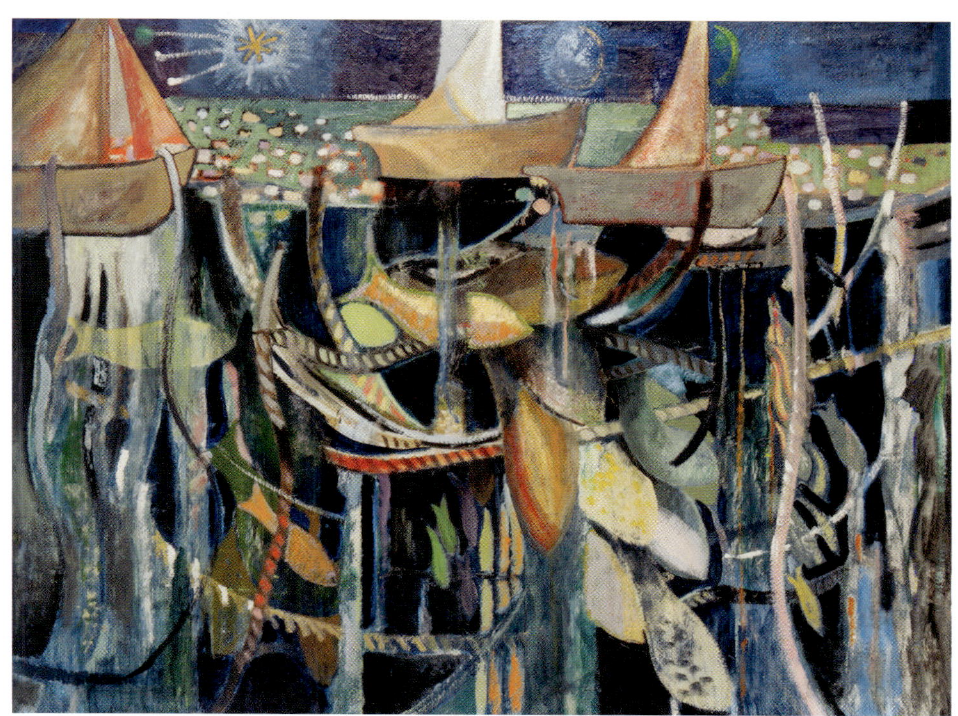

Fishing at Night
poss. mid-1970s, oil on board, 90 x 122 cm
private collection

Other post-war paintings have coastal settings. Much of the composition of the at once oceanic and cosmic painting *Fishing at Night* (above) explores an undersea world of fish of diverse colours, shapes and sizes swimming amongst an ineffable thicket of ropes and translucent nets descending from three orange, ochre and pink night-fishing boats. With shooting stars, one madly twinkling star and a crescent moon in the narrow top section of part-indigo-coloured sky — above the greenish, still surface of the sea, sparkling with little pointilliste jewels, as it were — every part of this picture is magically playful and otherworldly.

Two 1965 mixed-media pictures, *Brighton* [overleaf] and *Brighton Fashion* [p.113], show Gommon juxtaposing collaged newspaper images and snippets of text with painted imagery — a method he had utilised in making his *Book of the Dead*. However, these works, which convey the effervescent spirit of 1960s British youth culture, are radically different in tone.

In *Brighton Fashion* the forms of beachfront buildings are summoned up by blocks of newsprint. Newspaper images of fashionable young women — one modelling a trend-setting coat, another wearing a *risqué* backless swimming costume — are dispersed amongst joyous, simplified renditions of the sun, two fishing boats and their underwater nets and a number of multi-coloured fish. In a submerged newsprint cutting, a truncated headline — simply reading 'Teryle'— is set above a black-and-white photograph of a woman modelling a clinging mini dress (made from Terylene, the polyester-fibre fabric which then had a chic cachet). These works, unironic though with a Pop Art flavour, exude what W.H. Auden called 'the sexy airs of summer [and spring], The bathing hours and the bare arms'.[4]

The first mural paintings Gommon made came about through an introduction Lucy Wertheim gave him to some wealthy Americans who had moved in the

4. W.H. Auden, 'A Summer Night',
W.H. Auden Collected Poems (London:
Faber & Faber, London, 1976), p.103.

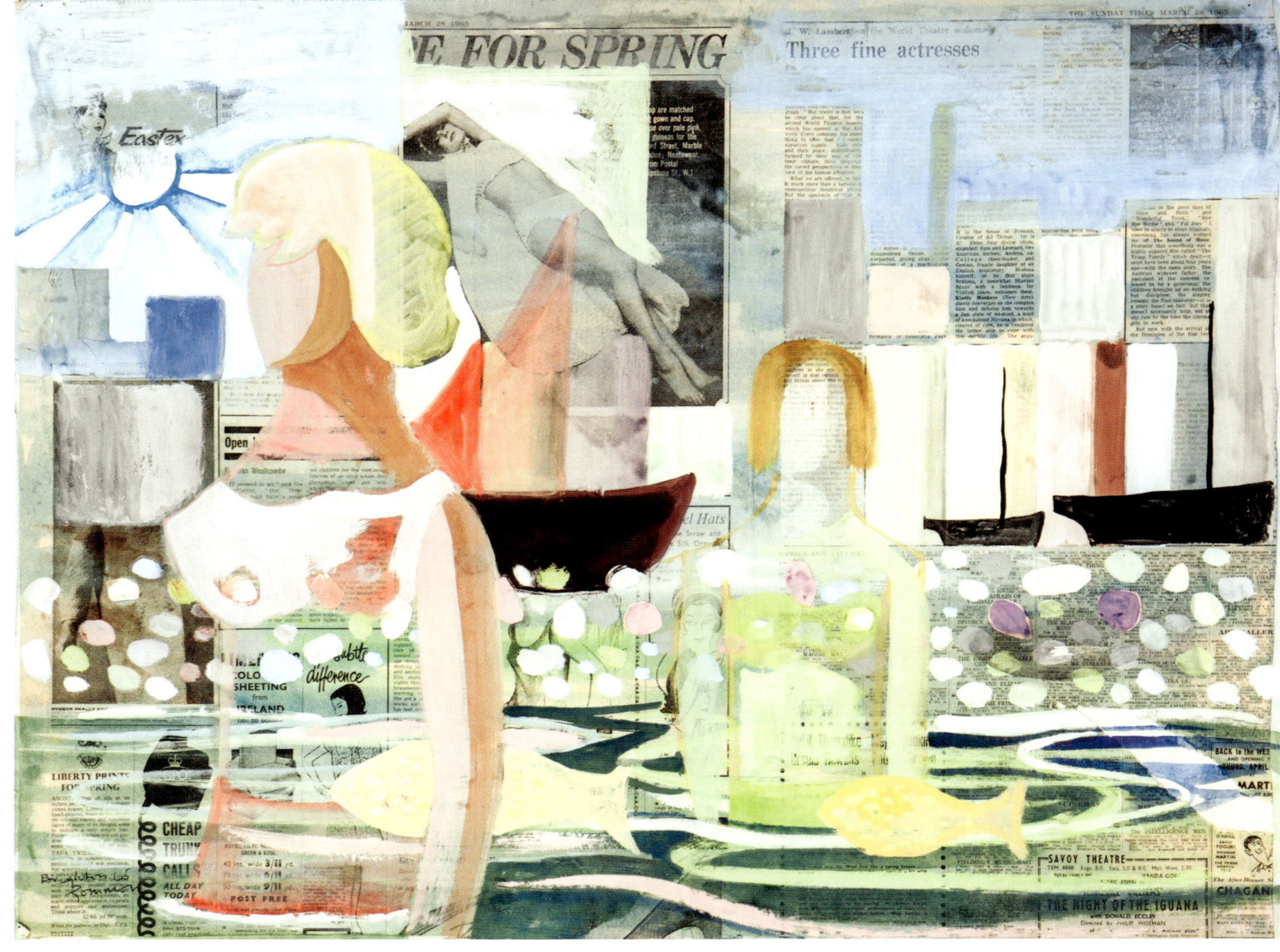

Brighton / 1965, gouache, pencil and collage on paper, 54 x 74 cm / private collection

early 1930s into a Park Street house in London's Mayfair. He then decorated the drawing room walls with images that, he recalled years later, were related to costumes and scenery that he designed for a ballet he had himself created (based on Beethoven's Ninth Symphony). The murals were particularly inspired by his study of Titian's painting *Bacchus and Ariadne* (1520—23) in London's National Gallery; the ballet itself was never performed.

The mural he painted at the Music Centre of Canberra Grammar School in Australia in late 1979 was based on abstract designs he had made of musical instruments with the aim, he said, of creating (quoting W.H. Auden's words) an 'attempt to present an analogy to the paradisal state in which Freedom and Law … are united in harmony' — whereby every good poem (or, by inference, every good painting) 'is very nearly a Utopia'.[5] (Sadly this mural is no longer *in situ*, after it subsequently sustained considerable water damage.)

The Crucifixion [p.114] was commissioned by Headmaster Paul McKeown in 1959 to be displayed on the western wall of the Chapel of Christ the King at Canberra Grammar School; Paul remained in this post at the school from 1959 to 1985. Peter Gommon recalls,

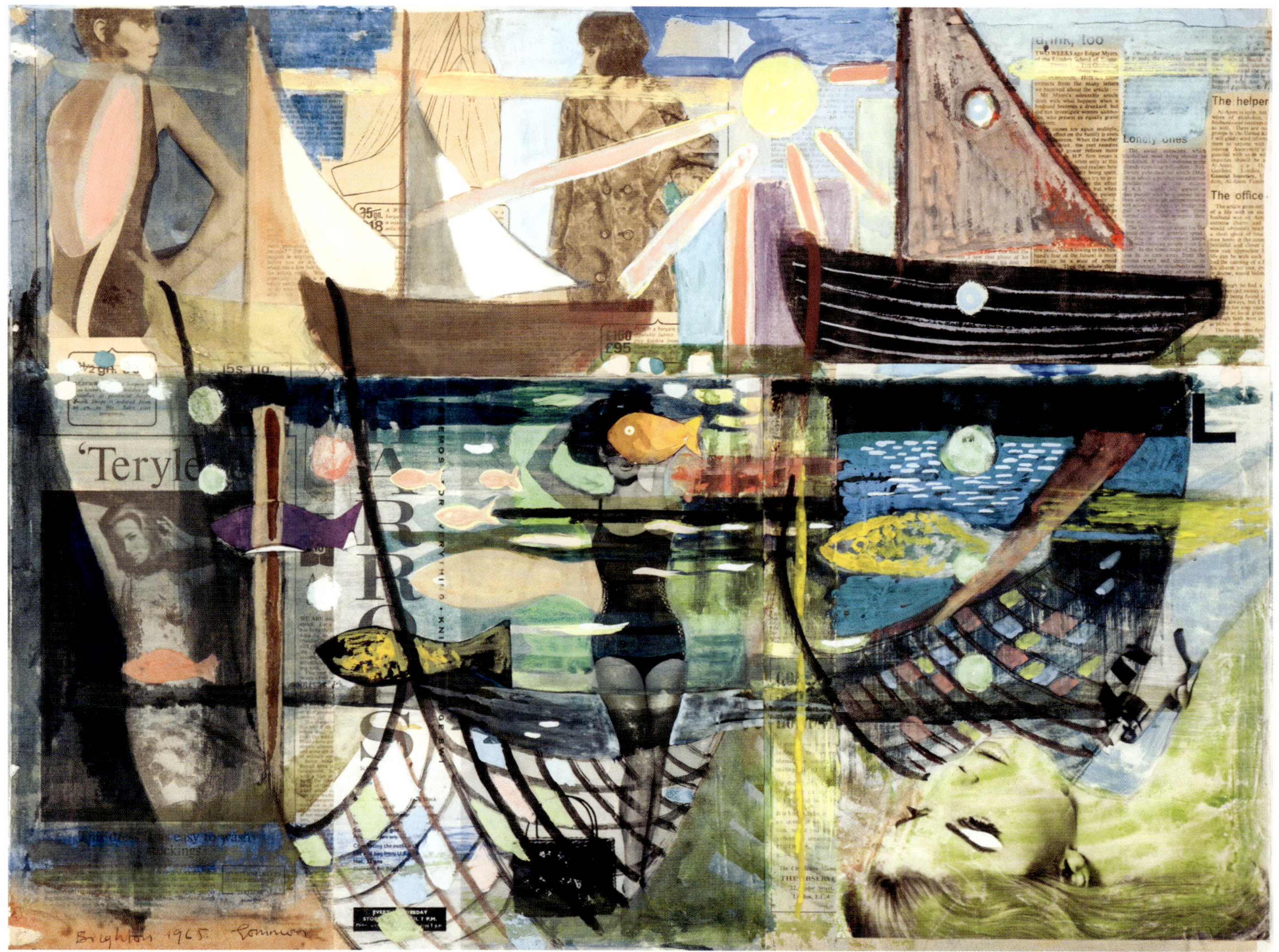

Brighton Fashion / 1965, gouache, pencil and collage on paper, 54 x 74 cm / private collection

Jean and David became good friends of Paul and Wilma [McKeown] in the 1950s when Paul was teaching at an Approved School quite close to the Grammar School in Northampton ... Paul was a man with immense moral strength. He found our class-ridden deferential society challenging. Paul and Wilma had a lot of David's paintings at their home in Canberra.

The Crucifixion carries a visceral power in its portrayal of the fallen, grieving woman in the foreground; the uncaring, carapaced soldiers with spears to the right; the rearing horse and imperious rider to the left (representing, Gommon said, the 'robustness [of] the physical world'); and the emaciated figure of the crucified Christ, whose agonised face and body he rendered as surprisingly youthful (based on drawings he made of a 16- or 17-year-old boy, a pupil at the school, 'posing in a gymnasium hanging from wall bars'). He related this figure's stylised head and feet to his study of the great German artist Matthias Grünewald, 'who painted one of the most horrific crucifixions [*c*.1512—16], with those great twisted hands and ... almost birdlike feet'.[6]

Interviewed in 1980, Gommon questioned 'whether it is possible to paint a religious picture today ... in [this] secular age'.[7] In 1933 he had painted a

5. W.H. Auden, 'The Virgin & The Dynamo', *The Dyer's Hand and Other Essays* (London: Faber & Faber, 1962), p.71.
6. 'An Interview with David Gommon, the Painter from Northamptonshire ...', p.45.
7. Ibid. p.44.

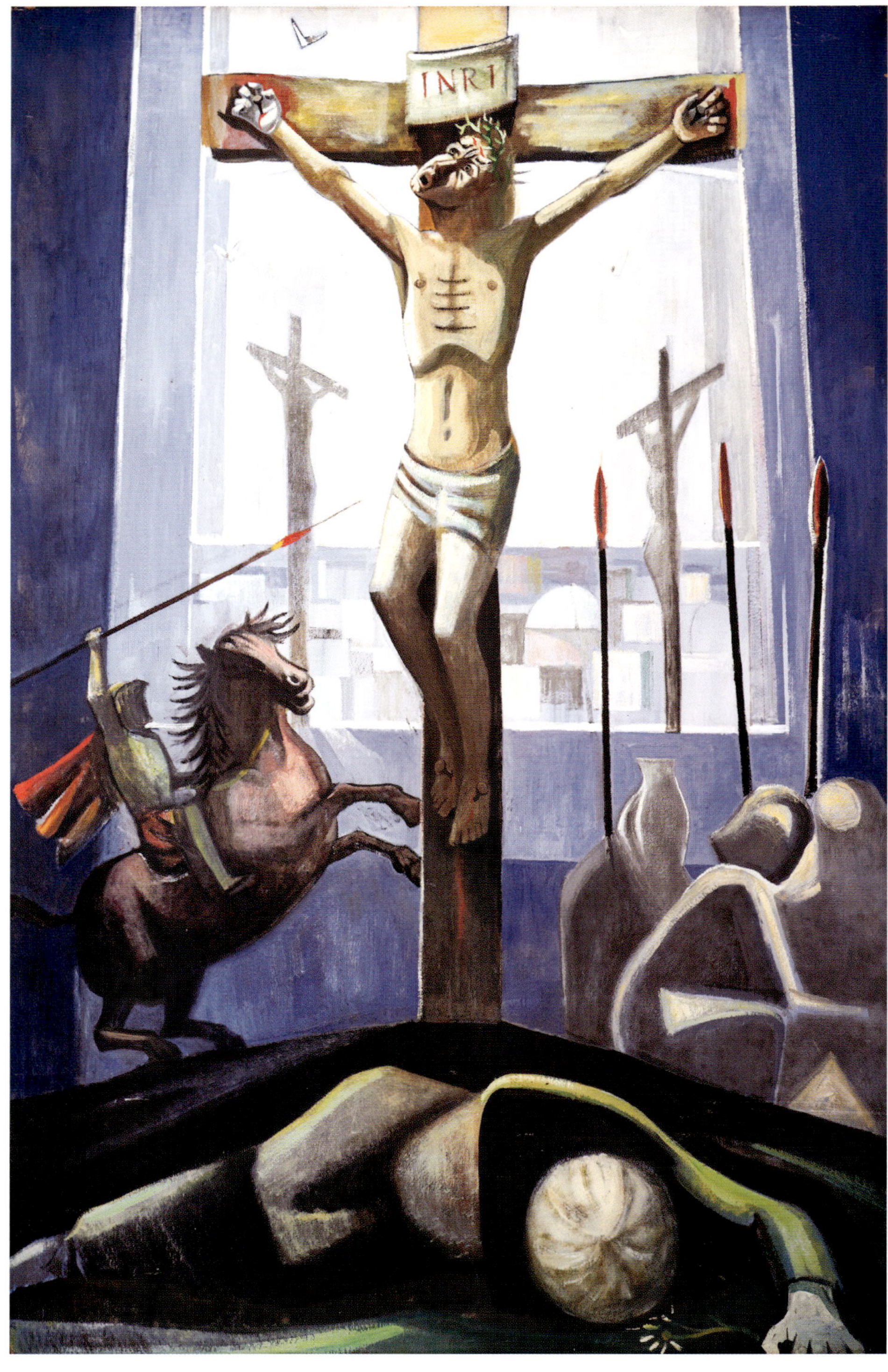

The Crucifixion
1959, oil on board, 181.6 x 123 cm
Canberra Grammar School, Australia

desolate *Crucifixion* scene (yet one still crowded with figures) [facing page]
which is more rawly and spontaneously elaborated than the 1959 picture; the
three crucified figures are portrayed with expressive austerity in black-and-
white, though individual facial expressions are absent. The disconsolate, tall
figure of Mary Magdalene in a long, maroon dress clings in piteous appeal
to the legs of Christ on the Cross.

Peter Gommon recalls that his parents would attend an Anglican church
from time to time, although in later years in Hardingstone 'they gradually
became pillars of the church; my mother would read the gospel and my

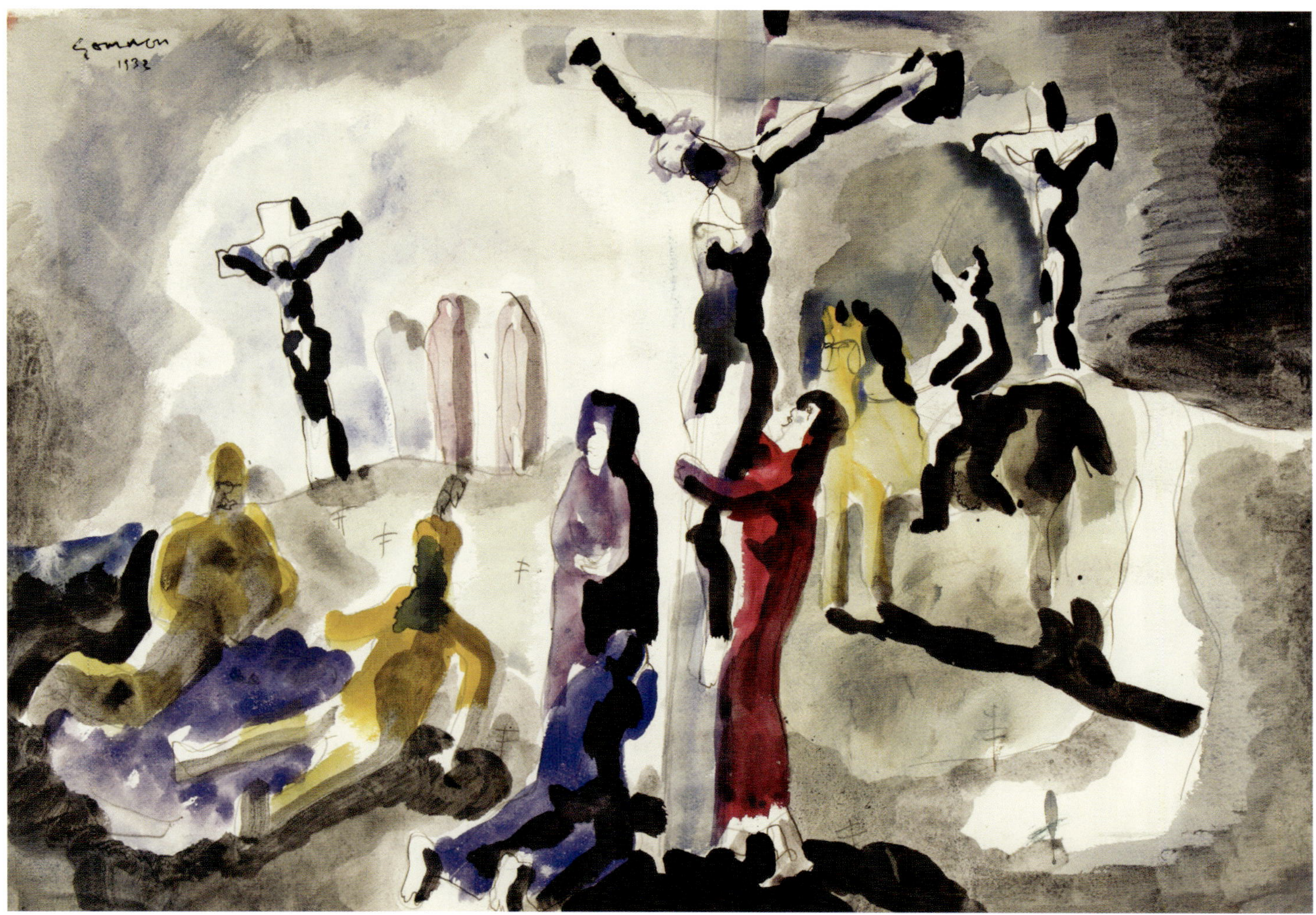

Crucifixion / 1933, pencil, pen and ink and watercolour on paper, 38.3 x 55.9 cm / The Whitworth, University of Manchester

father became a lay assistant'. Kate Currie says that when there was a performance (at St Matthew's Church, Northampton) of *Noye's Fludde*, the Chester Miracle Play (based on the biblical story of Noah's Ark) set to music by Benjamin Britten in 1957, her father played the part of God; 'I remember a friend saying, with a grin, "what a bit of type-casting!" — because he had a nice deep voice that filled the building.'

Around 1969 Gommon organised an impressive exhibition of religious art at St Matthew's, where the cultural legacy of Walter Hussey, a keen collector and connoisseur of modern art, and who was vicar there until 1955, remained a strong and inspiring influence. Hussey — who himself wrote how much he regretted that 'the arts had become largely divorced from the Church'[8] — was subsequently appointed Dean of Chichester Cathedral, for which he went on to commission works of art by (amongst others), Sutherland, Piper, Cecil Collins and Chagall. Pallant House, the Chichester gallery which opened in 1982, went on to inherit and show Hussey's significant and varied personal collection of modern art.

For the show he curated at St Matthew's, Gommon borrowed artworks by Graham Sutherland, Stanley Spencer, Rouault, David Jones, the Liverpudlian sculptor Arthur Dooley (1929—1994) and the Australian artist Roy De Maistre

8. See https://en.wikipedia.org/wiki/Walter_Hussey.

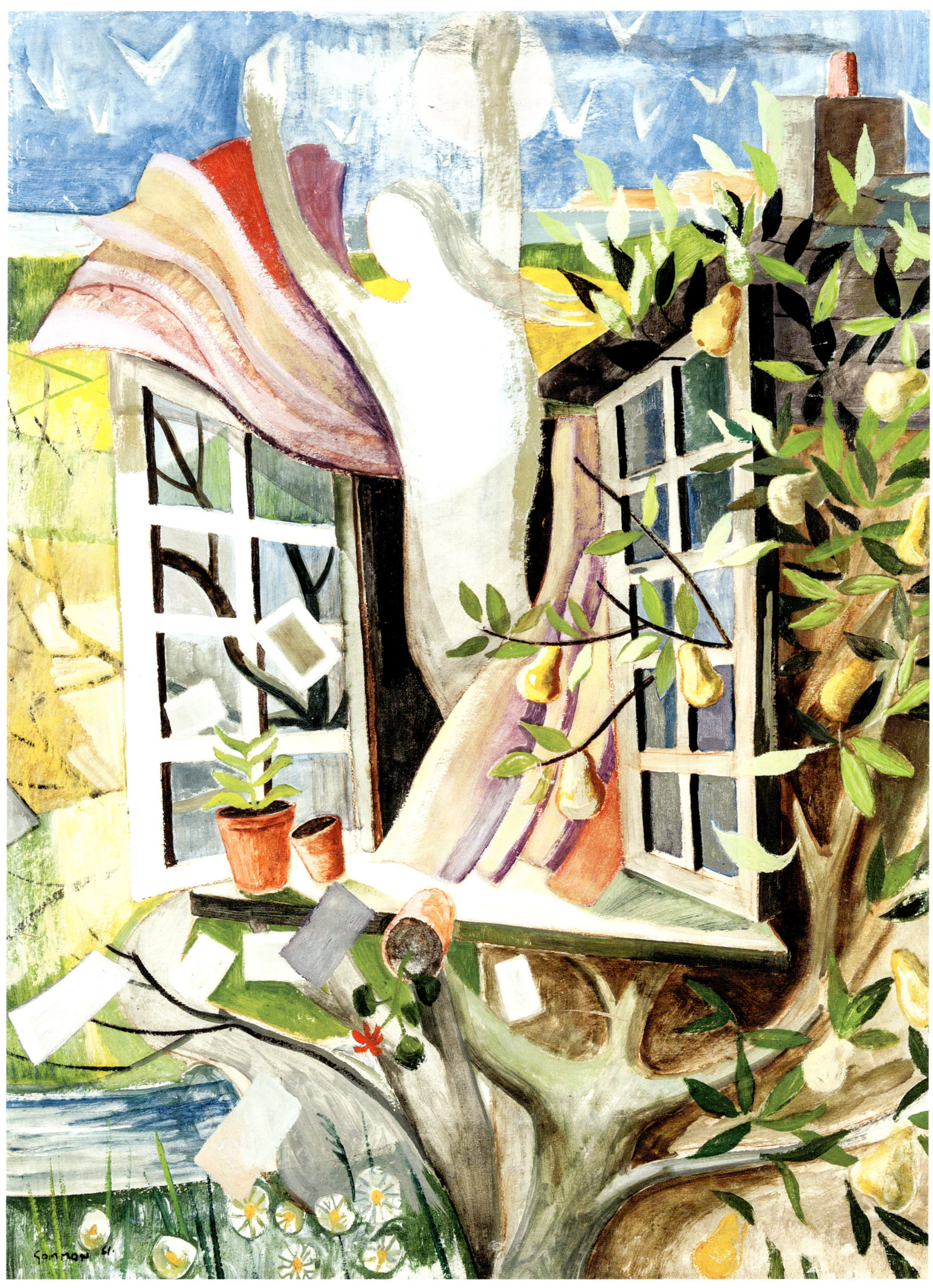

Mrs Pooley (Ascending to Heaven) / 1961, oil on board, 122 x 92 cm / private collection

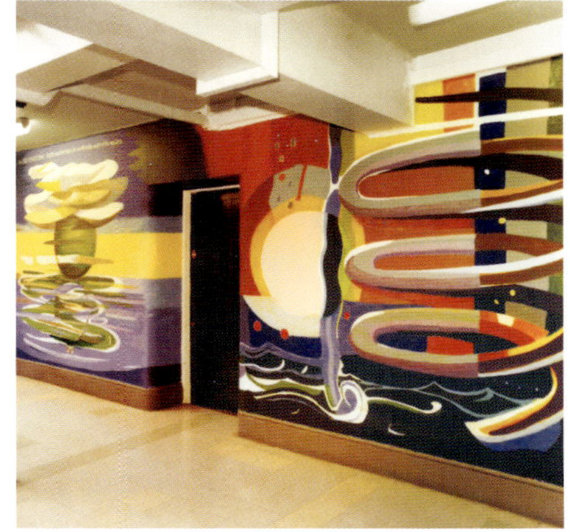

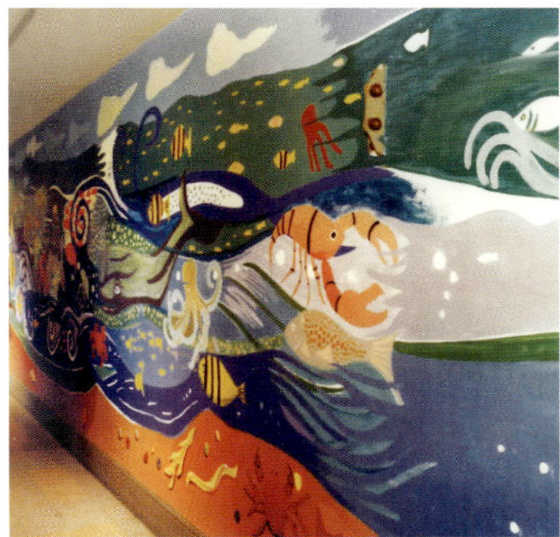

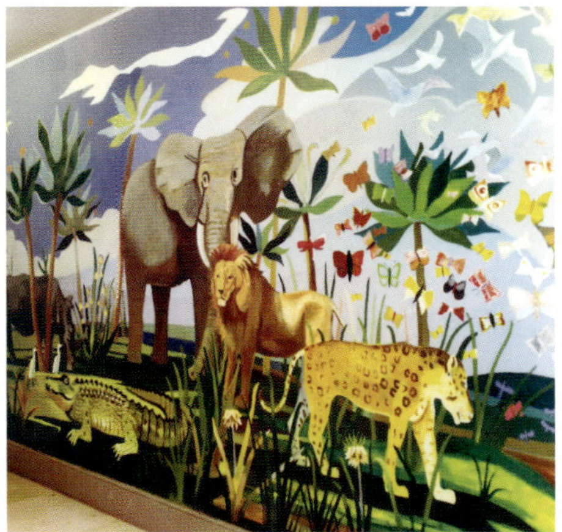

Details from the St Crispin Hospital mural
private collection

(1894—1968). Neville Wallis, *The Observer* art critic, had introduced Gommon to De Maistre, who was renowned for his early experimental, semi-abstract paintings — such as a serenely fluid landscape, *Rhythmic Composition in Yellow Green Minor* (1919) — which aimed to orchestrate varied hues on the colour spectrum and notes on the musical scale. Gommon later noted, 'What a charming and very kindly man Roy de Maistre was!'[9]

David's poignant 1961 painting *Mrs Pooley (Ascending to Heaven)* [facing page] was made following news of the death of the lady in whose house (in the Dorset village of Hartgrove) he had happily lived for a time as a young man. Peter Gommon says, 'David was fond of all the Pooley family. He must have heard of her death from her daughter Margaret, and according to Jean produced the painting quickly, as a heartfelt response to her dying.' This remarkable picture is infused with a spirit of buoyancy, lightness and metaphysical release as well as an almost festive brilliancy of colour as the late, now featureless and ageless Mrs Pooley is seen dynamically surging skywards from a bedroom window as a literal body of pellucid light (in the process knocking aside plant pots from the windowsill and letting what are presumably pages and papers of her life scatter in the air). Abundant golden pears on the tree to the right appear almost like bells ringing out her passing. There is an easy affinity here with the kind of paintings Stanley Spencer (1891—1959) was renowned for making of his own village in heaven — representing quotidian yet transfigured fellow residents of Cookham in Berkshire.

Gommon retired early from Northampton Grammar School in 1975. He had already been approached to undertake an ambitious scheme of mural decoration for corridors in St Crispin Hospital, a large psychiatric facility in Northampton. The idea was that a number of unemployed young people would be paid to be his painting assistants. He then spent about a year on this project. He said,

> On first sight of the mental hospital and the corridors ... which were usually busy with people and trolleys, often very drafty and worst of all very cold ... I shuddered and nearly decided not to do it! But I am very glad that I did ... it was an experience from which I learned a great deal.

He decided that these murals would be based on 'the story in Genesis of God creating the world in seven days. The corridor divided itself up very happily into seven definite areas, and the subject matter offered a splendid range of very colourful material.' In one section he depicted a sturdy-looking Adam and Eve in the Garden of Eden alongside various animals Adam had named: a Peaceable Kingdom in which keen likenesses of a bear, a cat, a stag, two camels, a bull, a duck, a cockerel, some hens, a cow and calf, a peacock and a donkey are seen to co-exist blissfully.

Gommon wrote, 'I finished up the seventh day with God [an unassuming man — with his hands behind his head — in blue shirt, grey trousers and a sunhat shading his eyes] sitting comfortably in a deck chair [under deliciously rendered abstract patterns of a pair of blossoming and fruiting trees], looking back down the whole length of the corridor admiring his work.[10]

9 David Gommon, from notes ... 1980, p.8.
10 Ibid, pp.8—9.

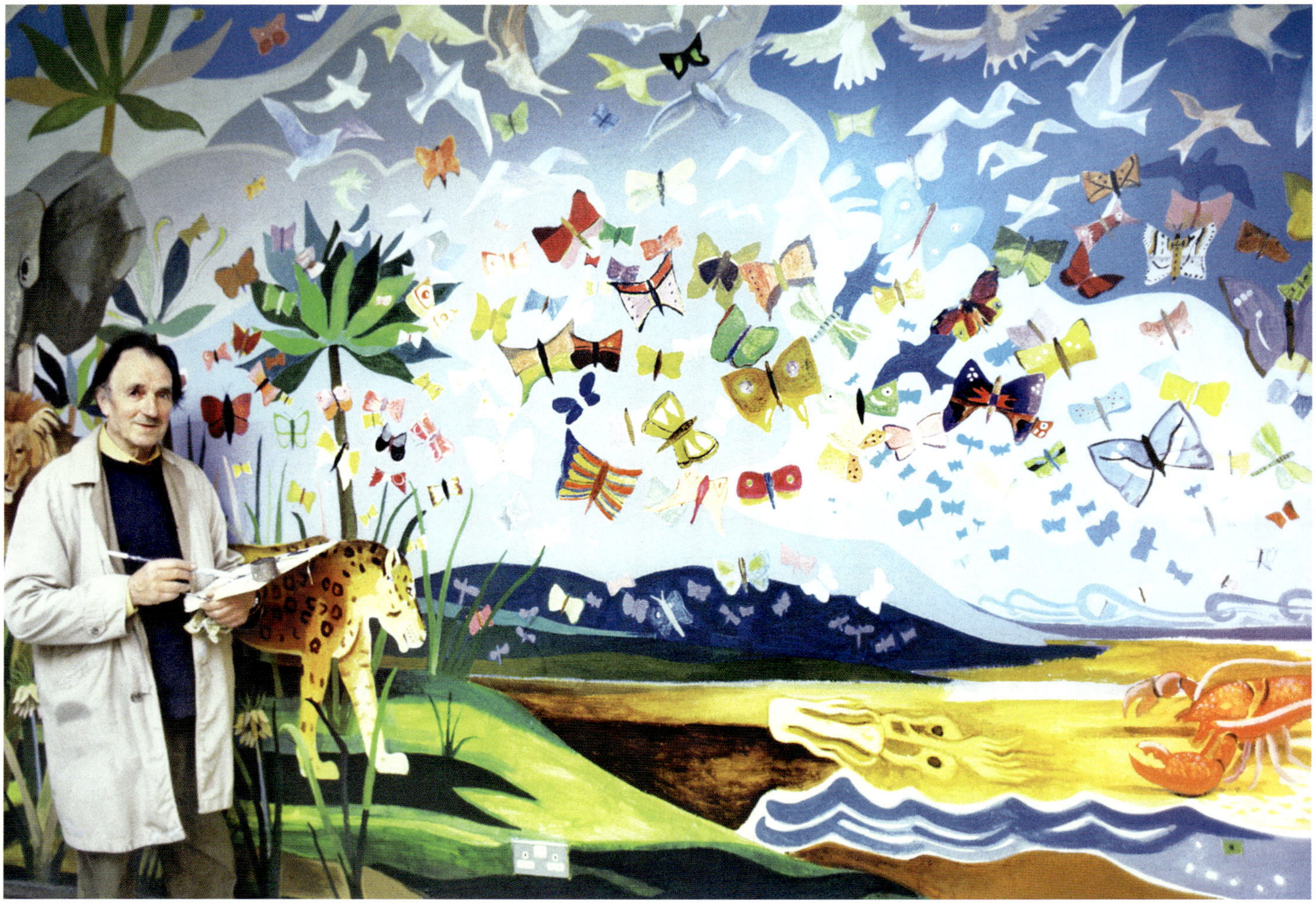

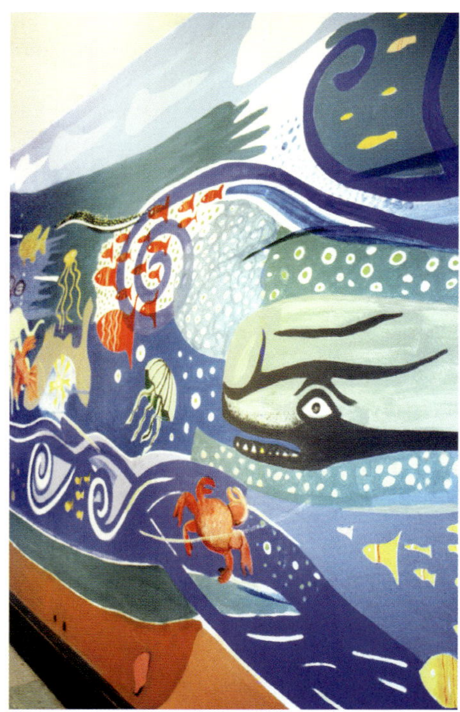

David and a section of the St Crispin Hospital mural
private collection

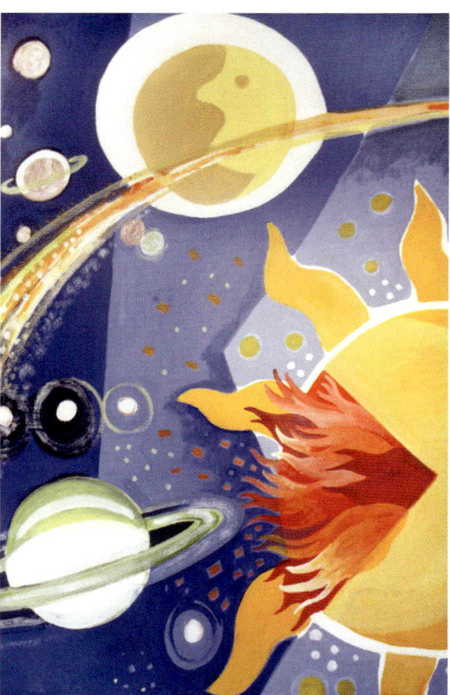

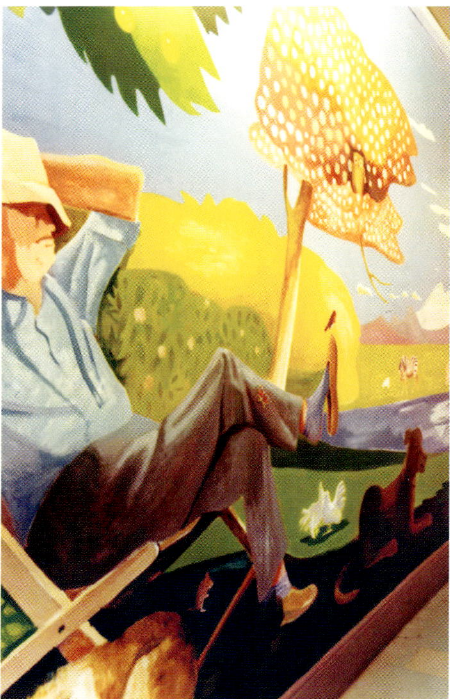

Details from the St Crispin Hospital mural
private collection

Creation on the wall

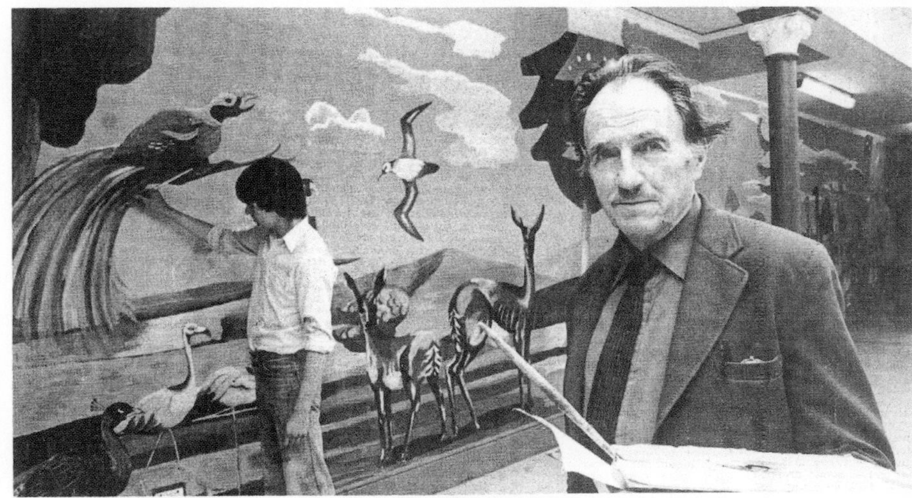

ARTIST David Gommon and helper Stephen Penger with one of the murals they are painting on the walls in St. Crispin Hospital.

David Gommon with assistant Stephen Penger, St Crispin Hospital, 1980, from the *Northampton Chronicle & Echo*

The hospital authorities then approached Gommon to paint further corridors. He spent about three years on this, working alone this time. These entrancing murals were based on the themes of 'Shopping' — portraying bustling market scenes, a florist's stall, a butcher's and a fishmonger's shop, a shoe shop interior in characteristic disarray — and 'The Seasons', which included radiant visions of a cricket match and apple pickers in an orchard, the latter scene imbued with a rapturous psalmist's joy.

These murals sadly no longer exist, as the hospital was closed in 1995 for housing redevelopment. They are now only known in some family photographs and also photographic studies in Sandra Bemrose's book *St Crispin Hospital 1876—1995: Memories from Staff, Past and Present.*[11]

11. Frustratingly, this is undated, but it would have been after 1995.

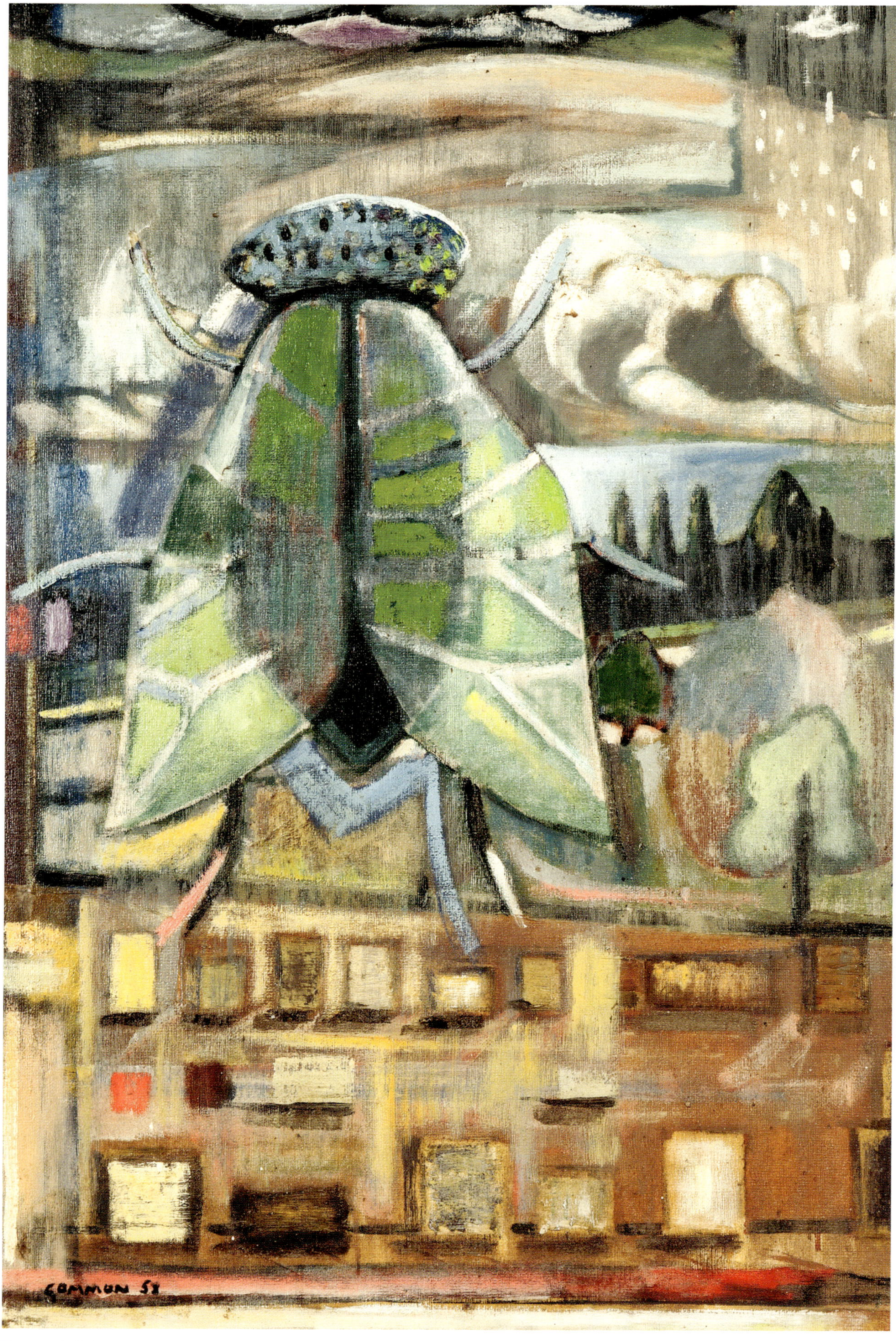

Fly on a Window / 1958, oil on board, 74 x 51 cm / private collection

Songbirds and a modernist poet

AN ATTITUDE OF REVERENCE FOR THE NATURAL WORLD IS AT THE heart of Gommon's painterly vision. In work from the 1930s the subtly symbolic figure of the horse predominates; after 1945 birds are at the forefront.

Interestingly, cats seldom appear in his art — a rare exception is a black cat appearing twice in his *Creation* series murals. His apparent aversion to cats — which later turned into mere tolerance — is explained by Kate Currie: 'He described as a child throwing stones at cats that came into the garden because cats were death to a London garden, pulling up flowers etc. He tolerated a cat in later years — when my brother brought one home from university.' In his poem 'The Firetails [sic] Nest', John Clare acknowledged the predatory nature of cats in relation to diverse species of birds whose habits and habitat he so keenly observed — and whose singing he listened to and described so precisely and affectingly:

> Tweet pipes the robin as the cat creeps bye
> Her nestling young that in the elderns [elder trees] lie
> And then the bluecap tootles in its glee
> Picking the flies from blossomed apple tree
> And pink the chaffinch cries its well known strain
> Urging its mate to utter pink again
> While in a quiet mood hedgesparrows trie
> An inward stir of shadowed melody
> While on the rotten tree the firetail mourns ...[1]

A similar kind of familiarity with circumambient birdlife informs Gommon's art as surely as it informed and enriched so many aspects of his life. A great disappointment in his later years was the intrusion of near constant traffic noise in his cottage garden and wider surroundings following the construction of the Expressway nearby in the early 1970s. This sullied for him what was often more or less the deep rural quiet in which birdsong had rung out so clearly (see pp.99—101).

Gommon's sense of kinship with fellow creatures extended to minute insects, as shown by the painting *Fly on a Window* (1958) [facing page]. With partly emerald green wings and pale blue and pink legs, this gorgeously delicate creature resting on a windowpane is viewed on a gargantuan scale — and with the kind of tender fellow feeling that William Blake evidenced in his 1794 poem 'The Fly'.

1. John Clare, 'The Firetails [*sic*] Nest', *John Clare: Major Works* (Oxford University Press, 2008), p.212.

It is curious to note that the Scottish painter John Maxwell (1905—1962) painted a series of four pictures (in the first three months of 1959) on the theme of butterflies, moths and flowers that bear some comparison with Gommon's 1958 painting. Maxwell wrote (on 2 September 1960) that 'the series started from two incidents — 1. Moths against the window at dusk; 2. a particularly lavish flowering of a large bush of Rosa Moyesii I have in the garden. Both seemed to suggest pictorial possibilities ...'[2] Maxwell's mystically resonant painting *Night Flowers* (Tate) highlights a purplish and red butterfly iridescent in splendid close-up against white flowers and a pitch-black sky.

Grossly magnified, sometimes full-page, visions of fleas and other insects had already appeared in Gommon's *Book of the Dead* (1939—1944) [eg. see facing page]. However, then they were represented as revolting symbols of a corrupt, aggressive modern society.

In March 1979 Gommon visited Durham University to attend a conference on the leading Modernist poet Ezra Pound (1885—1972); it was there that he met the Northumbrian poet Basil Bunting (1900—1985), another Modernist, and about whose 1966 poem *Briggflatts* his fellow poet Thom Gunn justif-iably wrote, '*Briggflatts* is one of the few great poems of [the 20th] century.'[3] It was then arranged that Gommon return there in July 1979, staying in one of the colleges to paint Bunting's portrait. He recalled, 'This I did. And it was for me a very happy experience getting to know Basil Bunting and hearing about his early days in Paris, and later in Italy, with Pound. He had such an attractive Northumbrian lilt. He was just eighty years old.'[4]

Like the poet David Jones, Bunting had been traumatised by events of the First World War — in his case, as a Quaker-inspired pacifist he was arrested in 1918 as a conscientious objector and, then refusing to make munitions, jailed for over a year (a time often spent in solitary confinement). His 1931 poem *Aus Dem Zweiten Reich* (*From the Second Reich*) sardonically evokes the lascivious yet sterile atmosphere and 'efficiently metropolitan chatter' of cafes in the Nollendorfplatz, then a beautiful Berlin square. The poem (whose acerbic tone and details bear comparison to elements in Gommon's *Book of the Dead*) ends with these shattering lines:

> ... notorieties
> contorted laudatory lips,
> wreaths and bouquets surround
> the mindless menopause.
> Stillborn fecundities,
> frostbound applause.[5]

Bunting later noted the main influences on his personal and artistic outlook as being 'Jails and the sea, Quaker mysticism and socialist politics, a lasting unlucky passion, the slums of Lambeth and Hoxton ...'[6]

In his portrait [p.125], Gommon portrayed Bunting sitting on a verandah or in what may be a garden room overlooking gently undulating fields, grazed by black cows (diminutively seen), with a far view of the River Tyne. The setting

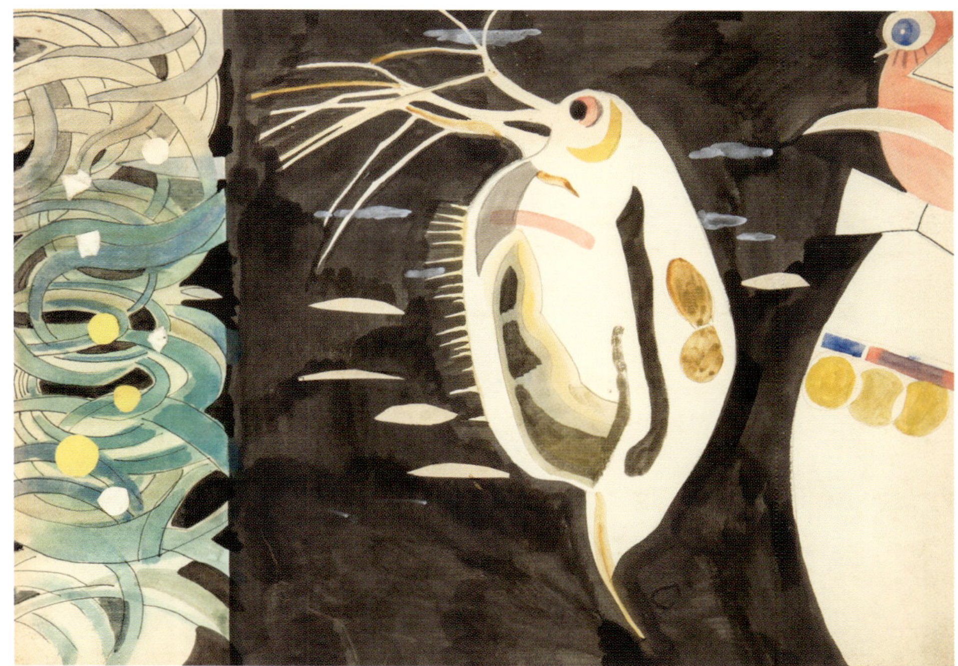

Mere Insects from
The Book of the Dead, a 'Comédie humaine'
1939—44, pen and ink, watercolour and
gouache on paper, 38 x 56 cm
private collection

is possibly the carriage house in the Northumbrian market town of Hexham, where Bunting lived simply in his later years. The subject's dispassionate ruminative air, his calm, upright dignity of demeanour, as he sits in profile, hands clasped together (casually attired in a jacket whose green hues and patternings — as in the crumpled folds in the sleeves — resonate with those of the natural world beyond), are movingly wrought. The thrush in the foliage behind him — facing the same direction — seems to be a symbol of Bunting's insistent belief that 'poetry, like music, is to be heard'.[7] Late recordings of Bunting reading his poetry aloud reveal (as Richard Caddel, one of the founders in 1988 of the Basil Bunting Poetry Centre at Durham University, wrote in 1999) 'a precise and measured speech which related to that of his Quaker schooling, rather than to the Celtic mists'.[8]

His essentially autobiographical long poem *Briggflatts* tells of his first love following his visit as a schoolboy to Brigflatts [*sic*] Quaker Friends Meeting House near Sedburgh in Cumbria; at this time he became strongly attached to a schoolfriend's sister living there. The opening lines help evoke the spirit of the zestful young poet (the 'sweet tenor bull') with a compact yet expressively varied musicality; as such they bear comparison to the expression of frisky, young, rustic love in Gommon's early paintings.

> Brag, sweet tenor bull,
> descant on Rawthey's madrigal,
> each pebble its part
> for the fells' late spring.
> Dance tiptoe, bull,
> black against may.
> Ridiculous and lovely
> chase hurdling shadows
> morning into noon.[9]

2. John Maxwell, in Mary Chamot, Dennis Farr and Martin Butlin, *Tate Gallery Catalogues: The Modern British Paintings, Drawings and Sculpture* (vol. II, M—Z) (London: Oldbourne Press, 1964), p.431.
3. See www.londonreviewbookshop.co.uk/ stock/briggflatts-basil-bunting.
4. David Gommon, from notes ... 1980, p.8.
5. Basil Bunting, 'Aus Dem Zweiten Reich', *Basil Bunting: Complete Poems* (Hexham: Bloodaxe Books, 2021), p.38.
6. Quoted in 'Basil Bunting Biography', www.poemhunter.com/basil-bunting.
7. Bunting quoted in 'Introduction', *Basil Bunting: Complete Poems*, p.11.
8. Ibid, p.12.
9. Bunting, 'Briggflatts', *Basil Bunting: Complete Poems*, p.61.

Richard Caddel has noted that one of Bunting's 'earliest memories was of his nurse singing Northumbrian folksongs'.[10] Gommon said that a significant early memory he had was 'of standing in front of a large class of Cockney children and reciting a Scottish poem, in what I thought was a Scottish dialect'.[11] His mother had introduced him as a child to Robert Burns's poems, and also to Border Ballads, which he always valued for their 'very visual poetry'.[12] These Ballads were a group of ancient songs (sung unaccompanied) which (as the pioneering folk song collector A.L. Lloyd pointed out) came from 'the bare rolling stretch of country from the North Tyne and Cheviots to the Scottish southern uplands'.[13] In this respect Bunting and Gommon had much in common.

The image of a song thrush appears in an untitled 1964 poem by Bunting which has an irony-steeped lyrical grace and shows an empathy with the bird's sorrowful predicament in the face of nature's savagery:

> A thrush in the syringa [a lilac bush] sings ...
>
> '... My sons
> by hawks' beak, by stones,
> trusting weak wings
> by cat and weasel, die.
>
> Thunder smothers the sky.
> From a shaken bush I
> list familiar things,
> fear, hunger, lust.'
>
> O gay thrush![14]

At this point, it is interesting to hear the artist Cecil Collins' personal account (from *Fools and Angels*, the 1983 BBC film on his art) of a moment of at once

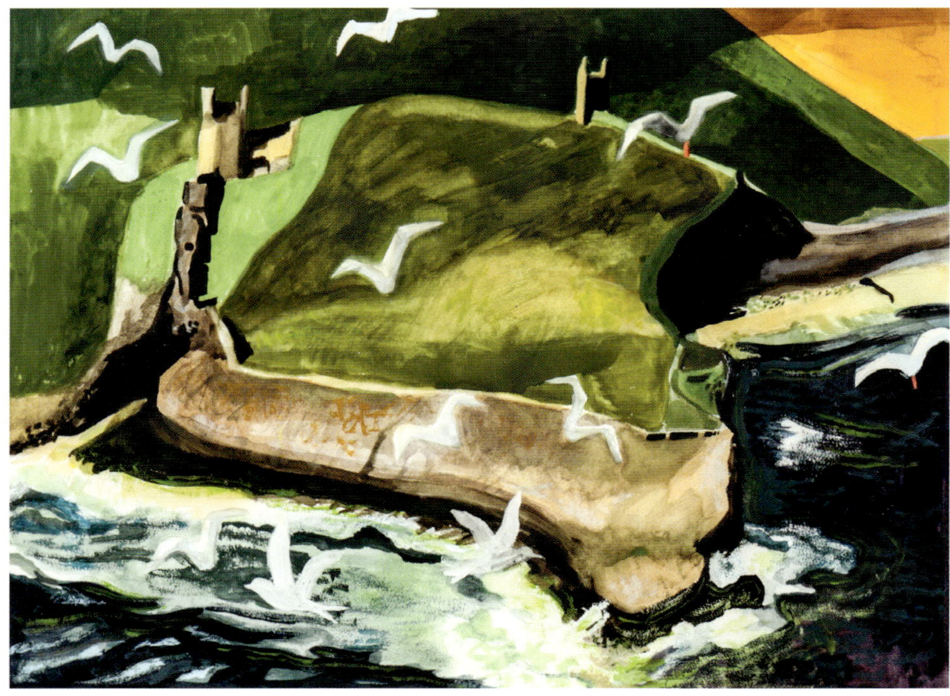

Dunstanburgh Castle
1984, gouache on paper, 51 x 71 cm
private collection

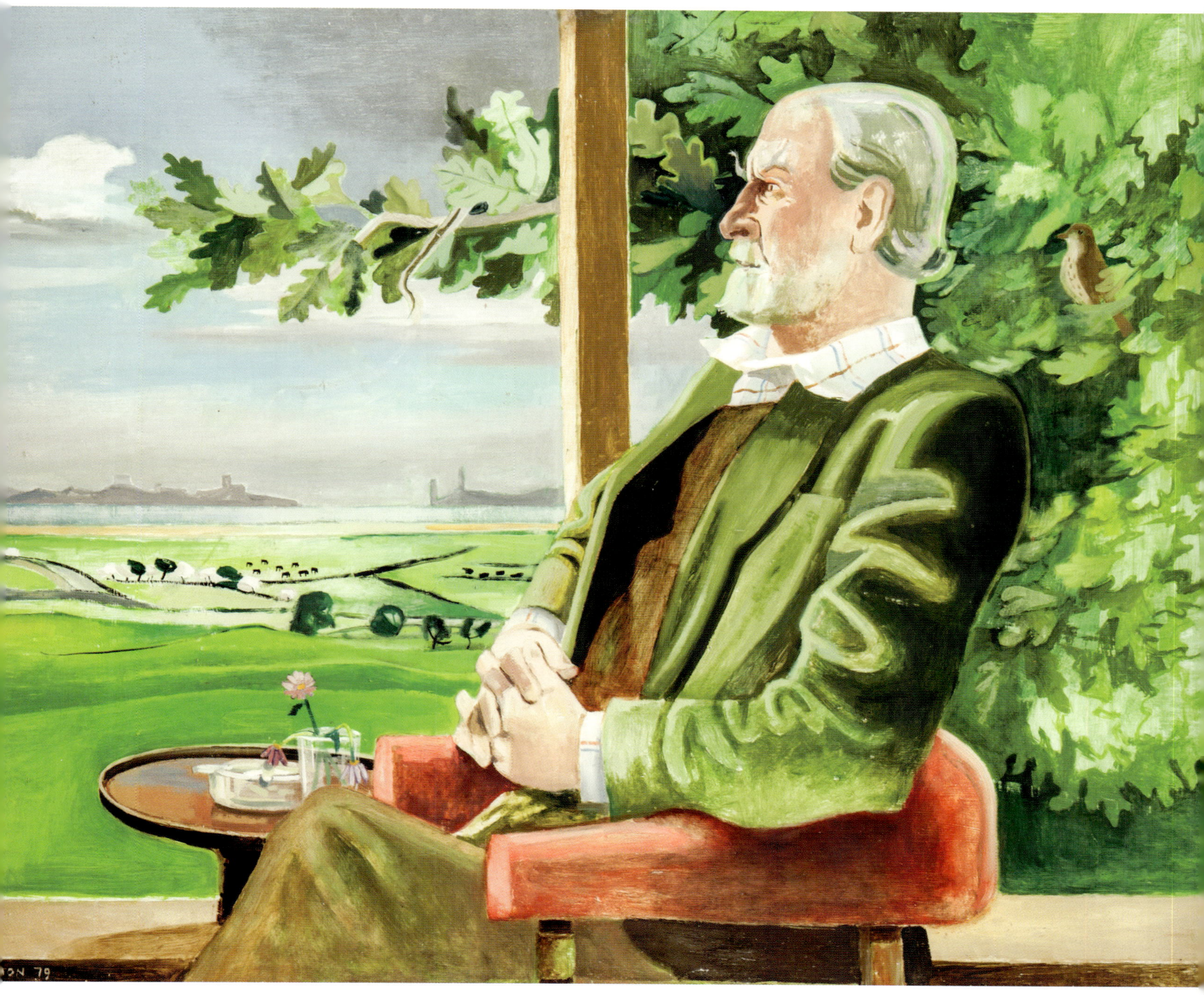

Portrait of Basil Bunting / 1979, oil on board, 76 x 101 cm / private collection

10. 'Introduction', *Basil Bunting: Complete Poems*, p.11.
11. 'An Interview with David Gommon, the Painter from Northamptonshire ...', p.38.
12. Ibid
13. A.L. Lloyd, *Folk Song in England* (London: Lawrence & Wishart, 1967) p.159.
14. Basil Bunting, untitled poem dated 1964, *Basil Bunting: Complete Poems*, p.135.

heightened vision and sound — of a kind that also characterises Gommon's own visionary sensibility:

> Just at the beginning of the War, an … afternoon, the light was coming onto the trees, a big bush, and on every leaf were drops of water shining just like diamonds, and on top of this bush was a thrush singing — and I suddenly saw that the bush was the shape of the thrush's song, that the song and the form were the same thing. And that was for me a moment of illumination as I had constantly in my childhood. It was a moment of vision.[15]

For Gommon, from an early age, a love and appreciation of poetry and music were intimately and inextricably linked with his visual sensibility. He would have agreed with Bunting's 1966 statement that 'Poetry, like music, is to be heard. It deals in sound — long sounds and short sounds, heavy beats and light beats, the tone relations of vowels, the relations of consonants to one another … Reading in silence is the source of half the misconceptions that have caused the public to distrust poetry.'[16] Peter Gommon recalls that the family enjoyed a 'collective experience of poetry' while listening to an LP of the Welsh poet Dylan Thomas's 1954 radio play *Under Milk Wood* — with the actor Richard Burton as a sonorous, wonderfully nuanced 'First Voice'.

Gommon painted a second portrait of Bunting in 1979 [facing page]; in this, the poet is seen dressed in the same attire, although, as the scene here is set (rather indistinctly) indoors, the luminous green jacket of the first portrait has become a more subdued olive tone. The first picture's somewhat fiercely detached pose in full profile (and strong sunlight) has become, in the second work, a more reticent-appearing 'brown study' in semi-profile — yet both works notably evoke aspects of the subject's noble-seeming demeanour and visionary clarity.

In a *c.*1968 *Sunday Times Magazine* interview Philip Norman described Bunting as 'a shy, prudent man with grey hair that spikes out at the back and baggy, clerical clothes … the brilliant contacts of his past — admiration and editing from [the great Modernist poet Ezra] Pound, the condescending interest of [the playwright Bernard] Shaw — seem to embarrass Bunting now almost as much as present admiration from people as spiritually far apart as [the American Beat poet] Allen Ginsberg and [the English literary critic and writer] Cyril Connolly … of his autobiographical poem *Briggflatts* Connolly said that every word shone "like hoarfrost".' In Gommon's second portrait, the achievement of Bunting's poem is tentatively but ineluctably acknowledged and celebrated in Gommon's faint yet elegant inscription of the word BRIGGFLATTS towards the top left of the portrait.

Gommon's own faith and development as an artist — one who felt a quite awestruck joy in the natural world, intuiting a sacred dimension as its ground of being — find parallels in certain passages in the *Journals* of the influential American religious writer, poet and Trappist monk Thomas Merton (1915–1968), who himself called the mystic Julian of Norwich 'one of the most wonderful of all Christian voices'.[17]

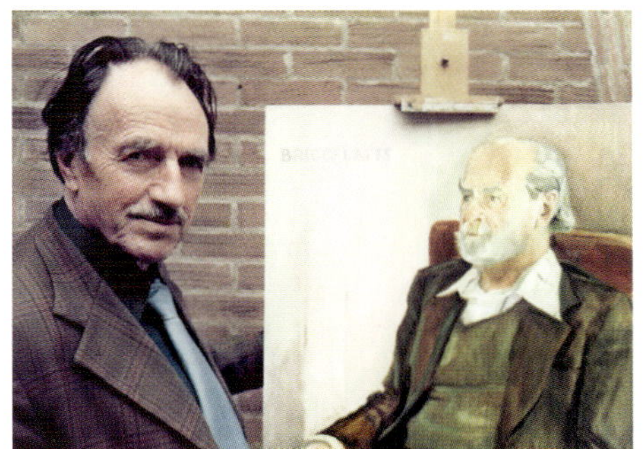

David painting Basil Bunting's portrait

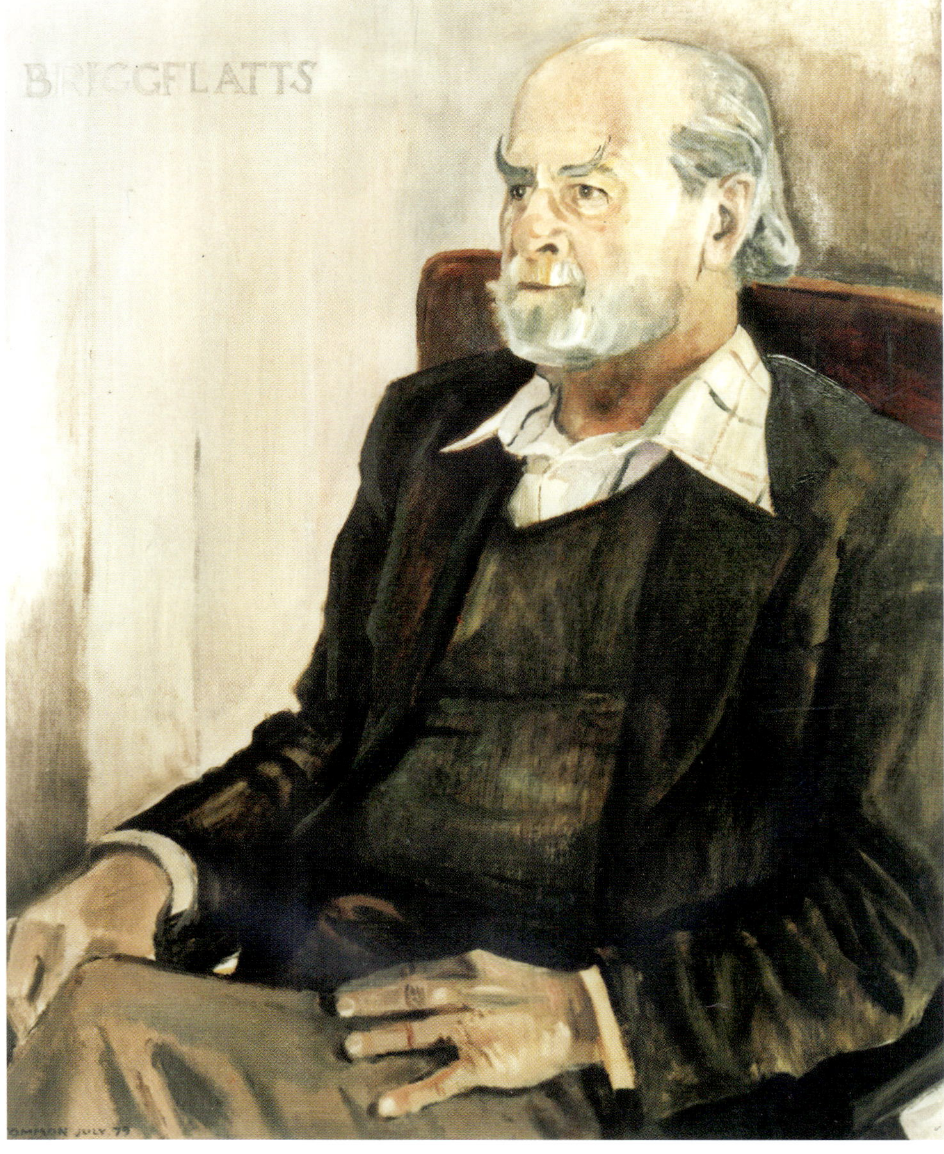

Portrait of Basil Bunting
1979, oil on board, 101 x 76 cm
whereabouts unknown

15. Cecil Collins, interviewed in *Fools and Angels*, a 30-minute film on the artist made for the BBC2 TV series *One Pair of Eyes* in 1983 and broadcast on 10 October 1986; www.youtube.com/watch?v=XTsocgoLril.
16. Basil Bunting, quoted in 'Introduction', *Basil Bunting: Complete Poems*, p.11.
17. 'Letters in a Time of Crisis', 'To Sister M. Madeleva', in Thomas Merton, *Seeds of Destruction* (New York: Farrar, Straus & Giroux, 1964), pp.274—5.
18. Thomas Merton, *The Intimate Merton: His Life from His Journals* (Oxford: Lion Publishing, 2002), p.151.
19. Ibid, p.234.
20. Ezra Pound, 'Henry James', in *Literary Essays of Ezra Pound* (London: Faber & Faber, 1954), p.297.

On 5 October 1957 Merton wrote about 'the beautiful, unidentified red flower or fruit I found on a bud yesterday. I found a bird in the woods yesterday on the feast of St Francis. These things say so much more than words.'[18] Then, on 23 October 1961, Merton wrote, 'Whatever happens to the world, its infinitely varied dance of epiphanies continues, or is perhaps finally transfigured and perfected forever.'[19]

Gommon's early patron, and lifelong friend, Lucy Wertheim had described (in her book) her own gallerist's journey into the unknown as an *Adventure in Art*. Gommon's own painterly voyage was also an Adventure in Art, one with undreamt-of detours, as for example when — following his 1930s portrayals of the wild natural world with its horses seen as apocalyptic as well as natural creatures — he jetisonned all that to explore the ominous, self-destructive stirrings of a world clearly at war with itself. The result was his prophetic and macabre *Book of the Dead* (1939—1944), showing him to be truly worthy of Ezra Pound's statement of universal import (made later in 1954) that 'Artists are the antennae of the race, but the bullet-headed many will never learn to trust their great artists.'[20]

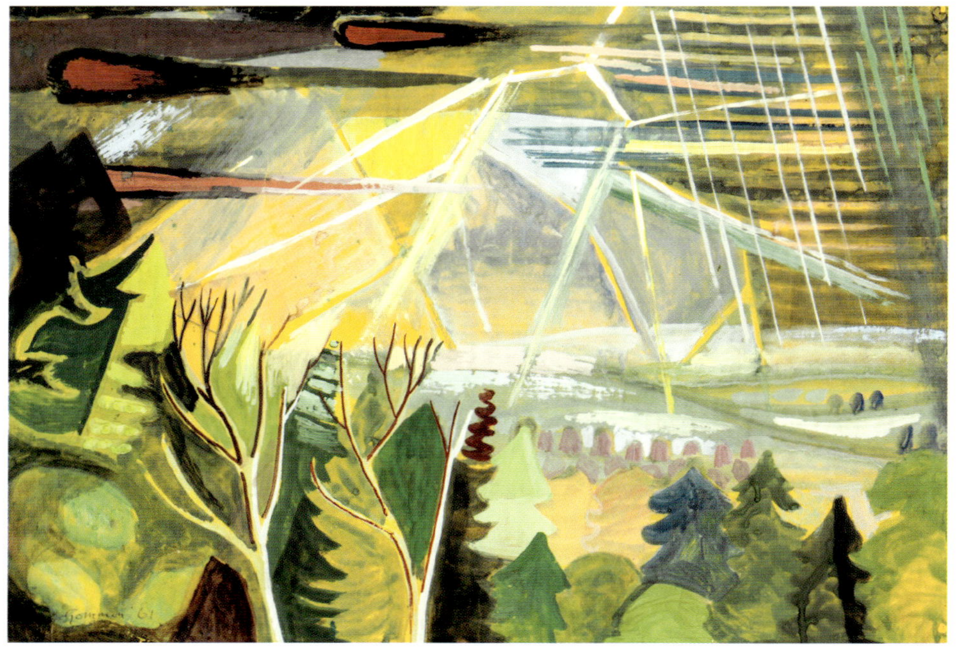

The Storm
1961, gouache on paper, 52 x 77 cm
private collection

It could be said that, by contrast, Gommon's post-1944 art forms as a whole a *Book of the Living*, in which he could look again with hope and wonder at (what the painter Roger de Grey once called) 'the world we inherit … [as] such a glittering marvel'.[21] Also, in his skilful post-war portraits he would come face to face with people whose imaginative, explorative yet sometimes vulnerable spirits he admired.

It is true that Gommon's post-war art also expressed grief at human weaknesses, strife and suffering — as, for example, in his harrowing 1959 painting based on the Crucifixion [p.114]. Sorrow is there too in a number of works, like his 1949 painting *War in the Caucasus* [p.57], and also in others describing

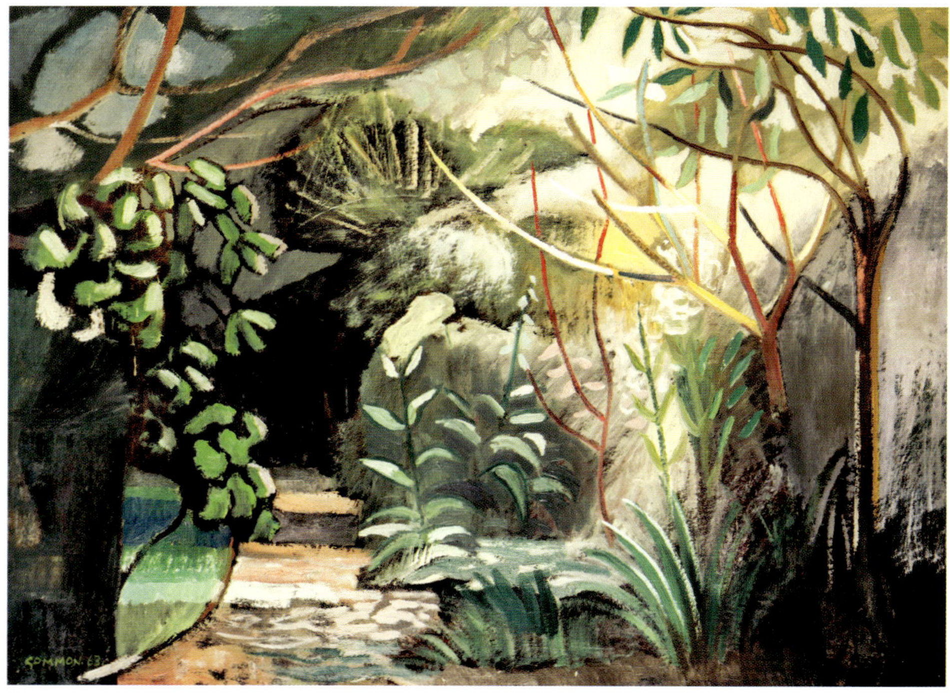

The Garden Path
1963, oil on board, 76 x 102 cm
private collection

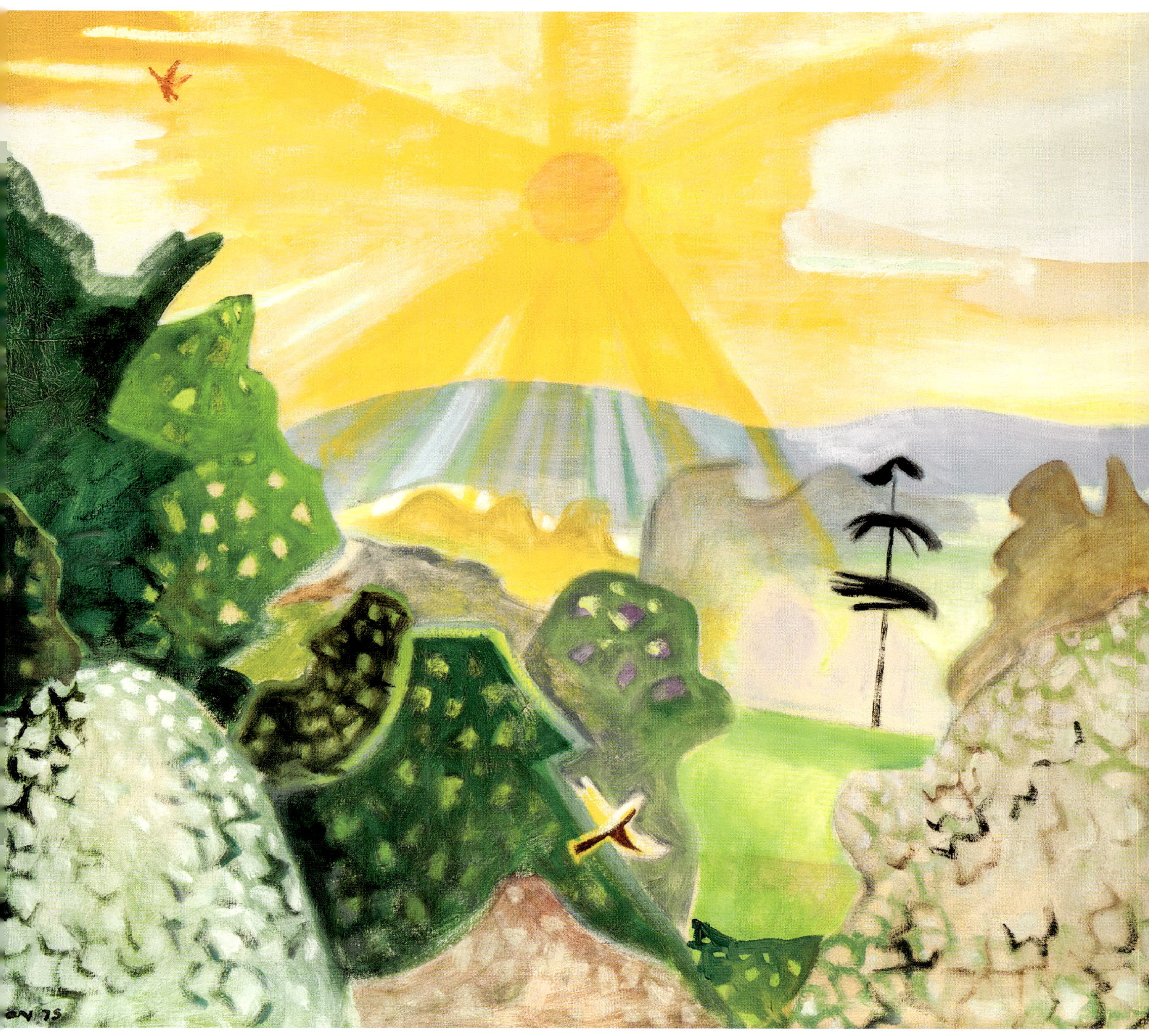

Dorset Landscape / 1975, oil on canvas, 78 x 94 cm / private collection

21 Quotation taken from a conversation
between Roger de Grey and Frank Whitford
in the series *Artists and Landscape* broadcast
on BBC Radio 3 on 21 February 1994, and
reproduced in the catalogue for the Roger
de Grey exhibition at the Royal Academy,
London, 1996, p.19

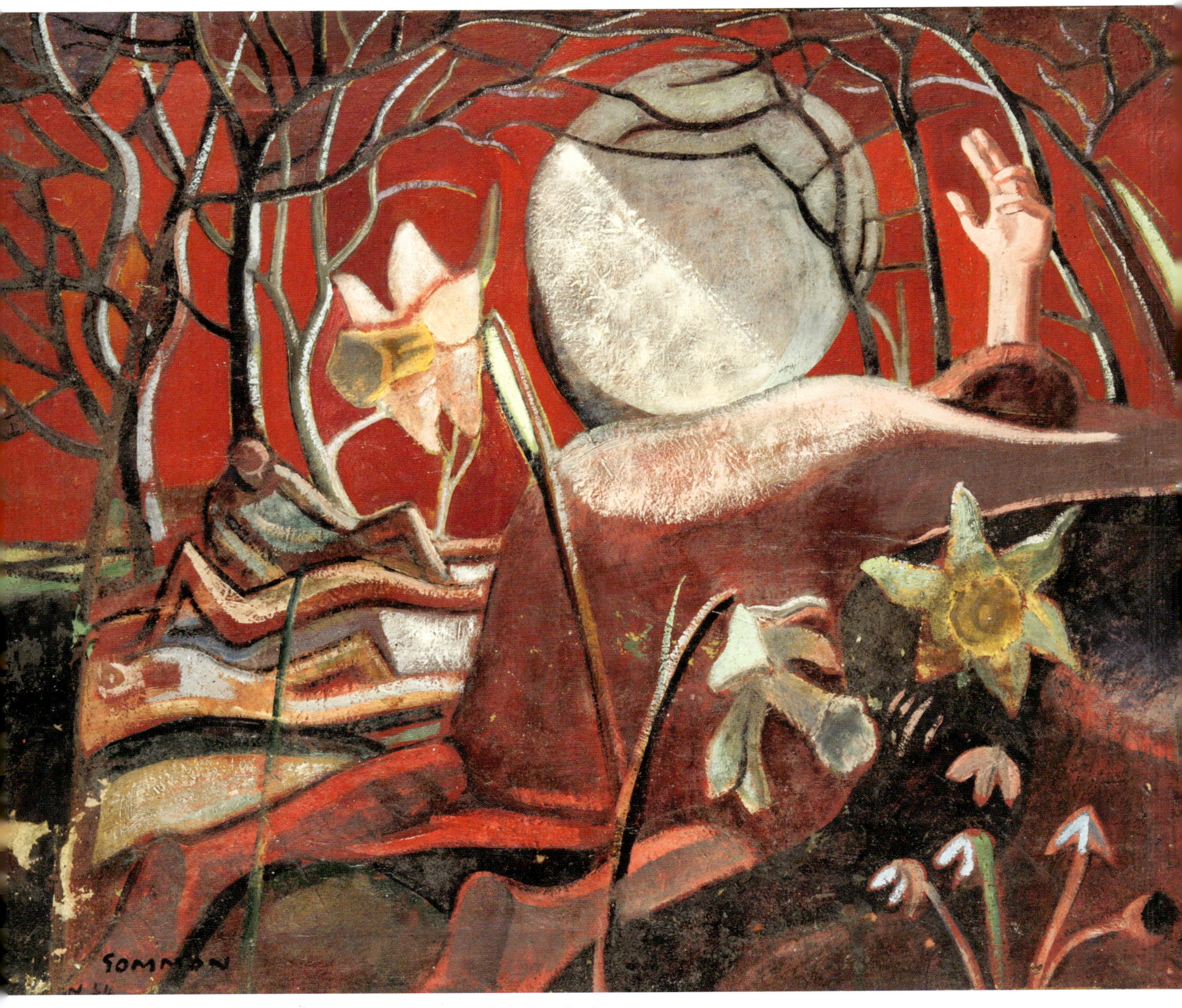

Agony in the Garden / 1954, oil on canvas, 70.5 x 91 cm / private collection

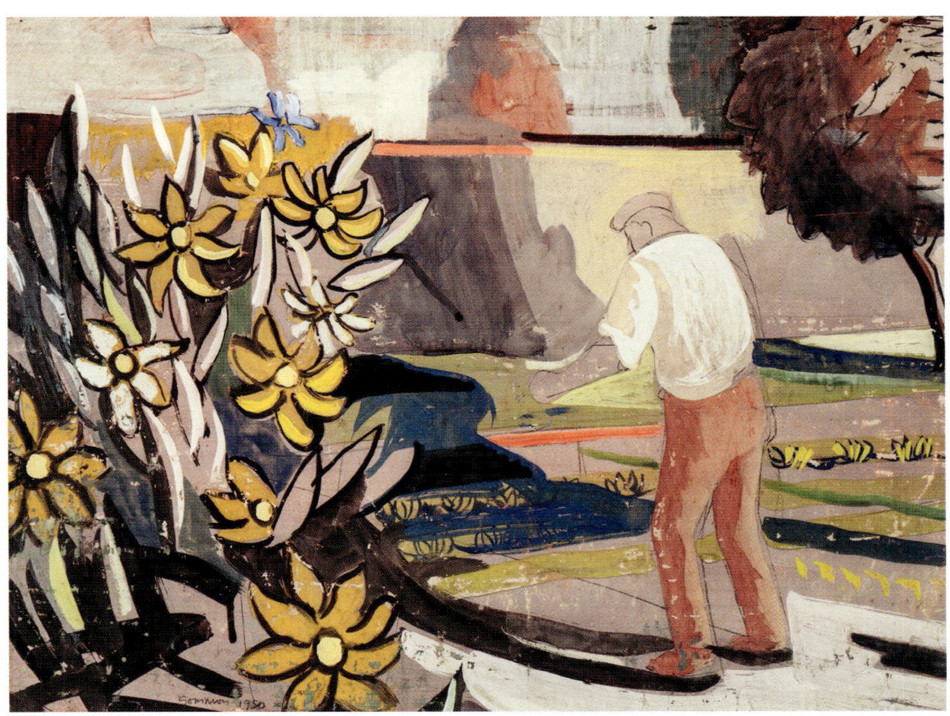

Sunset Garden (Little Billing)
1950, gouache on paper, 49 x 68 cm
private collection

the biblical *Agony in the Garden* [facing page] — dolorous scenes movingly embellished by the appearance of flowering sunflowers and daffodils.

Especially in his later years, Gommon found himself distressed and aggrieved by the increasingly widespread despoliation of the countryside — and by civic and corporate threats to wildlife. He would have been horrified by the prospect of a *Silent Spring*, a countryside devoid of birdsong as set out in the 1962 book of that title by the American ecologist and writer Rachel Carson (1907—1964). This book, one which helped initiate the modern environmental movement, is a brilliant study of the chilling consequences when the delicate checks and balances of the ecosystem are brutally overturned by the use of synthetic pesticides poisoning the land and rivers. Carson wrote, 'Over increasingly large areas of the United States [she also included the UK], spring now comes unheralded by the return of the birds, and the early mornings are strangely silent where once they were filled with the beauty of bird song.'[22]

In more recent years in the UK there has been a drastic diminution in numbers of songbirds, insects and other wildlife. In this era of global warming and environmental degradation, Gommon's paintings of the natural world continue to play a precious role in helping inspire us to enjoy and appreciate — and indeed find the impetus to safeguard — what Carson called the 'water, soil, and the earth's green mantle of plants [which] make up the world that supports ... animal life'.[23]

Gommon remained active as an artist — full of perennial curiosity about the world around him — to the end; he died suddenly on 20 January 1987. His *oeuvre* is astoundingly diverse, his imaginative versatility and agility remarkable, and his paintings over the years contain a beautiful and expansive range of musically modulated atmospheres, evoking (using Thomas Merton's felicitous phrase) an 'infinitely varied dance of epiphanies'.

22. Rachel Carson, *Silent Spring* (London: Penguin Random House, 2000), p.83.
23. Ibid, p.51.

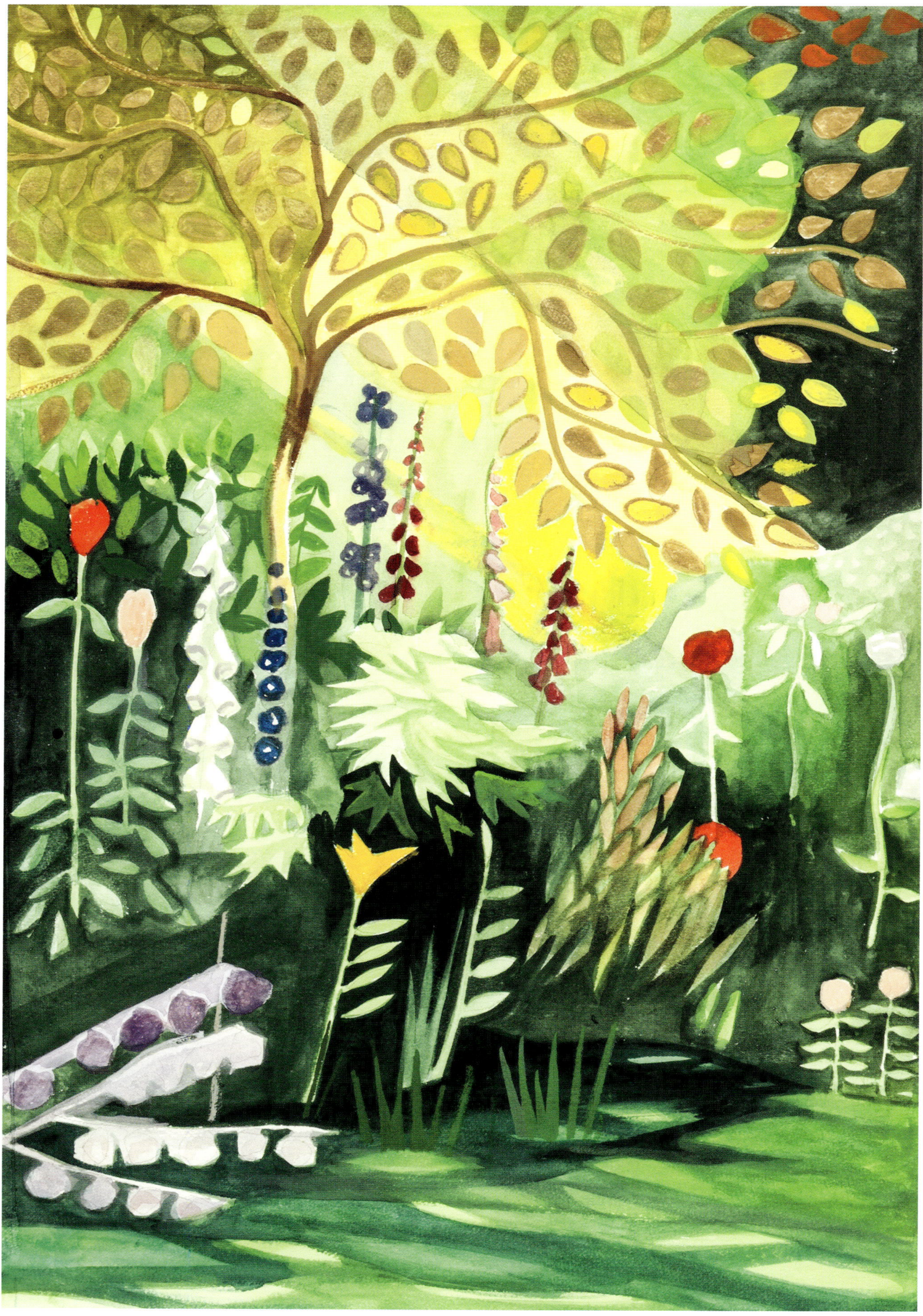

Autumn Garden / 1981, gouache on paper, 76 x 57 cm / private collection

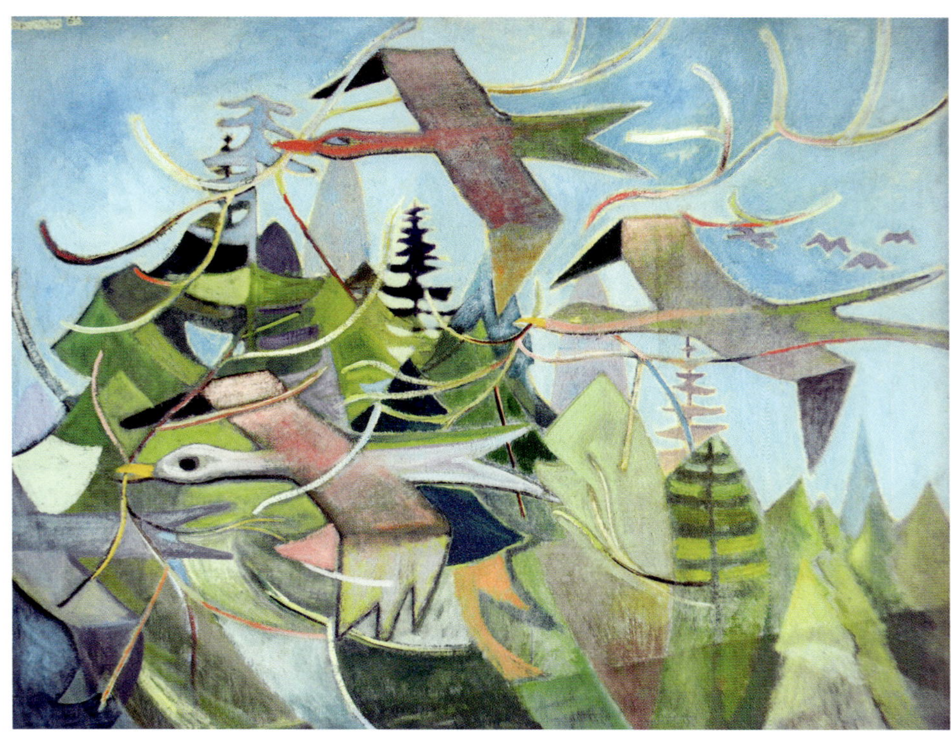

Nesting Birds
1965, oil on board, 92 x 122 cm
private collection

In a 1979 interview about his life and art, Gommon was asked what he was trying to express in his paintings. 'This is a very difficult question to answer' — but he then rose to the challenge:

> A delight, I suppose, an intense delight, an excitement and a desire to record what one sees. Not always what one sees in the visual world but what one sees in one's imagination or even from reading. It is almost an unconscious thing, ... something you just can't help doing — like breathing — or singing if you are filled with delight.[24]

24. 'An Interview with David Gommon, the Painter from Northamptonshire ...', pp. 40—41.

Exhibitions

Solo

1934 The Wertheim Gallery, London
1952 Committee Room 12, The House of Commons, London
(organised by R.T. Paget MP)
1959 Northampton Museum and Art Gallery;
The Crucifixion, Canberra Grammar School Chapel
1964 Luton Museum and Art Gallery
1965 Burton upon Trent Art Gallery;
Gainsborough's House, Sudbury, Suffolk;
Stafford City Art Gallery;
Northampton Museum and Art Gallery
1970 Liverpool School of Architecture foyer
1972 Vaughan College, Leicester
1975 Jeffreys, Gold Street, Northampton (Northampton Festival);
St Catherine's College, Oxford
1977 Northampton Museum and Art Gallery
1979 Derby City Art Gallery
1980 'Creation' mural, St Crispin Hospital, Northampton;
Eltham Gallery, Australia
1983 'Shopping' and 'The Seasons' murals, St Crispin Hospital,
Northampton
1991 Angel Row Gallery, Nottingham
1996 St Saviour Festival of Art and Life, Oxton, Birkenhead
2017 'Dreaming of Dorset', Art Stable, Dorset
2018 'Trafalgar', Greenwich Gallery, London
2019 'A Kind of Renaissance Man', Art Stable, Dorset
2023 'A Lifetime's Adventure in Art', Art Stable, Dorset

Group

1933 The Twenties Group, Wertheim Gallery, London
1934 The Twenties Group, Wertheim Gallery, London
1935 The Twenties Group, Wertheim Gallery, London
1936 The Twenties Group, Wertheim Gallery, London
1952 'Young Northampton Painters', Northampton Museum and
Art Gallery
1954 'Modern English Paintings from the Wertheim Collection',
Worthing Art Gallery
1963 The Herbert Art Gallery, Coventry (with Jonathan Adams)
1964 Kettering Art Gallery (with John Dee and Ralph Hartley);
Michael Jones Jewellers, Northampton (with John Dee)
1966 'Three Midland Painters', South London Art Gallery
(with Jonathan Adams and Ralph Hartley)
1967 Northampton Arts Association 21st Birthday show,
Northampton Museum and Art Gallery;
University Centre, Northampton
1979 Paris Salon (exhibits *Autumn* and *The Kissing Gate (Cherry
Orchard Field)*);
'The English Landscape', Durham City Art Gallery
1980 Northampton Museum and Art Gallery (with John Dee);
Fairfield Halls, Croydon; LYC Gallery, Brampton, Cumbria
1987 'British Art in the 20th Century', Blond Fine Art, London
1992 'A Century of Change', the Anderson Gallery, Broadway,
Worcestershire
2005 Williamson Art Gallery, Birkenhead
2014 'Treasures in MK', MK Gallery, Milton Keynes
2022 'A Life in Art: Lucy Wertheim — Patron, Collector, Gallerist'
and 'Reuniting the Twenties Group: From Barbara Hepworth
to Victor Pasmore', Towner Eastbourne

Works in collections

Note: all dates, media and dimensions are supplied by the institutions in question or, if not, are omitted.

Auckland Art Gallery Toi o Tāmaki, New Zealand
(gifted by Lucy Wertheim)
Boys Playing Cricket, oil on cardboard, 49.5 x 71.1 cm [1948/7/20]
Honolulu, pen and ink and pencil on paper, 38.4 x 56.1 cm [1948/7/77]
Honolulu, 1933, pen and ink on paper, 55.9 x 38.1 cm [1948/7/78]
Honolulu — Pen Portrait (possibly a self-portrait), 1933, pen and ink
    and wash on paper, 55.9 x 38.1 cm [1948/7/79]
Horse and Cart, oil on board [1950/2/17]
Horses and Riders, watercolour and gouache on paper, 38.2 x 55.9 cm
    [1948/7/80]
Jug and Fruit, oil on board, 61 x 86 cm [1948/7/22]
Portrait of My Mother, oil on canvas, 76.5 x 58.7 cm [1950/2/18]
Portrait Study (possibly of Gommon's grandmother), 1933, pen and ink
    on paper, 56.2 x 38.1 cm [1948/7/58]
Roses in a Jar, oil on board, 60.9 x 45.7 cm [1948/7/23]
Study, pencil on paper, 55.9 x 31.1 cm [1948/7/83]
Study, pencil on paper, 55.9 x 38.1 cm [1948/7/84]
Study, pencil and watercolour on paper, 56 x 38.4 cm [1948/7/85]
Tulips, oil on canvas, 76 x 55.7 cm [1948/7/24]
Untitled (Cart and Yellow Horse), watercolour and gouache on paper,
    38.5 x 55.9 cm [1948/7/76]
Untitled (Landscape), c.1934, watercolour and gouache on paper,
    38.3 x 56 cm [1948/7/82]
Winter Landscape, watercolour and gouache on paper, 38.2 x 55.9 cm
    [1948/7/88]

Durham University Library
Landscape, c.1931—9, watercolour on paper, 36 x 54 cm
Landscape v, c.1931—9, watercolour on paper 36 x 54 cm
Man and Dog Returning Home, c.1931—9, watercolour and pencil
    on paper, 36 x 54 cm
Musician, 1934, watercolour and pencil on paper, 36 x 54 cm
Pipe Smoking by the Lake, 1934, watercolour and pencil on paper,
    36 x 54 cm
Two Figures Skating, c.1931—9, watercolour on paper r, 36 x 54 cm
Two Figures Walking, c.1931—9, watercolour on paper, 36 x 54 cm
Two Figures Walking Dog, c.1931—9, watercolour on paper, 36 x 54 cm
Two Riders and a Man at the Hunt, 1933, watercolour and pencil
    on paper, 36 x 54 cm
Two Riders at the Hunt, c.1931—9, watercolour and pencil on paper,
    36 x 54 cm
Untitled (Dorset Farmer), c.1931—9, watercolour and gouache on paper
Walking up the Steep Hill, c.1931—9, watercolour on paper, 36 x 54 cm
Youth with Head Bowed, c.1931—9, watercolour on paper, 36 x 54 cm

Northampton Museums and Art Gallery
Portrait of Jon Adams, 1961, oil on board, 92 x 62 cm
Portrait of Ray Gosling, 1963, oil on canvas, 76 x 61 cm
The River Nene, 1970s, oil on board, 76 x 106 cm
The Malvern Hills, Autumn, 1984, gouache, 52 x 71.5 cm

Queensland Art Gallery (Qagoma), Brisbane, Australia
(gifted by Lucy Wertheim, 1951)
Horses, c.1931—9/poss. 1933—4, gouache on black card, 38.4 x 56 cm
    [1-0539_001]
Sunset, c.1933—4, gouache over pencil, 43.6 x 56 cm [1-0523_001]

Salford Museums and Art Gallery
(gifted by Lucy Wertheim)
A Ballet or *At the Ballet*, c.1933, oil on canvas, 81 x 68 cm [1947.230]
Boy, oil on cardboard [1947.178]
Downs, c.1933, watercolour, 38 x 56 cm [1939.29.101]
Flowers in a Jug, c.1933, oil on canvas, 92 x 67.5 cm [1939.15]
Head (possibly a self-portrait), c.1933, poss. watercolour on paper
    [1937.3]
Horses and Downs, c.1933, watercolour, 36 x 54 cm [1939.29.95]
Landscape, c.1933, watercolour and gouache on paper, 46.2 x 59 cm
    [1935.18]
Landscape [recto] and *Knight in Battle* [verso], oil on cardboard,
    38 x 51.3 cm [1947.215]
Portrait (1), c.1933, watercolour on paper [1939.29.43]
Portrait (2) (possibly of Gommon's mother), c.1933, poss. watercolour
    on paper [1939.29.47]
Portrait of a Man, watercolour on paper [1939.29]
The Bay, c.1933, watercolour on paper [1939.29.85]
The Farmer, c.1933, watercolour on paper, 35 x 56 cm [1939.29.62]
The Meet, c.1933, poss. watercolour on paper [1939.29.84]
**The Road*, c.1933, watercolour, on paper, 36 x 54 cm [1933.19]
    (purchase)
Theatre Study, c.1933, watercolour on paper [1939.29.63]
Woman and Child, c.1933, watercolour on paper [1939.29.86]

Towner Eastbourne
(gifted by Lucy Wertheim bequest, 1971)
Music Hall, c.1934, oil on canvas, 68 x 81.5 cm [EASTG 1253]

The Whitworth, University of Manchester
[The] Crucifixion, 1933, pencil, pen and ink and watercolour on paper,
    38.3 x 55.9 cm [D.1934.27]

Private collections
David Gommon's work has been widely collected over the years
and currently exists in many private collections, both in the UK
and worldwide.

Acknowledgements

Philip Vann would like to thank Peter and Moira Gommon, and Kate and Chris Currie, for all their kind, enthusiastic and knowledgeable support and hospitality during the period spent researching the art and life of David Gommon. Long conversations I had with Peter and Kate about their parents and David's life and art were, I found, fascinating and illuminating.

Appreciative thanks too to Ian Mayes for sharing his memories of his friend David and also of his own encounters with David's empathetic 1930s patron, Lucy Wertheim. I would also like to thank William Mayes for an invaluable early recollection of David, and Hannah Mayes for her kind hospitality on my visit to Hardingstone in Northamptonshire, where she managed to show me round Jasmine Cottage and its garden (where David and his wife Jean had lived) – though a place much changed now — and helped give me a real understanding of the history and background of the area.

Many thanks also to Philippe and Lucilla Garner: conversations with Philippe helped give me a good sense of Lucy Wertheim as both a courageous individual and a visionary and pioneering gallerist. In addition, I want to thank Karen Taylor, the Collections and Exhibitions Curator at Towner Eastbourne (where two complementary exhibitions in 2022, 'A Life in Art: Lucy Wertheim — Patron, Collector, Gallerist' and 'Reuniting the Twenties Group: From Barbara Hepworth to Victor Pasmore' — were revelations for many) for her help during the research period. And many thanks to Kelly Ross at her Dorset gallery, the Art Stable, for helping me with information and images. I would also like to thank Clara Hudson and Paul Deaton at Sansom & Co for all their kind support, interest and patience throughout this whole project.

Karen Taylor would like to thank editor Kelly Thompson for her invaluable assistance with helping to shape the text of her essay.

The Gommon family would like to thank the following variously for invaluable support of and belief in David's work and essential contributions to this book:

The DPC in Greenwich Ltd are specialist photographers of paintings and works of art; they specialise in expertly cleaning, restoring and framing paintings. The company photographed David Gommon's Trafalgar series of large oil paintings for a show in Greenwich.

R. Jackson & Sons of Slater Street in Liverpool restored, cleaned and framed many of the works illustrated in this book. Phil Jackson and his team have applied themselves assiduously to understanding the character of David Gommon's work so that the pictures could be faithfully restored.

Ian Mayes is a journalist and writer. At *The Guardian* he was the very first readers' editor, or resident independent ombudsman, later becoming President of the international Organisation of News Ombudsmen (ONO). Before going to *The Guardian* he was features editor of the *Northampton Chronicle & Echo*, where he first reviewed David Gommon's work in an exhibition at Northampton Museum and Art Gallery. While at *The Guardian*, he helped to launch the Hazlitt Society and was its inaugural Chair. As a writer on art he is known for his ability to see beneath the surface of a work and for his thoughtful and perceptive reviews.

Tom McEvoy, a friend and work colleague of Peter Gommon, took the initiative to set up a David Gommon Wikipedia page, which effectively launched the project that led to Kelly Ross's first exhibition at the Art Stable and through that to the creation of this book.

Kelly Ross Fine Art has developed a keen understanding and enthusiasm for David Gommon's work. She has hosted three successful shows at the Art Stable, her gallery in Child Okeford, Dorset; a fascinating coincidence because many of David Gommon's early paintings, under the patronage of Lucy Wertheim, were made in the immediate surroundings of the village.

Adrian Waine (of Photography for Industry) is an industrial photographer who took up the challenge of photographing paintings and finding ways of lighting them so that the colours and textures would be true to the original work. The majority of photographs in this book are his.

Index